D0205970

Bradley's Logic

For Jutta

Bradley's Logic

Anthony Manser

BARNES & NOBLE BOOKS
TOTOWA, NEW JERSEY

© Anthony Manser 1983

First published in the USA 1983 by
Barnes & Noble Books
81 Adams Drive
Totowa, New Jersey, 07512

Library of Congress Cataloging in Publication Data

Manser, Anthony Richards.
  Bradley's logic.
  Bibliography: p.
  Includes index.
  1. Bradley, F. H. (Francis Herbert), 1846–1924.
Principles of logic. 2. Logic—History—19th century.
I. Title.
B1618.B73P735 1983   160′.92′4   82–24407
ISBN 0–389–20379–3

Printed in Great Britain

Contents

Contents

Preface

Bradley's *Principles of Logic* is a neglected work, though from the number of references to it during the first forty years after publication, its influence on its time is obvious. This influence extends even to Bertrand Russell, who acknowledged his indebtedness many times. The *Principles* is also different from those writings of Bradley which have recently attracted the attention of philosophers. Hence it seems appropriate to re-examine it just one century after its original publication. In my time at Oxford after the war, I was frequently told that a great age of philosophy was one which devoted much attention to logic. Those who said this of course believed that it was Russell and Frege who had inaugurated such an age in sweeping aside the metaphysics of the Anglo-Hegelians. That Bradley himself was a logician, albeit of a rather different kind, was ignored. The History of Philosophy as then taught largely neglected the period between Kant and Russell; Hegel was mentioned only as a horrid example. Metaphysics was the enemy, and Empiricism the official style of English philosophy.

This is the background of my book. In the first chapter I sketch the actual history of how Hegel came to England, or at least to Oxford, for the official history seems not to account for the rise of Anglo-Hegelianism and its apparent domination of the philosophic scene for so long. In the second chapter I look briefly at what Hegel actually said about formal logic, for few writers seem to have examined this with any care. Most have been content to refer to the 'dialectic.' These two chapters are necessary for understanding Bradley's starting point. The major part of the book consists in a detailed examination of his views on logic as set out in the first edition of the *Principles,* though in the final chapter I examine the changes which took place in the second edition, published in 1920.

The abbreviations I use to refer to the works of Bradley are listed below, p. x. All other references occur in the notes at the end of each chapter.

In the text I have in general followed Bradley's spelling and conventions of punctuation in the interests of legibility.

Anthony Manser
University of Southampton

Acknowledgements

Many people have helped me to become clearer about Bradley and about contemporary philosophical problems, but I must particularly mention David Pugmire of Southampton and Guy Stock of Aberdeen, who have read much of the manuscript and saved me from many errors. For similar help with historical points for the first chapter, I am indebted to Fred Mather, of the Department of History, Southampton.

In the preparation of the text I owe an enormous debt to the Departmental Secretary, Heather King, both for her efficient typing and for assistance and encouragement. Also, I owe a great deal to the University Computing Service, in particular to Andy Schulkins and Andy Cotton for their unfailing helpfulness and patience with two amateurs using a computer for the preparation of text. Without their assistance the manuscript would have taken much longer to prepare.

An earlier version of chapter VII was delivered to the Royal Institute of Philosophy as part of the lecture series on Idealism.

I am grateful to the University of Oxford for permission to reproduce the examination papers in the appendix to Chapter I.

Abbreviations

I have referred in the text to the works of Bradley in the following manner:

AR	*Appearance and Reality,* Oxford, 1946
CE	*Collected Essays,* Oxford, 1969
ES	*Ethical Studies,* Oxford, 1935
ETR	*Essays on Truth and Reality,* Oxford, 1944
PL	*Principles of Logic,* Oxford, 1950

I include as an appendix a comparison of the pagination of the first and second editions of the *Principles of Logic.* Bosanquet and Russell both use the first edition, as did many of the earlier commentators on Bradley.

I

The Revolution in English Philosophy

What might be called the 'official story' of recent British philosophy, largely written in the 1950s, refers to a 'revolution' which occurred at the beginning of the century. The revolution is associated with the names of Russell and Moore. It is implied that the present distinctive style of British philosophy is due to the acceptance of their doctrines and their methods. It is also implied that what had preceded Russell and Moore was similar to what occurs in Europe today, and that consequently there is no need for the 'analytic' philosopher to pay much attention to figures who have large followings on the Continent. This 'official story' also suggests that the Europeans had failed, in spite of the brief flourishing of the Vienna Circle, to grasp where philosophy was going; they were still in a pre-revolutionary period. Now, in the 1980s, this view is less widely held; no apology is needed to quote Heidegger or Sartre in a philosophic paper or to discuss the views of Hegel. This attitude was not properly enshrined in philosophical writings in a formal manner; it was more a matter of emphasis, of what was said in conversation. Some may have wished to make a stark contrast, as Ayer in his talk of 'pontiffs' (bad) and 'journeymen' (good), with its echoes of a long British tradition stemming from Locke and his idea of the philosopher as an 'underlabourer.' Others were more aware of the actual history, as Gilbert Ryle in his careful and typically non-manifesto-like introduction to the Third Programme talks entitled *The Revolution in Philosophy*.[1] Nevertheless in the 1950s the idea of a revolution, a radical change in the style of philosophizing, was in the air. Moore and Russell were the founders; their immediate predecessors were almost members of a different species, metaphysicians, not philosophers. In addition, they were self-confessed 'idealists,' sometimes referred to as 'Anglo-Hegelians,' which made their oddness even more apparent, for the 'revolutionaries' could appeal to the English tradition of empiricism as a partial validation of their 'revolution.' The new philosophy was the heir to Locke and Hume, had its roots deep in English soil and could thus be legitimated against a temporary continental aberration.

I do not have the knowledge to rewrite the intellectual history of the years 1850–1950, and perhaps the time is not yet ripe for this to be done. Nevertheless it is necessary to say something about this period, to endeavour to explain why Hegel should have become influential in England some twenty years after his death and at a time when he was beginning to be forgotten in his native country. Though the British Idealists were much less Hegelian than has sometimes been thought, it is odd that they should have found his work a basis for their thought and that they could apparently dominate the philosophical scene for some forty or fifty years. The reasons are complex and include both philosophical and non-philosophical elements; I will pick out two for attention here, for I think there was a drastic change in English philosophy, but that it took place some fifty years before the time of Russell and Moore. This change could be called the real revolution in English philosophy, and the work of Russell, Moore and later of Wittgenstein could only have occurred within this new tradition which was established in the middle of the nineteenth century. However, even if this thesis is not accepted, these two factors are necessary to understand the thought of Bradley. They are, first, the rise of a class of professional philosophers in England and second, the fact that the problem of meaning became central to philosophy. Ryle saw the latter point clearly:

Finally, in the hands of both Frege and Bradley the notion of Meaning became, what it has remained ever since, an indispensable, if refractory, instrument of philosophical discourse.[2]

Ryle was right to date the turn to meaning prior to the date of Moore and Russell. I will have more to say about it when I come to deal with Bradley himself; in this chapter I want to look at the philosophical history of the period and, in particular, at the way in which changes in the method of teaching philosophy affected the philosophy taught. Hence I want to cast a sceptical eye on what I have described as the 'official story' of recent British philosophy.

When I studied philosophy at Oxford after the war, the dominant school was that of 'analysis' which, as I have already indicated, took as its starting point the work of Russell and Moore. And the belief was in the air that from the time they first published, English philosophy had been analytic in character. Hence it was with surprise that I encountered an undergraduate from Merton who was writing an essay on the 'Concrete Universal' as a philosophical exercise, not as a piece of history. In fact the consolidation of the analytic school only took place in the late 1940s, at least as far as Oxford was concerned. Cambridge, with fewer philosophy teachers, was different; Oxford dominated the philosophic scene in terms of the number studying the subject. As far as the provincial universities were concerned, the immediate post-war expansion was largely staffed by Oxford products. Above all, it had been the return of the young men after the war that made the difference; they taught the 'new' philosophy. The extent of the change can be seen by comparing the examination questions; in 1942–43 they were such as could have been answered by those trained in 1900. By 1946 a very different attitude was needed. I reproduce two illustrative Oxford examination papers at the end of this chapter. The attitude of those who had learnt their philosophy at that period was a missionary one; we felt we were engaged in a twofold battle, against the surviving philosophers of the older persuasion and against the educated public. As a young philosopher in a provincial university I was forced to defend what I then took to be the correct view of philosophy against my non-philosophical colleagues, who believed that English philosophy had lost its way and had become preoccupied with trivial questions. That my experience was neither peculiar nor unique can be seen by similar defensive semi-popular articles and talks on the Third Programme. *The Revolution in Philosophy* is an example. It was felt by many philosophers that the public did not appreciate what had happened in philosophy, that it had changed its direction and that the new was both important and a legitimate heir to what had previously been studied under that name. For it did provide solutions to all legitimate philosophical problems and show that the rest were either to be answered by empirical means or were only pseudo-problems.

We, the brash disciples of the analytic gospel, did not realize the extent to which the public were justified in their belief that this philosophy was new and radical, were unaware of the number of both books and articles in the 'older' tradition that had been published through the twenties and thirties and that these had formed the staple of philosophy teaching in those years in Britain. *Analysis* had been founded (in Southampton) in 1933, but it was the organ of young rebels, and made little impact on philosophy at the time. It is salutary to go through the articles in *Mind* or the *Proceedings of the Aristotelian Society* for the inter-war years to see what was thought worthy of discussion. To us Idealism had died in 1903; the evidence indicates that it was still flourishing thirty years later. There were figures who straddled the boundary between old and new, like R. G. Collingwood. He was an anomaly, a man who flirted with Idealism and yet produced work which could not be ignored by analytic philosophers. Nevertheless, he was regarded with suspicion by them.

Like so many intellectual changes, the analytic movement had one of the characteristics Kuhn attributes to scientific revolutions; the young men adopted the new ideas and eventually succeeded to the chairs of the older generation. In this case the process was interrupted by the six-year moratorium on new appointments imposed by the war; the change in 1945 was consequently more drastic and more conspicuous. If we had been asked what the change consisted in we would have said that it was a growing professionalism and a concentration on detailed questions instead of large issues. The vehicle of philosophy had become the article in the philosophical journal, which, as Ryle said, left no room for 'a crusade against, or a crusade on behalf of, any massive "ism".'[3] I was certainly taught to believe that everything of philosophic importance was contained in articles published since 1903, though exceptions were made for two books, the preface and first chapter of Moore's *Principia Ethica* and Wittgenstein's *Tractatus Logico-Philosophicus*. I understand that Oxford later became even more restrictive; one university lecturer attributes his first-class degree in the late fifties to a diet of material all of which had been published subsequent to 1950.

These views were not formally taught; they constituted a background to our study of philosophy. We were not greatly interested in the history of the subject, though we read the necessary texts for examination purposes. We did not notice that, in the history of English philosophy, the first person who can be properly considered a professional, i.e. one who made his living from teaching philosophy, was T. H. Green. Nor did we realize that, in conventional history of philosophy, the only professional to be studied was Kant.

By the 1950s philosophy had become a profession and was taught, like any other academic subject, in departments of universities, to students who were expected to be specialists. Ryle, in the introduction to *The Revolution in Philosophy,* talks of this growing professionalism as one of the major features which led to a change in the content of philosophy.[4] Amateurs, and this included most major figures in the English canon up to J. S. Mill, had published their work in general journals, and their books were read by the whole educated public. Though only few might have the ablity to philosophize well, it was accepted that what they had to say was relevant to the general intellectual life. The fact that the majority of intellectuals in the early nineteenth century were either clergymen or involved with theological questions was also relevant. Ryle thought the decline of interest in religion was of importance in changing the philosophical scene, in altering the image of a philosopher from one who brought wisdom to bear on the issues of the day to that of a 'philosophers' philosopher'[5] concerned with technique, rather than 'edification.' In fact, the decline of clerical dominance at Oxford probably began in the 1860s, so the process was concurrent with the rise of Anglo-Hegelianism; Green did not take orders.

Perhaps an extreme version of the analytic view is that of Geoffrey Warnock; it could be taken as exemplifying the Oxford attitude at the time I was studying there:

Are there not questions of a quite non-technical sort, questions about life in general and attitudes to life, which historically have been at any rate touched on by most philosophers, and which furthermore are vastly more interesting to people in general than are the highly abstract, highly 'professional,' and frequently minute disputations in which philosophers currently engage?

This is not, I believe, an impressive point. No doubt one would not wish to deny that there are very vital and interesting questions of this sort. But does it follow that philosophers ought to discuss them? Have they not perhaps, like physicists or philologists, their own special and specialized concerns in which in fact, for what the point is worth, they are evidently more interested? Is it really any use exhorting or instructing them to do something else? Their position after all is not usually such that they have any great interest in pleasing the public or pursuing mass audiences; they would not be much put out if those whom their work did not attract should pay simply no further attention to it. Even if, as in fact is not perfectly clear, their present concerns are somewhat more confined than the concerns of philosophers historically have been, it is not clearly improper nor in the least degree unusual for such progressive specialization to occur. Finally, is it certain that those philosophers who have dealt largely in *Weltanschauung* have done so to any great purpose or profit? And could it be any more certain that, if those questions were now to be more frequently mooted among philosophers, the outcome would be particularly valuable? A marked capacity for abstract thought is compatible with an 'attitude to life' entirely ordinary, or even dull. A philosopher's views in this area might be expected to be consistent and reasonably clear; but they might well, while fulfilling those conditions, be absolutely uninteresting. If so, one need not complain if he should keep them to himself.[6]

I have quoted it at length because it is important to capture not only the sense but also the tone of the passage. The use of rhetorical questions, not at all typical of the book as a whole, indicates an unease about what is being said. 'Abstract thought' seems to become the content, as well as the medium, of philosophy. At the same time there is, implicit in the passage, a rejection of the 'continental' tradition, a rejection which is similar to that implied by Ryle. In many cases it was made more explicitly – Sartre and Heidegger were said to be 'metaphysicians' and hence unworthy of consideration by serious philosophers. But those who wrote and spoke in this way seem to have ignored the fact that changes analogous to those which had occurred in England must have taken place on the Continent; both Sartre and Heidegger were obviously 'professionals,' albeit at that time not actually employed in universities, and there were plenty of similar figures who were willing to discuss large general issues in their classrooms. Hence another explanation seemed to be needed to account for the difference in the two traditions. One such lay to hand; England was the country of empiricism; I have already mentioned the way in which the 'revolutionaries' claimed that their rejection of idealism was partly a return to more native ways of thought. And the very name 'Anglo-Hegelian' had something of a condemnation about it; Green and his followers should not have needed to go outside their homeland for inspiration.

But this could not be the whole story; the figure of Mill would seem adequate to demonstrate that a philosopher could be an influential public figure. And, in any case, few of the great philosophers had regarded 'technical questions' as trivial. Mill's *System of Logic* was concerned with just such, and yet was addressed mainly to a lay public. Perhaps another feature, one peculiar to Oxford and Cambridge, had as much influence on the radical difference in style and content between Britain and Europe. I mean the tutorial method of teaching, in contrast to the professorial lecture, the main or only method employed on the Continent or traditionally used in Scotland. The professor is a dominant figure who establishes a 'school' of philosophy. His lectures are the initiation into that school; time is available in a lecture course to develop a *Weltanschauung,* to set out a 'philosophy.' In a tutorial it is possible to deal only with a single question which can be discussed exhaustively. What forms ideal subject-matter for a tutorial will also constitute an article in a journal. A book cannot sensibly be discussed in an hour; an article can. Hence the style of teaching may well influence its content; analytic philosophy is more appropriate to the tutorial than is a 'system,' where it is the articulation of the whole which is of central importance. The medium may become the message, or at least may determine what message can be delivered.

So far I have been concerned with undermining what may be called the official account of the history of English philosophy, one that makes 'idealism' a foreign interlude within the prevailing empiricism, but which gives no explanation as to why a whole generation of philosophers should start whoring after strange gods. I have already implied that I want to date the real 'revolution' in philosophy considerably earlier. I agree that the coming of professional philosophers was essential to the change, but think that the figure of T. H. Green, the first of these, is more important in the transformation of English philosophy than those usually considered the 'revolutionaries.' It is, I claim, no accident that 'professionalism' and a form of Hegelianism should accompany one another, but to see the connection it is necessary to look, at least in outline, at the process which transformed Oxford from a kind of finishing school for the gentry into something approximating to a university on the continental or Scottish model. Whether it is historically accurate or not, Newman certainly thought he was describing the university at the turn of the century when he wrote:

I protest to you, Gentlemen, that if I had to choose between a so-called University, which dispensed with residence, and gave its degree to any person who passed an examination in a wide range of subjects, and a University which had no professors or examinations at all, but merely brought a number of young men together for three or four years, and then sent them away as the University of Oxford is said to have done some sixty years since, . . . I have no hesitation in giving preference to the University which did nothing.[7]

By the 1840s teaching was still at a fairly low level. The college system meant that each college tried to teach its own undergraduates. Given that the majority of fellows were appointed for life and had no formal obligation to take part in instruction, this frequently meant that one man was employed to cover all topics. (It should not be forgotten that Bradley, considerably later, was a life fellow and never taught or lectured to undergraduates though he continued to be a member of Merton until his death in 1924.) Pattison, who was opposed to it, says that in 1846 'there was unquestioning satisfaction in the tutorial system, *i.e.* one man teaching everybody everything. . . .'[8] Green began his teaching career by lecturing at Balliol on Greek History for Greats, and on English and early European History for the schools of law and modern history. The result of this wide range was that the average tutor offered little in the way of real learning or inspiration. Pattison quotes from one who refused such a post:

I could certainly keep ahead of my pupils, *which was all that many tutors ever did.* I could come round my class by questions they were not prepared for. I was sure always to hear mistakes which it would be easy to correct. In matter of fact a tutor often did no more than half the class could have done quite as well. Though the method of instruction was very effectual, yet it was easy sailing.[9]

He also mentions a colleague:

Bode was also a good general Latin scholar, according to the measure of those days, and knew one book – namely, Horace's *Odes*.[10]

The result was that those who wished to attain honours in the examinations had to supplement college teaching by attending private lessons with a coach for which the student paid in addition to his college fees. The reform of the university was twofold; it involved the improvement of college teaching and the introduction of university lectures given by professors. The latter innovation was probably modelled on Germany, for although Scotland had always had a professorial system in its universities, Oxford was unlikely to follow a provincial model. The attempt to establish professors was unpopular in many quarters; in a widely proclaimed satire on the commission of 1850, Mansel, later Waynflete Professor of Moral and Metaphysical Philosophy, has Commissioner-Socrates, 'the model instructor of Youth,' reply to a request to tutor someone:

> Tutor! benighted wretch! didst thou say Tutor?
> Who talks of Tutors now? The coin's not current.
> Professors, man, Professors are the thing.
> They'll mould and model English education
> On the best German plan: 'tis quite delightful
> To see how German Students learn of them.
> No bigotry, no narrow-minded feeling,
> Nothing sectarian.[11]

The passage also reveals the religious dimension to the arguments about the reform of university teaching. Professors are non-sectarian, presumably a piece of High Church special pleading by Mansel. However, Hegelian terms are linked to biblical criticism in the next passage. Perhaps more relevant is the fact that professors are Hegelian; the chorus is invoked by Hegelian language, and enters with a mention of both Kant and Hegel:

> Ye who scan
> The Universe of Being, and reveal
> How Werden, eldest born of Seyn and Nichts,
> Gave birth to Daseyn, whence in long succession
> The world of Thought and Substance. Ye who fathom
> The hidden myths of Scripture and the essence
> Of Worship, Function of Psychology, –
> I summon you, appear.
> *Enter* Chorus of Professors.
> Professors we,
> From over the sea,
> From the land where Professors in plenty be;
> And we thrive and flourish, as well we may,
> In the land that produced one Kant with a K
> And many Cants with a C.
> Where Hegel taught, to his profit and fame,
> That something and nothing were one and the same;
> The absolute difference never a jot being

'Twixt having and not having, being and not being,
But wisely declined to extend his notion
To the finite relations of thalers and groschen . . .
    Bacon, be dumb,
    Newton, be mum;
The worth of induction's a snap of the thumb.
    With a bug, bug, bug, and a hum, hum, hum,
    Hither the true Philosophers come.[12]

The introduction of Hegel into England is often attributed to Stirling; *The Secret of Hegel* was published in 1865. Passmore talks of him as having 'first presented Hegelianism to Great Britain in a relatively intelligible and coherent form.'[13] But that such a satire could be written shows that Hegelian language and ideas were recognized by an educated audience much earlier. I suspect that Passmore, like Muirhead in *The Platonic Tradition in Anglo-Saxon Philosophy*,[14] has been misled by a reliance on published material. As often in Oxford, the oral tradition may be in advance of the written. Hegel was known in England before 1850. German thought was becoming influential; Mansel also mentions Strauss, Bauer and Feuerbach in the satire.

Credit for much of the reform of Oxford teaching and for the first proper introduction of Hegel into England must go to Jowett. His part in the former is well known; his role in the latter is seldom mentioned. In 1844 he made a tour of Germany with H. M. Stanley, of which one object was to meet Erdmann, then considered Hegel's chief disciple and interpreter, in order to consult him upon 'the best manner of approaching' his master's works.[15] It is not entirely clear what led Jowett to study Hegel, though it is perhaps significant that the two travellers took with them the text of *Der Kritik der reinen Vernunft*. Kant had been introduced to this country by Coleridge, and the influence of German romanticism was later strengthened by the works of Carlyle. The intellectual ferment of Germany must have seemed attractive to young men at this time. Further, Jowett may have felt that the philosophic basis of this ferment would be helpful in combating the dominant empiricism, which itself had, at that time, a religious dimension. The separation between philosophy and theology was not so absolute as it is now; Mansel, whom I have quoted above, was successively 'Fellow and Tutor of St. John's College; Waynflete Professor of Moral and Metaphysical Philosophy, Magdalen College; Professor of Ecclesiastical History; Canon of Christ Church; Dean of St. Paul's.'

Jowett's trip to Germany took place at the height of the Tractarian controversy, and in the following year Newman was converted to Rome. It has been argued by J. M. Cameron [16] that Newman was, contrary to Pattison's judgment, an empiricist rather than a Kantian. It seems to me that Cameron has made out his case. There are many echoes of Hume in Newman's works, none at all of Kant. Perhaps the disaster of the Tractarian movement led some to consider seeking a philosophical basis for Christianity that would prevent such events in the future. Certainly Stirling later praised Hegel as a defender of religion.[17] And whatever the opinions of Strauss and Feuerbach, there was no difficulty in finding ostensibly Christian passages in Hegel. I only suggest that it might have been such a motive that encouraged Jowett to seek a firmer foundation for his belief, one that was not liable to lead to atheism or to Rome. I say this because it is puzzling that a foreign philosophy should have been so eagerly adopted by many, though by no means all, of those who became professional philosophers in the thirty years following Jowett's trip.

In the first number of *Mind* (1876) Mark Pattison, briefly a follower of Newman, gives an account of 'Philosophy at Oxford.' Although not sympathetic to Hegelianism, his definition of the topic is interesting: 'A philosophy must be the concentrated expression of the life of the period.'[18] Hence the earlier periods of the nineteenth century were not philosophical; the first, 1800–1833, was 'neither a philosophy nor a school of thought, but a vague state of inquiry . . . blind groping, working its way out of the mist of insular prejudice in which the French universal empire had enveloped the "nation of shopkeepers".'[19] In the second period, 1830–1848, though the terms of the controversy were religious, there was yet a philosophical principle at stake:

The controversy on 'private judgment' involved, if it did not elucidate, the question of reason *v.* authority. The dispute as to the merits of the Reformation was not a mere theological quarrel, it inevitably carried the thoughts of the disputants to the ultimate criterion of belief.[20]

Newman had erred because he could find no resting place between reliance on the private judgment of the individual, the principle of

Protestantism and of empiricism, and acceptance of the authority of the Church:

In an honest endeavour to get nearer to the truth of things than the conventional Philistinism of 'liberal' politicians, Dr. Newman dug down and found a little below the surface the disused principle of 'authority.' Disgusted with the cant phrases of reform oratory of his day, he missed the deeper principle of Reason, which all the while lay below the surface of the Whig political tradition. He broke not only with the constitutional principles of 1688, but with Reason. He threw off not only the scum of democratic lawlessness, but the allegiance which the individual understanding owes to the universal reason, and too hastily concluded that authority could supply a basis for a philosophic belief. Long before Dr. Newman gave in his adhesion to the Papal Church, the philosophic basis of his mind had anticipated the Syllabus and the Encyclical.[21]

Unfortunately Pattison says little about that 'reason' which he refers to, but it is clear that he thinks philosophy can only exist under conditions of freedom; he attacks the Scholastic period because it produced only 'chicane and mystification;' speculation may have been free, but it had no effect on the holders of real power. Genuine freedom requires that philosophy should be socially or politically effective. At the same time, he believed that there must be something beyond the individual's private thoughts, which he called 'universal reason.' The theological argument foreshadows, perhaps, later debates about 'private language;' although the topic may appear different, the substance of the arguments is similar. Interestingly, Jowett himself saw the new modes of philosophizing as leading to a freedom from reliance on authority, though he did not mention Hegel in this connection. In a letter to Florence Nightingale he writes:

And there is a great change in education at the Universities, especially at Oxford. When I was an undergraduate we were fed upon Bishop Butler and Aristotle's *Ethics,* and almost all teaching leaned to the support of doctrines of authority. Now there are new subjects, Modern History and Physical Science, and more important than these, perhaps, is the real study of metaphysics in the Literae Humaniores school – every man for the last ten years who goes in for honours has read Bacon, and probably Locke, Mill's *Logic,* Plato, Aristotle, and the history of ancient philosophy. See how impossible this makes a return to the old doctrines of authority.[22]

In his *Memoirs*, Pattison makes the point about authority even more strongly:

More than this, the abject deference fostered by theological discussion for authority, whether of the Fathers, or the Church, or the Primitive Ages, was incompatible with the free play of intellect which enlarges knowledge, creates science, and makes progress possible. In a word, the period of Tractarianism had been a period of obscurantism, which had cut us off from the general movement; an eclipse which had shut out the light of the sun in heaven. Whereas other reactions accomplished themselves by imperceptible degrees, in 1845 the darkness was dissipated, and the light was let in in an instant, as by the opening of the shutters in the chamber of a sick man who has slept until mid-day. Hence the flood of reform, which broke over Oxford in the next few years following 1845. . . . In these years every Oxford man was a Liberal. . . .[23]

Nevertheless, he is willing to admit that the raising of the issues by the Tractarians had an intellectual aspect; their discussions were 'yet water from the well of the mind.'[24] Two relevant events occurred in 1845; Newman's conversion to Rome and the condemnation by the Convocation of Oxford of W. G. Ward's *Idea of a Christian Church*. These led to the dissolution of the 'Oxford Movement' as a dominant party in university affairs. Pattison suggests that beneath this theological controversy a philosophical principle was at work; he is referring to the conflict between reason and authority. But it was not a simple conflict; Newman was not against reasoning. Having largely written Whately's *Logic*, he was no stranger to it. But it is in the way he uses reasoning that the trouble arises. Hume said about belief in the external world:

Nature has not left this to his choice, and has doubtless esteemed it an affair of too great importance, to be trusted to our uncertain reasonings and speculations. We may well ask, *What causes induce us to believe in the existence of body?* but it is in vain to ask, *Whether there be body or not?* That is a point which we must take for granted in all our reasonings.[25]

We have to assent, even though reasoning does not compel us. Similarly, Newman finds himself forced to believe in God, but the assent that men give as a result of the proofs is merely, like all such assent, notional. Real assent to the existence of God must come from experience, but for knowledge of God's attributes in detail only the authority of revelation as interpreted by a Church can be the source. Without this we are at the mercy of private interpretations of the scriptures. Pattison's implicit claim is that this mode of thought was inherent in Tractarianism; my point is somewhat different. I am suggesting, contrary to the more usual view, that in spite of Tractarian opposition to Benthamite Utilitarianism, there were elements of empiricism in some Tractarians, notably Newman. Certainly he was no follower of Kant. Hence Hegel's different approach to religion and to human experience in general might have seemed attractive to some opponents of Tractarianism.

Pattison, no friend to German thought, sketches the change in philosophical thinking as follows:

In the '30s, when the revolutionary enthusiasm rose to a height . . . in these years Whately's Logic, or some form of nominalism, predominated in the schools. When Tractarianism had made the clergy aware of their own strength, and high sacerdotal doctrines were openly proclaimed, we fell off from Whately, and vague, indefinite, realistic views under the influence of Coleridge and Sir William Hamilton slowly occupied the schools. They established themselves there in a more explicit form when Mansel, a Tory leader and arch-jobber, became the logical legislator of the school, and first introduced Kant into Oxford. But the High Church party received in Newman's secession a blow which for the moment seemed fatal to their cause. Coincident with this, was the appearance of Mill's great work, and Oxford repudiated at once sacerdotal principles and Kantian logic . . . . For more than a quarter of this century Mill and nominalistic views reigned in the schools. But gradually the clerical party rallied their forces, and since the Franco-German war have been advancing upon us with rapid strides. This fresh invasion of sacerdotalism had been accompanied by a renewed attempt to accredit an *a priori* logic, though in a less cumbrous form than the Kantian, bristling as that does with postulates and assumptions. . . . What is curious is that this new *a priori* metaphysic, whoever gave it shape in Germany, was imported into Oxford by a staunch Liberal, the late Professor Green. This anomaly can only be accounted for by a certain puzzle-headedness on the part of the Professor, who was removed from the scene before he had time to see how eagerly the Tories began to carry off his honey to their hive.[26]

Pattison writes as an opponent of the High Church, and his account is hence somewhat distorted. Whately's *Logic* was published in 1826, and Tractarianism was formally established in 1833. There seems no reason to connect it with the neo-Kantian views of Sir

William Hamilton, nor does it seem that he had great influence on Oxford philosophy, though Mansel certainly was his follower. Part of the difficulty here is the fact that Mansel had little philosophical significance, however great his influence may have been during his life. Pattison does not mention Jowett's contribution, and he is wrong to claim that Idealism was Tory in character, or that it served the High Church party; Tractarianism had tried to solve the spiritual and religious problems of the day by a return to older modes of thought. Idealism coped with the same problems by looking forward. In much of what he says here, Pattison is engaged in fighting the battles of Oxford; as Jowett's rival he could hardly give him much credit. Indeed, part of the article on 'Philosophy in Oxford' is concerned with an attack on the teaching of the subject and its results in the examination room. Given the extent to which this improvement in standards was due to the work of Jowett, Pattison was unlikely to approve. It is significant that some of his charges could apply still; for example, that those answers to questions in the final examinations which seem most impressive when first read on closer attention turn out to be the result of a memory 'charged with generalized formulas, with expressions and solutions which are derived ready-made from the tutor. . . . The utmost that the student can acquire from the system is that he has learned to write in the newest style of thought, and to manipulate the phrases of the last popular treatise.'[27]

Though Jowett brought Hegel to Oxford, it is T. H. Green who is normally considered the first of the Anglo-Hegelians. There are several reasons for this, of which the chief is that Jowett has not been regarded as a philosopher, but rather as a classicist and educationalist. There is doubt about his central role in the reorganization of Oxford teaching. But a reading of the nearest thing to a philosophic work that he produced, the introductions to his translation of the dialogues of Plato, reveals familiar Anglo-Hegelian themes, and a detailed history of the movement would have to investigate those writings closely. Many of the arguments which occur in Green's ethical works are foreshadowed, sometimes in striking ways. Jowett seems even to be willing to contemplate the disappearance of the institution of private property:

There may come a time when the saying, 'Have I not a right to do what I will with my own,' may appear to be a barbarous relic of individualism.[28]

Hegel he sees as the successor to Plato:

But the nearest approach in modern philosophy to the universal science of Plato, is to be found in the Hegelian 'succession of moments in the unity of the idea.'[29]

Jowett's main achievement was the elevation of Balliol to the foremost rank of Oxford Colleges, an elevation which was not unconnected with his espousal of Anglo-Hegelian doctrines. From the books published by Oxford writers after about 1860 it certainly appears as if the philosophical scene was dominated by Anglo-Hegelianism, though this domination was by no means complete. There was the long-standing quarrel between Jowett and Mark Pattison, which ensured that the latter was against both the reform of teaching methods and the new philosophical tendencies, as the quotation on p. 15 above demonstrates. That an undercurrent of the old empiricism persisted in Oxford can be seen by the fact that Bradley and Nettleship both failed to obtain first-class degrees in 1869, apparently because the examiners were shocked that they should discard the language of Mill for that of Kant, Hegel and Green.[30]

Green went up to Balliol in 1855, and became a fellow in 1860; he died in 1882, though in that period he had an enormous influence both on philosophical thought and on the structure of education. There is no space here to discuss his educational reforms, though it is perhaps a pleasing irony that one of the staunchest opponents of the Anglo-Hegelians, Cook-Wilson, only obtained a place in Oxford as a result of a scholarship scheme instituted by Jowett and Green.[31] But his educational views, his belief that all should be able to obtain an education suited to their talents regardless of their financial situation, were integrally linked to his philosophic ones. There was no divorce between philosophy and the rest of his thought. Collingwood remarks:

The school of Green sent out into public life a stream of ex-pupils who carried with them the conviction that philosophy, and in particular the philosophy they had learnt at Oxford, was an important thing, and that their vocation was to put it into practice. This conviction was common to politicians so diverse in their creed as Asquith and Milner, churchmen like Gore and Scott Holland, social reformers like Arnold Toynbee. . . . Through this effect on the minds of its pupils, the philosophy of Green's school might be found, from about 1880 to 1901, penetrating and fertilizing every part of the national life.[32]

I think it is impossible to understand the influence of the Anglo-Hegelians unless the social dimension of their thought is grasped. It was a philosophy that could be, and was intended to be, put into practice, and as such contrasts strikingly with the attitude later expressed by the self-styled 'revolutionaries,' whose effort to restore the subject to its empiricist roots led to an apparent neglect of philosophy's influence on society. This is ironic, in that Mill himself had been a reformer. A full history of the thought of the period would involve a detailed consideration of the complex relations between philosophy and politics.

There is no doubt that Green believed that real change could only come with the acceptance of Hegelian ideas. In a lecture entitled 'Popular Philosophy in its relation to Life,' he argued that thinking men were bound to find the doctrines of empiricism deficient, for they failed to deal with 'higher' feelings. Hence a sense of bafflement and weakness afflicts them. They can only find satisfaction in

a philosophy like that of Hegel, of which it was the expressed object to find formulae adequate to the action of reason as exhibited in nature and human society, in art and religion.[33]

He even harked back to Cromwell; he quoted Vane's words on the scaffold:

The people of England have long been asleep. I doubt they will be hungry when they awake.

adding:

They have slept, we may say, another two hundred years. If they should wake and be hungry, they will find their food in ideas which, with much blindness and weakness, he [Cromwell] vainly offered them, cleared and ripened by a philosophy of which he did not dream.[34]

He was not averse to contemplating revolutionary action:

It was partly no doubt as a symptom of warlike feeling that he disliked the formation of the volunteer rifle corps, but also because he regarded it as hostile to the people. 'Fools talk at Oxford of its being desirable in order that the gentry may keep down the chartists in the possible contingency of a rising. I should like to learn the use of the arm that I might be able to desert to the people if it came to such a pass. After all we do not know what may arise from the hunger produced by a European War.'[35]

It is sometimes argued that Green was not really a Hegelian. In his philosophical writings, Kant is cited more often than Hegel, and he is reported to have said of the latter's work that it would all have to be done over again. He even described some of the writings as a *'Wirrwarr'* or chaos, and advised readers to 'sit loose to the dialectical method,' though he prefaced this by saying that readers cannot 'drink too deep of Hegel.' We of the present generation of philosophers are accustomed to accept Kant and reject or ignore Hegel. The Anglo-Hegelians tended to regard them as closely related, though it is probably not quite correct to gloss *The Secret of Hegel* as 'Read Kant,' as is said to have been done by one baffled reader. It is clear that Green felt that Hegel was the more important figure, however many difficulties he discovered in him, and however attractive he found the thought of Kant. In a sense, it might be said that it was the idea of Hegel, rather than his actual doctrines, which was important to him. In 'Philosophy at Oxford,' Pattison commented at length on the Green and Grose edition of the works of Hume. He was critical of the format of the book, saying that Green's 300 pages of introduction out of a total of 560 was disproportionate, and was so hostile and destructive as to convince the reader he need never look at the *Treatise* again. But, he continues, a closer examination reveals that Green's aim in demolishing Locke, Berkeley and Hume was really to attack 'the theory of our popular logic,' represented by Mill. He concludes by saying that Green, under the 'disguise of an introduction,' has in fact issued a declaration of war 'from an idealist point of view, against the reigning empiricist logic.'[36] It is noteworthy that Pattison realized that logic was the area in which the main philosophical battle was to be fought.

Green had been teaching in Oxford for five years before the publication of Stirling's *The Secret of Hegel,* a book which is often thought to mark the beginnings of Anglo-Hegelianism. Its main effect may well have occurred outside Oxford, which has always been more influenced by the spoken word of its own teachers. In any case, it was not a book that was likely to be popular; many found it unreadable, and it is certainly written in a spirit of enthusiasm which often conceals the author's sense. It was early said: 'Whatever Hegel's secret was, Stirling succeeded in keeping it.' Certainly Kant played an important role; Stirling talks of Hegel as having made explicit the concrete universal which was implicit in Kant, and of Hegel as being probably the only man who thoroughly understood him. He also had no doubts about the real purpose of Kant and Hegel:

Further, to preclude at once an entire sphere of objections, I remark that Kant and Hegel are the very reverse of the so-called 'German Party' (with which in England they are very generally confounded). It is the express mission of Kant and Hegel, in effect, to replace the *negative* of that party, by an *affirmative:* or Kant and Hegel – all but wholly directly both, and one of them quite wholly directly – have no object but to restore Faith – Faith in God – Faith in the Immortality of the Soul and the Freedom of the Will – nay, Faith in Christianity as the Revealed Religion – and that, too, in perfect harmony with the Right of Private Judgment, and the Rights, or Lights, or Mights of Intelligence in general.[37]

By the 'German Party' Stirling is referring to those influenced by the work of Strauss, Feuerbach and Bauer, the 'Tubingen School.' George Eliot had translated Strauss's *Leben Jesu,* published in 1835, in 1846, and Feuerbach's *Das Wesen des Christentums,* published in 1841, in 1854. It is interesting that the books of two of Hegel's students should precede the arrival of the works of their teacher, particularly when Feuerbach could be seen to oppose Hegel in many ways. It is clear that Stirling's 'Hegel' was a rather different figure from that of Green and his followers. Bosanquet actually says in a letter:

I should not like to say it in public, but I am convinced that Stirling never understood Hegel. I remember something of his attitude towards the Logic wh. makes me feel sure of this, though I do not know his [Stirling's] writings as well as I ought. Apart from this old superstition of the 'other world' I can see no earthly reason for placing the raison d'etre of our life in some of the organa by which it is known.[38]

Thus there was an ambiguity in the way Hegel was seen by those who looked to him as a solution to problems both of philosophy and of the Victorian Age, an ambiguity which is invisible to those who look back on the period from the point of view of Moore's and Russell's attack on the Anglo-Hegelian tradition. The position is complicated by the growing professionalism of philosophy. It has been said that Green was 'certainly the first Fellow of his College and possibly the first of his University to conceive of himself as a professional philosopher.'[39] The foundation of the journal *Mind* in 1876 is evidence of this growing professionalism, though it should be remembered that it was a journal of philosophy *and* psychology, and then published as many articles on the latter as on the former topic. (Though *Mind* perhaps did not in its early years have quite the influence it later achieved; Bradley writes that in 1883 'he did not see *Mind* regularly.')[40] Ensor remarked: 'Whatever be the thought of the English Idealist school, which Green did so much to found, they at least conceived their task as one for fully trained and organised professionals, not for gifted but isolated amateurs.'[41] Nevertheless, T. M. Lindsay, in a review entitled 'Recent Hegelian contributions to English Philosophy' which discusses Caird on Kant and on Descartes, and Green and Grose on Hume, in *Mind* 1877, stressed the general nature of their view of philosophy. It is worth quoting him at length:

For, in spite of our practical character, English speculation has commonly found vent in the creation of a system or in the invention of theories rather than in the patient contemplation and description of a course of history. The fact that our English Hegelians write upon the history of philosophy rather than propound metaphysical theories for discussion may be an accident, but it reveals very clearly that in their eyes philosophy is not philosophy simply, but something more, that it is related to poetry, politics, history and science in a way that earlier English thinkers scarcely dreamed of. This relatedness of knowledge is coming to be a commonplace, and men far removed from Hegelian modes of thought are ready to declare that philosophy cannot be isolated as it was when Hamilton and Mill ruled over rival systems. The books I am now speaking of do not reveal this fact so openly as Dr Hutchinson Stirling's Secret of Hegel, where every now and then a side allusion, or a rapid paragraph, or a page of kaleidescope [sic], showed how philosophy was to the writer the one foundation of all the arts and sciences of human life.[42]

It is noteworthy that Lindsay regards the empiricist tradition as involving systematization, and the Anglo-Hegelians as in the opposite mould, that of 'patient contemplation and description.' It is also curious that he thinks of empiricism as a philosophy isolated from the real concerns of the world, though I presume this was how at least some of the Anglo-Hegelians regarded it. Perhaps this was due to the decline of its influence in philosophical circles. In Anglo-Hegelianism professionalism and a concern for 'questions about life in general and attitudes to life' were combined – a sufficient reason for later generations of 'minute philosophers' to ignore them. Thus though it may be true, as Collingwood claims, that the 'movement never in any sense dominated philosophical thought and teaching in Oxford,'[43] nevertheless their contribution both to philosophy and to public life was much greater than that of their more traditional contemporaries. Their influence in Oxford was diminished by the early deaths of some major Anglo-Hegelians which left an intellectual gap to be filled by their opponents. Green died in 1882, aged 46, Nettleship ten years later at the same age, and Wallace was killed in a bicycle accident in 1897 aged 53. Of course it could be argued that the non-Hegelian fellows of Oxford were the more typical, in that they represented a tradition that had long existed, of being philosophers concerned with the subject and not with any influence it might have on the world outside. 'Professionalism' is normally thought of as a way of ensuring standards of integrity among practitioners whose expertise cannot easily be judged by the public they serve. There is an ambiguity in the claims of Ryle and Warnock for philosophic professionalism, because it is not clear what 'service to the public' they expect philosophers to provide. It sometimes seems that the 'growing professionalism' involved an exclusive attention to the internal concerns of the subject.

For the Anglo-Hegelians and their ideas had a public influence, and to see why this was it is necessary to look again at the tangled religious story of the nineteenth century. I have already mentioned the shock of Newman's conversion to Rome. This, together with the difficulties for all Christian denominations in coming to terms with the changes in life caused by the rapid industrialization of Britain, led some to seek another path. One option was that of science; the success of the physical sciences led to the growth of what has become known as 'Victorian Naturalism,' a belief that the universe was explicable in purely physical terms. This belief received a powerful stimulus from the publication of Darwin's *Origin of Species* in 1859, which removed one of the last defences of the standard theistic view. For many the evidence of science against

Christianity was joined by the influence of the German school of biblical criticism, springing from Strauss's pioneer work. This claimed that the Bible was a book which could be studied like any other historical document and contained the kinds of errors to be expected in an earlier and less cultivated age. Jesus was 'naturalized' in the same way that the living world had been by Darwin. For some the transition to atheism was accomplished without any great feeling of loss; the thought of 'rational improvement,' unhampered by outworn dogmas, seemed a sufficient substitute. For others the evidence either of science or of Strauss and his followers was overwhelming, but the loss of faith in a traditional Christianity left an unsatisfied demand for spiritual consolation.

It was to this group that Hegel, or at least his thought as interpreted by the Anglo-Hegelians, mainly appealed. An important contemporary document of this is Mrs Humphry Ward's novel *Robert Elsmere*. The hero's spiritual guide is Mr Grey, a thinly disguised Green. Elsmere, a country parson, loses his faith in orthodox Christianity as a result of contact with the local squire, Wendover, a figure probably modelled on Mark Pattison. Wendover uses analysis of the nature of evidence and testimony to destroy the literary and historical basis of biblical faith. Grey convinces Elsmere, in the hour of his crisis, that a philosophical faith, which cannot be disproved on evidential grounds, is what he needs. The message could be put in the form 'the spiritual world is within the natural, not beyond it.' A classic exposition of this view is found in the later paper by Bosanquet, 'On the True Conception of Another World.'[44] Supernaturalism was rejected by the Anglo-Hegelians because, in Caird's words, 'the world of intelligence and freedom cannot be different from the world of nature and necessity; it can only be the same world seen in a new light, or subjected to a further interpretation.'[45] Bradley himself expressed respect for Christianity in several places, but seems not to have believed in 'life after death' (cf. 'The Evidences of Spiritualism', *CE,* pp. 595–617, and *AR,* pp. 444–52). Idealism of the Anglo-Hegelian form hence found no difficulty in justifying action in the world as a form of spirituality.

It also found no problem in reconciling Darwin with its philosophic outlook. Wallace finds the key to the problem of logic to be the same that led Darwin to his theory of the origin of species: 'Philosophy, in short, is to the general growth of intelligence what artificial breeding is to the variation of species under natural conditions.'[46] In the passage from which I have quoted, Wallace gives a brief summary, in Darwinian terms, of Hegel's logical system. Just as the variation in domestic species of animals which are induced by the breeder give a pointer to the process of natural selection in the wild, so the 'history of philosophy is the conscious evolution of what for the far greater part is transacted in the silent workshops of nature.' Earlier systems of philosophy are stages on the way to the present and hence encapsulate the development of human thought in general. Wallace thus interprets the structure of Hegel's logical writings as in essence historical. The reason why the *Science of Logic* begins with the concept of 'Being' is that this is the simplest and most primitive idea, one appropriate for the first thinkers, the pre-Socratics. Subsequent philosophies are developments and elaborations of it, and the task of the logician lies in showing what elements are preserved and what rejected in the evolution of logic, the major part of philosophy, up to the present. Although Hegel himself did not accept the idea of natural evolution for the world of non-human living things, the Anglo-Hegelians found no difficulty in 'darwinizing' him, because as far as human development was concerned, he did accept evolution. Perhaps the high point of this reconciliation was marked by the publication in 1893 of a book by D. G. Ritchie under the title *Darwin and Hegel.* A more contemporary version of the attitude to religion adopted by the Anglo-Hegelians is provided by the work of the 'Swansea School,' although their starting point is different. 'Victorian Naturalism' had another direct effect on philosophy; it encouraged its assimilation to natural science, with standards of mathematical rigour. There is, however, no reason to believe that this latest attempt to 'set philosophy on the sure path of a science' has been any more successful than earlier ones. I will only remark that the abandonment or rejection of Anglo-Hegelianism was not the result of the discovery of fallacies in its arguments; these were seldom directly confronted by the self-styled 'revolutionaries.'

There is more to be said on the relations between the thought of the later Victorian era and the Anglo-Hegelians; I have merely tried to indicate something of its actual history in order to show that it was no accident that Hegel came to Britain when he did, nor that his work was enthusiastically received. More central to the purpose of this book is the way Hegelianism and professionalism went together, and, as I will show in the next chapter, logic was central here. I have concentrated on the situation in Oxford for two reasons. First, Anglo-Hegelianism did not substantially affect Cambridge, with its more scientific tradition and hence distance from the major theological quarrels of the century. Second, until the time of Russell and Moore, Cambridge philosophy had little influence on Oxford. Also, the importance of philosophy was greater at Oxford, as can be seen from the number of philosophy teachers there, both then and now.

APPENDIX

I reproduce here two examination papers, both from the Second Public Examination for the Honours School of Philosophy, Politics and Economics. The first was set in 1942, the second in 1948. In each case candidates had to answer four questions. The title of both papers is 'General Philosophy from Descartes to the Present Time.'

SECOND PUBLIC EXAMINATION

Honour School of Philosophy, Politics, and Economics

GENERAL PHILOSOPHY FROM DESCARTES TO THE PRESENT TIME

[Candidates are recommended to answer **four** *questions.]*

1. 'Oh what a dusty answer gets the soul
   When hot for certainty in this our life!'
Was Descartes' search for infallible certainty a mistake ?

2. Why did Descartes treat space and time so differently ?

3. How far is Locke's criticism of innate ideas a criticism of Descartes ?

4. 'Leibnitz was preoccupied by the part played in the new physics by degrees of quality.' Explain and discuss.

5. Examine the problem with which Leibnitz was concerned in the distinction between the principle of contradiction and the principle of sufficient reason.

6. Was Locke's plain historical method as plain and as purely descriptive as he made it out to be ?

7. Discuss Spinoza's view of the relation between mind and body.

8. 'Berkeley turned the simple fact that we cannot see a thing without seeing it into the unwarranted assertion that by seeing a thing we bring it into being.' Discuss this criticism.

9. If we argue that the mind is not so creative as Berkeley maintains or so passive as Hume maintains, is there a tenable via media ?

10. What is Hume's doctrine in regard to space, and what difficulties does it present ?

3 K 14   **Turn over.**

11. What in Berkeley's view is the *esse* of time, and what answer to this question do you think his doctrine requires ?

12. 'If Kant limited reason to make room for faith, Hume limited reason to make room for "nature".' What is the difference ?

13. 'What is wrong with most so-called empiricists is not their empiricism but their *a priori* account of the facts of perception.' Does this apply to Hume ?

14. Discuss the influence on modern philosophy of the prevalence of the historical rather than of the scientific point of view.

15. Examine the importance of system in scientific thought.

[*T. T.* 1942.]

SECOND PUBLIC EXAMINATION

Honour School of Philosophy, Politics, and Economics

GENERAL PHILOSOPHY FROM DESCARTES TO THE PRESENT TIME

*[Candidates are recommended to answer **four** questions.]*

1. What light does a study of economics throw on the part played by deduction in an empirical science?

2. What is mysticism? Is it always reprehensible in a philosopher?

3. In what sense is it correct to say that we cannot know anything about substance?

4. Is it important to distinguish time from duration?

5. Could statistics provide any evidence as to whether you will be a smoker or a non-smoker in June 1949?

6. 'The phrase "the self" hardly occurs in ordinary speech.' Has this any relevance to the philosophical problem of the self?

7. Can I see anything without having a sense-datum?

8. 'There exist no certain marks by which the state of waking can ever be distinguished from sleep' (DESCARTES). How do you know that you are awake now?

9. Was Descartes right in maintaining that the mind is more easily known than the body?

10. 'The greatest part of the questions and controversies that perplex mankind depend on the doubtful and uncertain use of words' (LOCKE). Should clarification be the primary aim of philosophical thinking?

11. 'Berkeley degraded bodies to mere illusion' (KANT). Is this a fair criticism of Berkeley's view?

12. 'It is not true that two substances may be exactly alike and differ only numerically' (LEIBNIZ). Can this be proved?

13. 'Every simple idea has a simple impression that resembles it' (HUME). What is the importance of this contention?

4 Q 12   [*T. T.* 1948.]

NOTES

1 London, 1956.
2 *The Revolution in Philosophy,* London, 1956, p. 7.
3 Ibid., p. 4.
4 Ibid., pp. 3–4.
5 Ibid., p. 4.
6 *English Philosophy since 1900,* Oxford, 1958, pp. 168–9.
7 *The Idea of a University,* London, 1889, p. 145.
8 *Memoirs,* London, 1885, p. 244.
9 Ibid., p. 93.
10 Ibid., p. 232.
11 H. L. Mansel, *Phrontisterion or, Oxford in the 19th Century,* in *Letters, Lectures and Reviews,* ed. H. W. Chandler, London, 1873, p. 400.
12 Ibid., p. 401.
13 *A Hundred Years of Philosophy,* London, 1957, p. 49.
14 London, 1931.
15 G. Faber, *Life of Benjamin Jowett,* London, 1957, p. 178.
16 *The Night Battle,* London, 1962.
17 *The Secret of Hegel,* London, 1898, p. xxii.
18 *Mind,* 1876, p. 84.
19 Ibid., p. 86.
20 Ibid., p. 86.
21 Ibid., p. 85.
22 Letter of 31 August 1865, E. Abbott and L. Campbell, *Jowett,* London, 1897, vol. I, pp. 412–13.
23 *Memoirs,* pp. 238–9.
24 *Mind,* 1876, p. 86.
25 *Treatise,* bk I, pt IV, sect. ii.
26 *Memoirs,* pp. 165–7.
27 *Mind,* 1876, pp. 92–4.
28 *The Dialogues of Plato,* Oxford, 1871, vol. II, p. 142*.
29 Ibid., p. 158*.
30 Cf. A. E. Taylor, *Proceedings of the British Academy,* 1926.
31 *Statement and Inference,* ed. A. S. L. Farquharson, Oxford, 1926, pp. xxiii–xxiv.
32 *Autobiography,* London, 1944, p. 17.
33 *Works of T. H. Green,* London, 1980, ed. R. L. Nettleship, vol. III, p. 125.
34 Ibid., p. ix.
35 Nettleship in ibid., p. xxiv.
36 *Mind,* 1876, pp. 93–6.
37 *The Secret of Hegel,* p. xii.
38 *Bernard Bosanquet and his Friends,* ed. J. H. Muirhead, London, 1935, pp. 52–3. The letter was written in 1886.
39 Melvin Richter, *The Politics of Conscience,* London, 1964, p. 140.
40 *Principles of Logic,* p. 516.
41 *England 1870–1914,* Oxford, 1936, p. 162.

42 *Mind*, 1877, p. 477.
43 *Autobiography*, p. 16.
44 *Essays and Addresses*, London, 1889.
45 *Hegel*, London, 1883, p. 131.
46 *Prolegomena*, Oxford, 1874, p. cx.

II

Hegel and Formal Logic

It is significant for the development of philosophy in Britain in the nineteenth century that it was Hegel's logical writings which first commanded attention among philosophers, rather than his other works. Jowett, the most important figure in this importation, tried to translate the *Science of Logic* with the aid of his friend Temple. He talks of the work as 'in sight of being finished' in 1849, though the translation was abandoned in that year, for reasons which are not clear. The manuscript subsequently disappeared.[1] The first published translation of Hegel in English, though it was from a French version rather than the original German, appeared in 1855; it was entitled *The Subjective Logic of Hegel.*[2] In spite of the claim on the title page, it turns out to be a free rendering of the second volume of the *Science of Logic,* rather than a translation in the strict sense. In the preface, the translator Sloman talks of it as:

cette analyse de Hegel, qui devint alors une véritable traduction dans laquelle toutes les idées, sinon toutes les phrases du philosophe, sont fidèlement et scrupuleusement reproduites.

The words and phrases are Hegel's, but their ordering is not; it is a simplified version of the original. Without a detailed comparison, it would be hard to realize this, for the book begins with the apparent author talking in *propria persona.* However, it is perhaps historically important, for it contains the unfortunate rendering of *'Begriff'* as 'notion,' though at least the word is not capitalized, as soon after became the custom. This translation has done much philosophical harm, for although 'notion' can be legitimately used to render the German, it carries in modern English overtones of vagueness which are quite foreign to Hegel's use of the word *'Begriff.'*

Stirling's *The Secret of Hegel* also contains translations from the *Science of Logic,* with some additional material from the *Encyclopaedia.* The whole of section 1 of the first volume of the former, entitled 'Quality,' is translated and accompanied by a detailed commentary. Then there is a 'summary or translation, commented and interpreted' of section 2. The first scholarly and complete version of any portion of Hegel's writings on logic is the *Logic of Hegel,* published by Wallace in 1874; this comprises the first part of the *Encyclopaedia,* together with 'Prolegomena' of 184 pages, which 'seek to remove certain obstacles and to render Hegel less tantalizingly hard to those who approach him for the first time.' A second edition, with the 'Prolegomena' increased in size and published separately, was produced in 1894. It remains among the better introductions to Hegel. In the preface, Wallace explains that he found the *Science of Logic* too formidable to translate, though it was the 'more valuable and comprehensive work.' The only other text of Hegel available in English at this time was Sibree's translation of the *Lectures on the Philosophy of History,* published in 1857. Bradley's first published work was a pamphlet entitled 'The Presuppositions of Critical History,' but the earlier Anglo-Hegelians did not pay much attention to the topic.

Hegel was regarded in Britain primarily as a logician; this determines the ground on which the philosophical battles were fought in the second half of the century. Its importance can perhaps be seen by comparing the situation in England with that in France, where Hegel arrived much later, in the 1930s and as the author of the *Phenomenology.* This text fitted well with another German influence which was growing, the phenomenological, in Husserl's sense of the term. Hence there arose the 'existentialized' Hegel of Sartre and Merleau-Ponty. The French neo-Hegelians, if they can be called such, paid little attention to the *Science of Logic* or to the *Encyclopaedia.* In England the *Phenomenology* appears to have been somewhat neglected by those interested in Hegel, and was not translated until 1910.

The study of logic had already been raised to a central philosophical position by the appearance of 1843 of Mill's *System of Logic.* Its popularity is shown by the fact that it went through eight editions in Mill's lifetime. He made it clear in his correspondence and later in his *Autobiography* that the aim of the book was to put 'metaphysical and moral science' on a 'basis of analysed experience' in opposition to the German school:

The German or *a priori* view of human knowledge and of the knowing faculties is likely for some time longer . . . to predominate. . . . But the 'System of Logic' supplies what was much wanted, a textbook of the opposite school – that which derives all knowledge from experience. . . .[3]

This refers to an earlier importation from Germany, the neo-Kantian philosophy made popular by Coleridge and Carlyle. Mill appears to have been ignorant of Hegel, or not to have regarded him as of any importance, at this stage of his career. However, when he did read him, he found him contemptible:

Besides these, I have been toiling through Stirling's *Secret of Hegel*. It is right to learn what Hegel is and one learns it only too well from Stirling's book. I say too well because I have found by actual experience of Hegel that conversancy with him tends to deprave one's intellect. . . . For some time after I had finished the book all such words as *reflexion, development, evolution* etc., gave me a sort of sickening feeling which I have not yet entirely got rid of.[4]

The necessity encountered in pure mathematics and pure physics seemed to establish that *a priori* knowledge existed. Mill attempted to explain this necessity in terms of experience, relying on the doctrine of association of ideas. Because of the increasing import-ance of science and the manner in which he provided its foundation, his work had great influence. Wallace later expressed the position:

So the advancing sciences of modern times looked upon the Inductive Logic of Mill in the light of a new revelation. . . . The enormous influence of the physical sciences saw itself reflected in a distinct logical outline: and the new logic became the dominant philosophy.[5]

Wallace thought that Hegel's logic would replace that of Mill. Wallace was writing in 1873, but it seems that his motive was the same as led an earlier generation of Anglo-Hegelians to concentrate on Hegel's logical writings. Mill's reply to the Kantians consisted in a denial that logic was formal. Curiously, his criticism of Kant is not so remote from Hegel's, though Mill is hardly likely to have realized this from a reading of Stirling's book.

Kant has, however, an importance in the history of logic which has seldom been realized. For he made the distinction between form and matter central to his philosophy, and hence gave formal logic a dominant role in philosophy. A section of the *Kritik der reinen*

Vernunft was entitled 'Transcendental Logic.' He also published in 1800 a textbook on logic. For him logic was no longer a mere organon or instrument, but part of the essence of mind. Leibniz was clearly a greater logician; indeed, Kant was not really interested in its formal aspect. But Leibniz's logical works were not widely known until the beginning of the twentieth century, so he has no place in the history of logic in the nineteenth century.

The title of this chapter may have struck some readers as odd, for it is often thought that Hegel substituted 'dialectics' for the traditional logic. There is no space to spell out the erroneous nature of such a view here; it springs from a failure to attend closely to Hegel's writings. The conventional view of dialectic states that all thought is organized in triads. Some of Hegel's chapters are divided into three parts, but others are not; the discussion of judgment has four sections. Both in the *Science of Logic* and in the corresponding sections of the *Encyclopaedia,* he devoted much attention to the old logic and by no means rejected it *in toto.* He agreed with Kant on the 'Mistaken Subtlety of the Four Syllogistic Figures' as the latter entitled an early essay, and also on the importance of logic for philosophy. His aim was to substitute logic for metaphysics:

Logic in our sense coincides with metaphysics, the science of things in a setting of thoughts.[6]

Kant, he thought, had revolutionized philosophy, but had not succeeded in solving all problems, for he was left with an apparently unbridgeable gulf between the subject, the knower, and the real object, the 'thing-in-itself.' Part of the aim of the *Science of Logic* is to show that there is no such gulf.

The book itself has a twofold structure, being divided into three parts and also into two volumes. The parts are entitled 'Being,' 'Essence' and 'Concept.' The first volume, 'Objective Logic,' contains the sections on 'Being' and 'Essence.' The second volume is called the 'Subjective Logic.' It is in this section that the discussion of formal logic occurs. Though it is no part of my intention to give a commentary on the whole work, it is perhaps worth pointing out that the first volume is called 'Objective' because it traces, though without detailed references to named thinkers, the history of philosophy up to the time of Kant. It is for this reason that it begins with 'Being,' the first concept dealt with in pre-Socratic thought. When the subject, or knower, becomes central to philosophy as it does with Kant, the stage of the concept has been reached.

The justification for the inclusion of this chapter in the book is that Hegel's treatment of formal logic is followed by both Bradley and Bosanquet. Here it is only this element of the *Science of Logic* that concerns me; there are numerous other features of his treatment that would need to be considered in a full discussion. Bosanquet is closer to Hegel in detail, but it is often hard to see why Bradley says what he does without being aware of the Hegelian background. It is also clear that Bradley has no truck with 'dialectic' conceived as the 'identity of opposites' (cf. *PL,* p. 410), and that the major part of his treatment of logic involves no special apparatus. The same applies to Hegel's treatment of formal logic. In both cases there are normal philosophical arguments about problems of inference, etc. Like other philosophical arguments, it is seldom possible to formalize them. As with other philosophers, the reader is going to disagree from time to time; Hegel and Bradley are no more immune to error than anyone else. But because the argument cannot easily be put into standard forms, either of the old or of the new logic, there is no reason to believe that a new method is employed.

Hegel agreed with Locke that men were able to reason before the invention or discovery of formal logic, just as they breathe and digest their food without any knowledge of anatomy or of physiology. Logic is implicit in everyday language, which is also the 'essence of mind:'

The forms of thought are, in the first instance, displayed and stored in human *language*. . . . Into all that becomes something inner for man, such as a thought or idea, into all that he makes his own, language has penetrated . . . logic is his natural element, indeed his own peculiar nature. If nature as such, the physical world, is contrasted with the mental sphere, then logic must be said to be something above nature which permeates every relation of man to nature, his sensation, intuition, desire, need, instinct and by doing so transforms it into something human. . . .[7]

Hence there was something correct about the traditional logic, in spite of the subtleties that rendered it 'universally tedious and disgusting,' to use Hegel's expression. These subtleties are the result of attempting to 'mechanize' thought, to make it into something to be learnt by rote, just as mathematical tables are. Hegel thought that mathematics was entirely different from logic:

> In concrete philosophical studies, philosophy must take its logical element from logic, not from mathematics. It is only a makeshift of philosophical incapacity which, instead of finding the logical element in philosophy, looks to the forms it takes in other sciences. Such forms are only presentiments or atrophied versions of the logical. Further, the use of such borrowed forms is purely external. Their use needs to be preceded by an awareness of their meaning and value, which can only come from reflecting on them, not from the authority of mathematics.[8]

Mathematics is of little use in education; it is possible to construct calculating machines, which shows that calculation is itself mechanical. Logic, as Hegel conceived it, involved mental activity. If it was to replace metaphysics, it could not be something to be learnt by rote.

Hegel thinks that 'formal logic' involves an unsatisfactory division between 'form' and 'content.' We are accustomed to the distinction expressed in this way; earlier it would have been between 'form' and 'matter.' Farquharson, in a note to Cook-Wilson's *Statement and Inference,* suggests that 'content' is a 'translation-word,' a rendering of the German *'Inhalt'* and is hence 'likely to be found in the later English Idealists.'[9] The normal English form was 'contents.' The *Oxford Dictionary* lists it as first occurring in this sense in 1845, oddly enough in a work by Mark Pattison. In the Introduction to the *Science of Logic* Hegel regards the distinction between form and content as equivalent to a separation between truth and certainty. The reference is to Kant and the notion of the Categories as 'forms' which can be 'filled' with the 'material' of intuition. Hegel regards this as a 'mechanical' method of combining two 'constituents.' It can give certainty, but cannot, on Kant's own admission, give truth, because things-in-themselves are unknowable. A logic which will enable men to reach truth needs to be of a different kind, and this is what Hegel aims to provide.

Here, however, I am only interested in the way in which he deals with formal logic. The 'Subjective Logic' is primarily concerned with the nature of conceptual thought. Readers of English translations may be misled by over-pedantic translations; it appears that Hegel frequently talks of 'the concept' as if there were just one. In fact, *'der Begriff'* can often be rendered 'a concept.' It is noteworthy that he does not deal with words or concepts in this section, as did most previous writers on Formal Logic. Here he departs from Kant, whom he otherwise seems to follow. And in this he is copied by Bradley, who begins the *Principles of Logic* with a chapter entitled 'The General Nature of Judgment.'*

Hegel distinguishes between judgments and sentences or propositions. The latter are isolated assertions or bare facts, perhaps mere reports of sense-experience. A judgment, on the other hand, is a pronouncement that has a wider basis, the result of a process of investigation. One paradigm would be the judgment delivered by a judge after weighing up the evidence presented in court. Logic is concerned with judgments, not with propositions, i.e. with what someone is prepared to assert after thinking about a topic. That a set of words constitutes a judgment cannot be discovered from examining just its grammatical structure; attention must be paid to its connection with other judgments. In the last resort, there is no great gulf between judgment and inference. A judgment gains its significance from its context. Hegel extends this version of the 'contextual principle' to individual terms; if words have meanings on their own, it becomes hard to see how they can be combined to make significant wholes. A judgment is a unity, something which is concealed by the 'linear' pattern of previous logicians, who believed that words existed independently of judgments, and judgments independently of inferences. What can be understood is a piece of discourse as a whole.† If, as Hegel claims, meaning depends on a larger unit than the single word it is difficult to find a stopping place; the search extends ever wider. Ultimately only totality, 'Absolute Knowledge,' makes sense. It is a logical principle, the search for meaning, that forces Hegel to the conclusion that many have found 'metaphysical.' Bradley accepts that Absolute Knowledge is an ideal, though he finally says in the *Principles of Logic* that it is unattainable.

Traditional logicians thought of the copula as a device for uniting words into propositions; it was the source of their unity. Hence the

---

* Bosanquet begins his *Logic* with a discussion of concepts, but he introduces what he has to say by remarking that it is impossible to separate the formation of concepts from their use in judgments, and he spends some time in criticizing Lotze for his failure to realize this.

† This point is discussed at greater length in connection with Bradley in chapter IV below.

talk of 'ascribing a predicate to a subject,' which implies that it is something we do. Hegel objects:

When we say 'This rose is red' or 'The picture is beautiful,' we do not mean that from the outside we attach redness or beauty to the rose or the picture, but that these characteristics belong to the objects.[10]

Judgment is a determination of the object itself, not the result of our actions. The simplest form of judgment, such as 'This rose is red,' has the form 'The individual is the universal,' which is an analysis rather than a synthesis. This leads him to make the surprising remark:

Every thing is a judgment, i.e. an individual with a universal as its inner nature, or, alternatively, a universal which is individualised. Its universality and its individuality can be distinguished, but they are one and the same.[11]

He denies that the form 'The individual is the universal' implies that the subject is concrete and the predicate abstract. The subject must possess other qualities besides that mentioned by the predicate, and therefore must be richer and wider. On the other hand, the predicate is a universal and so exists whether or not the particular subject does. So it could be seen as more real. A substance is sometimes considered to be that which can only appear in the subject position in a proposition. Hegel suggests that the predicate may be more substantial, have a higher ontological status:

The word God is by itself a senseless sound, a mere name; only the predicate says what He is and fills the name with content and meaning; the empty beginning only becomes actual knowledge at the end.*

If the game of superiority can be played either way, it is a sign of its unimportance.

Judgments can be arranged on a scale, from the simplest, such as 'This rose is red,' up to 'conceptual judgments.' Hegel takes his classification from Kant's *Logic,* though most philosophers will be

---

* *Phenomenology of Mind,* S, vol. 3, pp. 26–7. Hegel says that proper names are 'meaningless in the sense that they express no universal, hence they appear to be imposed arbitrarily. Indeed, proper names can be assumed, bestowed and even altered at will' (S, vol. 5, p. 126).

more familiar with the table in the *Critique of Pure Reason* (A.70). The difference between them is that Kant thought every judgment could be classified in respect of one of the three moments falling under each of the four divisions of Quantity, Quality, Relation and Modality. Hegel alters Kant's order by putting Quality first. More important, he regards each of the four heads as constituting a distinct type of judgment, and the three Kantian moments under each head as species of those genera. Thus there are twelve different 'forms' of judgment, ranging from the lowest to the most complete. He also differs from Kant in thinking that form cannot be discovered by grammatical inspection; there is a logical difference between 'This wall is green' and 'Gold is a metal.' The latter comes higher in the scale because mere sense-experience is adequate for the discovery of the truth of the former. The latter is a piece of scientific knowledge whose verification involves other facts; it does not rest only on sense-experience. Hegel makes a similar point by contrasting the 'correctness' of propositions with the 'truth' of judgments. 'This wall is green' can be correct, but not true, whereas 'Gold is a metal' can be described as 'true.' He sometimes calls the former 'untrue' though never 'false.' Facts are relevant both to correctness and to truth, but the way in which they are relevant and the type of facts involved differs. His major criticism of the traditional logic is that, by relying on mere grammatical form, it failed to mark important differences between judgments, or between them and mere propositions.

'This wall is green' is low on the scale because the wall also has other properties, and other things are green. In such cases the subject and predicate touch, as it were, only at a single point; their relation is external. A negative judgment shows this, because 'The wall is not red' depends on the fact that it has some other colour, which implies a further judgment of the same kind. Thus these judgments are 'correct but untrue;' they do not express the essential nature of the subject. The same applies to the other two examples he gives, someone is sick or has committed a crime. The concept of the human body involves its proper functioning, sickness is a deviation. In disease the body is 'untrue to its essence;' explanation of disease requires reference to something external to the body. 'Real' judgments have an internal connection, a necessary link between their parts. It is for this reason that judgment and inference cannot be ultimately separated. Hegel rejects Kant's class of 'infinite' judgments, such as 'The mind is not an elephant.' They are as trivial as 'A lion is a lion.'

Singular judgments of reflection are of the form 'This plant is wholesome,' 'This body is elastic,' 'This punishment is deterrent.' They cannot rest on sense-perception, because to make them it is necessary to refer to other objects; mediation is already involved. To say of a plant that it is wholesome implies that others are not, so the singular judgment is connected with the particular, whose traditional form is 'some x's are y.' Similarly, a singular judgment may lead to a universal, as in 'Socrates is mortal,' the truth of which depends on mortality belonging to men as such. Here we are talking of the 'universal or kind (*Gattung*) without which these individuals would not exist at all.' The word '*Gattung*' is perhaps best translated as 'genus,' but in English versions of Marx it is often rendered 'species,' as in 'species-being' for '*Gattungwesen.*'

There is a natural transition from this type to Judgments of Necessity, for generic qualities which belong to all of a species can be expressed by 'Man is . . .' or 'The plant is . . .'. The necessary connection is shown by the fact that 'The tiger has four legs' is not refuted by the production of a three-legged tiger. Such an animal is deficient, which implies that a conceptual element was present in the original judgment. Judgments of Necessity are divided into Categorical, Hypothetical and Disjunctive. The categorical is of the form 'Gold is a metal.' Hegel thinks it the result of bad logical training to place this judgment on the same level as 'Gold is expensive.' He says: 'Gold remains the same as it was, though that external reference changes or passes away.' Gold would still be gold, and a metal, if it became as cheap as iron. Its price is a contingent feature, its metallicity a necessary one.

The inadequacy of categorical judgments arises from their incompleteness; there are other metals besides gold. Here it is possible to see that Hegel's idea of the systematic nature of knowledge is not imposed on the facts, but comes from the development of a science. If we discover that gold conducts electricity, we want to find whether all metals do, and then to discover what it is about metals that gives them this property. The scientist is not content with isolated facts, he strives to connect them. The logical forms of this connection are hypothetical and disjunctive judgments. Hegel expresses the hypothetical in the form 'If A exists, then B exists;' it is 'the connection of the two elements that is postulated, not their existence.' An example is 'If anything is a metal, then it conducts electricity.' We should not be misled by the appearance of the word 'exists' in Hegel's formulation, for the hypothetical is equivalent to an unrestricted universal, a point developed by Bradley. 'All men are mortal' looks as if it results from an examination of instances; 'if anything is a man then it is mortal' makes it obvious that a connection of attributes is at issue. Causal judgments are special cases of hypotheticals. Hegel claims that causal connections are necessary. The Hegelian sense of 'necessary' is not that of traditional logic. He does not argue that effects can be deduced from causes *a priori*. What he means by 'necessary' is to be gathered from a study of what he writes. All too often critics import their own meaning into the discussion. There is no space to expound the full sense Hegel gives to the word, but Bradley's discussion of inference is not unlike Hegel's, and so can serve to illustrate it. A hypothetical judgment is seen to be necessary when it is fully understood. Hegel admits that there are hypothetical judgments whose necessity we do not see, as when we know that *x* is always followed by *y*, so that we can predict *y*'s occurrence but cannot say why it occurs. But this is, for the scientist, not a position in which he can happily remain; he wants to discover the reason, or what makes the connection necessary.

Surprisingly Hegel completes this ascending series with disjunctive judgments. He takes their form to be '*A* is either *b* or *c*,' as in, to take a low-level example, 'The murderer is either Smith or Jones.' The evidence rules out all other possibilities, but does not point conclusively to either. Hegel rejects a truth-functional analysis; '*p* or *q*' is true because either *p* is true or *q* is true or both *p* and *q* are. The truth of the judgment about the murderer depends on the evidence as a whole, and it cannot be divided into two separate judgments. In its full form, a disjunctive judgment expresses the relation between genus and species (and vice versa). It contains all the species on the one hand, and the genus on the other. A judgment such as 'Metal is either tin or lead or. . .' presents an exhaustive analysis, in which the disjuncts are mutually exclusive and include all possibilities. When we are entitled to assert such a judgment, then the full concept of 'metal' has been achieved. Bosanquet developed Hegel's argument at length; he says:

The disjunction is therefore the only judgment-form that in strict theory can stand alone. All connection is within a system; and only that judgment is self-sufficing which affirms at once the system and the connections within it. I do not say that every disjunction is thus ultimately self-dependent, but relatively to the number of hypotheticals which have their truth within it every true disjunction has a substantive character.[12]

Hegel's final group are conceptual judgments. They are so named because they involve systematic wholes of the kind involved in disjunctive judgments. To understand something fully is to have grasped its concept. Hegel's treatment is unsatisfactory, and it is difficult to avoid the conclusion that he included them to correspond with the class 'Modality' in Kant's table. Kant thought that '*A* may be *B*' says less than '*A* is *B*.' Hegel, however, puts the assertoric form below the problematic, because bare assertion reduces a judgment to the level of subjective opinion. 'This action is good' is a possible expression of a conceptual judgment. It is inadequate because the reason for its goodness is not included in the expression of the judgment. Hence it can be regarded as equivalent to a bare assertion, though one at a different level, and consequently of a different logical form, to 'The wall is green.' He gives no example of a problematic judgment, and what he says about it is so obscure that it can be omitted. It would be possible to make the same point about apodeictic judgment; there is a sense, as so often with Hegel, that he has said all he wants to say about one topic and is anxious to get on with the next.

However, as Hegel claims it is the highest type of judgment, it is necessary to examine it:

The subject of the apodeictic judgment ('The house, if of such and such a character, is good;' 'the action, if of such and such a character, is just.') contains first the universal which it *ought* to be and second its character; the latter is a ground or reason why the predicate of the conceptual judgment belongs, or does not belong, to the whole of the subject, that is whether the subject does or does not correspond to its concept. Now this judgment is truly objective, i.e. is the truth of judgment in general.[13]

It is significant that Hegel uses teleological examples. A house can be viewed in many ways, as a collection of bricks, mortar and other material, as a physical object possessing a certain size and shape, etc. It can only be seen as a house by those who possess the concept 'house,' and this concept necessarily involves its purpose or function, i.e. what a house ought to be. This point receives further development in the chapter on Teleology later in the 'Subjective Logic.'* In Hegel's sense, apodeictic judgments are of a different logical form, though it is hard to see them as an improvement on other types. It is also difficult to see how a disjunctive could be transformed into an apodeictic judgment. The kind of necessity seems to have changed. Hegel thinks they form a link with inference; he says unity of subject and predicate has been made explicit in a concept, and so the copula has virtually disappeared. By this he means that it no longer even looks as if we were arbitrarily applying a predicate to a subject; the connection between the two terms of the judgment can be clearly seen. The unifying link is now a concept.

This is the middle term, the element which mediates between two others. Inference, Hegel says, is the rational and the whole of rationality. In the *Encyclopaedia* he even calls it 'the definition' of the Absolute.† He is critical of the traditional syllogisms. Of the (German) standard form:

Caius is a man,
All men are mortal,
Therefore Caius is mortal,

he remarks 'boredom immediately descends when such a syllogism is encountered.'[14] Nevertheless:

> Everything is an inference (or syllogism), a universal which is tied to individuality by particularity. But of course everything is not a whole consisting of three propositions.[15]

He renders the form of syllogisms by the letters *U, I* and *P*, standing for Universal, Individual and Particular. Thus the traditional first

---

* I have discussed this point in my 'Hegel's Teleology', Southampton University Philosophy Department Notes, 1980 (copies available from the Philosophy Department).

† There is a translation issue here; all the English translators of Hegel seem to translate '*der Schluss*' as 'syllogism.' There are grounds for this in some places, where Hegel is discussing the syllogism of traditional logic, but in other places it would seem better to use 'inference,' which is the wider term. All syllogisms are inferences, but not all inferences are syllogisms. I have used whichever translation seemed appropriate to the context.

figure becomes *I–P–U*. He is interested in the order of mediation only, and not in the distribution of terms. Bosanquet points out[16] that this way of expressing an argument is similar to Locke's:

If we will observe the actings of our own minds, we shall find that we reason best and clearest when we only observe the connection of the proof, without reducing our thoughts to any rule of syllogism.

Locke's examples are 'Homo–Animal–Vivens,' 'Punishment–Just–Guilt.'[17] So *I–P–U* could be rendered, in the case of Caius, 'Caius–Man–Mortal.' This brings out the nature of the connection, i.e. that everything exists is individual, but any individual is a particular sort of individual, a member of a species, and the species is a member of a genus. It is as a member of the species 'man' that Caius is mortal.

Hegel's detailed treatment of the traditional doctrine parallels that he gave for judgments. The Qualitative Syllogism is the one in logic books. The first figure, *I–P–U*, represents a normal mode of reasoning; its disadvantage is that different middle terms can be found for a given subject, as is apparent from what goes on in the law courts or scholastic disputations. He calls such uses 'ceremonious syllogising;' they are of little help in the search for truth. His criticism is partly epistemological; inference is a method of discovery, not a mere reformulation. He puts the traditional third figure in second place and renders it *U–I–P*, accepting that it only gives particular conclusions. The third figure, the normal second, he renders *P–U–I*, giving negative conclusions. He rejects the traditional fourth figure, as did many others, though substitutes for it the quantitative or mathematical syllogism, which is 'If two things are equal to a third, they are equal to each other.' He represents this as *U–U–U*, and claims it is not an axiom, but can be derived from logical principles.

In the traditional treatment the second and third figures are reduced to the first to be validated; it was felt to need no proof. Hegel finds the subsumptive structure unsatisfactory. The middle term in the old doctrine operates formally; it was regarded as a 'mark' rather than a genuine feature of the object or objects under discussion. The traditional syllogism is abstract. To remedy this he turns to Reflective Inference, of which the first form appears to be our old friend Caius repeated, with the additional criticism that we can only know that all men are mortal if we already know that Caius is, an objection that is also made by Mill. Hence we must pass to inductive inference, whose schema Hegel gives as:

$$
\begin{array}{c}
I \\
I \\
P\text{–}I\text{–}U \\
I \\
I \\
\vdots \\
\vdots
\end{array}
$$

'I' stands for the particular instance. If we conclude that all metals conduct electricity because lead, tin, etc. do, there is a doubt whether all metals have been considered; the problem of induction is to ensure complete enumeration. Hence he turns to Analogical Inference. His example is 'In all planets hitherto discovered this law of motion exists, consequently a new one will exhibit the same law.' Here the difficulty is to find the right mediation. It is easy to suggest wrong ones, as in arguing that the earth is a celestial body and inhabited, so the moon is also inhabited. What makes the earth habitable is the possession of an atmosphere and of water, not its being a celestial body. He adds that the so-called Philosophy of Nature is a good source of foolish arguments. To use analogy correctly involves knowledge of what are accidental and what necessary features of the subject of the analogy.

Necessary Inference overcomes this problem; it has the three forms, Categorical, Hypothetical and Disjunctive, with the particular, the individual and the universal respectively as middle term. His treatment, however, is confused and lacks examples. He claims that at this stage we no longer impose concepts on facts, but the inference develops out of the facts; we have achieved the level of necessity. If inference is considered something done in accordance with rules, it appears to be unrelated to the world, to be the result of the structure of our minds or of our language. If it is to be 'true,' it must arise out of the facts, not be imposed on them. A proper concept of x is something which actually applies to real x's, but this can only be discovered by scientific investigation. The discovery of a necessary connection is evidence that a genuine concept has been found. Only at an elementary level is a scientist concerned with mere 'allness;'

what he seeks is true universality, in other words, a real or conceptual connection, where the two terms are strictly equivalent. The Hegelian philosopher is engaged in a formal study of what scientists do, not doing their job for them. This, I think, is the significance of Hegel's attempt to replace metaphysics by logic. The metaphysician is a person who tries to construct an *a priori* account of the world; the logician analyses how scientists proceed. He cannot initiate knowledge of facts. Hegel began by saying that a concept was thought to be abstract, just as the pre-Socratic idea of Being was abstract, so abstract that it could not be distinguished from nothing. The history of science has been a history of increasing concreteness. As a result of developed atomic theory, a physicist can say what a metal is, and he understands it by his theory of atomic structure, by concepts. He is in a better intellectual position than the craftsman who knows empirically that metals have the characteristic of ductility. The logician follows the scientist's progress. When all has been discovered, this would be Absolute Knowledge, where the search for knowledge would have to stop.

Thus what Hegel means by 'logic' is different from what is meant by the term today. He claims that grammatical form is not a guide to logical form, but what he meant by it can only be seen by the way he uses it. Hence he regarded the formal manipulations of traditional logic with contempt; it did not deal with the acquisition of knowledge, nor assist in the understanding of the work of scientists. Because scientific or philosophical thinking is at issue, it is impossible to model logic on mathematics.

Hegel's discussion lies behind many of Bradley's arguments, and will, I hope, help to make sense of his project. At this stage I make no pronouncement upon the validity or usefulness of this conception of logic, which is so different from that of the present. Hegel may have made mistakes. But he developed a view of logic which is worth studying even if it is found necessary to reject his conception of logic and its Anglo-Hegelian development. In this chapter I have only expounded Hegel. The philosophical issues I have left to be dealt with in my discussion of Bradley.

NOTES

1 G. Faber, *Life of Benjamin Jowett*, London, 1957, p. 184.
2 Translated and edited H. Sloman and J. Wallon, revised by a Graduate of

Oxford, to which are added some remarks by H. S. [presumably Hutchison Stirling], London, 1855.

3 *Autobiography,* New York, Doubleday, n.d., pp. 169–170. Cf Mill to Gomperz, 19/8/1854.

4 Mill to Bain, 4/11/1867.

5 *The Logic of Hegel,* Oxford, 1874, pp. lxxvi–lxxvii.

6 *Encyclopaedia,* para. 24.

7 *Wissenschaft der Logik,* Surkhamp, Frankfurt am Main, 1969, vol. 5, p. 20. Henceforth this edition will be referred to as 'S'.

8 Ibid., p. 248.

9 Oxford, 1926, vol. I, p. 63.

10 *Encyclopaedia,* para. 166Z.

11 Ibid., para. 167.

12 *Logic,* Oxford, 1888, pp. 346–7.

13 *Wissenschaft der Logik,* S, vol. 6, p. 349.

14 Ibid., p. 358.

15 Ibid., p. 359.

16 *Implication and Linear Inference,* London, 1920, pp. 105–8.

17 *Essay,* bk IV, ch. xvii, sect. 4.

III

Ideas

I intend to take Bradley's discussion in a somewhat different order from his own. There is no reason to think that he would regard such an alteration as significant. At the beginning of the *Principles of Logic* he states that there is no accepted order in logic, and hence he will commence with judgment. He adds 'if we incur the reproach of starting in the middle, we may at least hope to touch the centre of the subject' (*PL,* p. 1). Most readers have taken this as a throwaway remark, but it is significant and already embodies part of Bradley's views on the nature of logic, views which differ from those of most of our contemporaries. He is more explicit in the 'Terminal Essays' appended to the second edition. Though these must be treated with care because his later metaphysical views affected his views on logic, in some cases they can illumine the text. In the second of these essays, he says:

> any one of the three, judgment, inference and ideas, can be plausibly shown as preceding the others. But really, here as elsewhere, what in every sense comes first is the concrete whole, and no mere aspect, abstracted from the whole, can in the end exist by itself. (*PL,* p. 640)

One of the targets of Anglo-Hegelian thought was 'linear inference,' to an attack on which Bosanquet devoted his last book.[1] All the Anglo-Hegelians claimed that logic was a 'circular' discipline; it had no 'foundations,' no necessary starting point. This view might be seen as a specification of their general criticism of empiricism, with its stress on the origin of thought and reasoning in 'simple ideas.' No doubt this view originated from Hegel's *Science of Logic,* which concluded with a chapter on the 'Absolute Idea;' this turned out to be about method and claimed that logic was a 'circle of circles;' both Bradley and Bosanquet argue for this position from their own points of view. The opposition to 'linear inference' has a further significance; modern logicians tend to think of complex sentences or propositions as built out of simple or elementary ones, and of the latter as formed from basic units or words. The symbolism used in the propositional calculus is designed to make this point. Part of the thrust of Bradley's attack on 'external relations' was directed against this notion, as will be shown below in chapter VI. For Bradley a judgment is one symbol, not a concatenation of several, and unless it were such it would not have the unity that a judgment requires. The doctrine that logic is circular implies that there are no 'atomic' or elementary propositions, nothing which has necessarily to be grasped before anything else can be. Bradley does not deny that, as a matter of fact, simple judgments are used by most human beings before they use complex ones, but this is a fact about human beings, not a necessary feature of language or thought. There is no logical reason to disbelieve the reported first words of Macaulay; 'Thank you madam, the agony has abated somewhat.' To insist that atomic propositions must precede complex ones is to confuse temporal and logical order; Bradley is careful to distinguish them.

The danger of starting with ideas is that it may mislead the reader into forgetting this point; its advantage lies in its greater familiarity. Bradley's discussion of 'idea' is the opening of his criticism of empiricism. From the time of its introduction by Locke, the 'new way of ideas' had been a source of confusion in philosophy, for it was uncertain whether 'idea' referred to a particular mental content, normally thought of as an image in one person's mind and hence private, or to the meaning of a word, something which was public. Bradley thought these two were radically different, and the confusion between them was the source of philosophical muddle. For a mental image has two sides, a 'that' and a 'what,' existence and content, which need to be distinguished for philosophical purposes. In the case of symbols there is a third dimension, that of meaning; the ideas of interest to logic are all symbols, whether or not they are also mental existents. A word is similar; it is a pattern of sounds or of marks on paper and can be considered as such, as an idea can be considered by a psychologist interested in the contents of the mind. But when a word is so regarded, it is merely another part of the furniture of the world; it has no more meaning than the pen used to write it. When it is considered as a symbol, as having a meaning, it takes on its true character as a word. It points beyond itself. Bradley expresses it:

> For logical purposes ideas are symbols, and they are nothing but sym-bols. And, at the risk of common-place, before I go on, I must try to say what a symbol is.
>
> In all that is we can distinguish two sides, (i) existence and (ii) content. In other words we perceive both *that* it is and *what* it is. But in anything that is a symbol we have also a third side, its signification, or that which it *means*.
>
> . . . and by a sign we understand any sort of fact which is used with a meaning. The meaning may be part of the original content, or it may have been discovered and even added by a further extension. Still this makes no difference. Take anything which can stand for anything else, and you have a sign. Besides its own private existence and content, it has this third aspect. Thus every flower exists and has its own qualities, but not all have a meaning. Some signify nothing, while others stand generally for the kind which they represent, while others again go on to remind us of hope or love. But the flower can never itself *be* what it *means*. (*PL*, pp. 2–3)

The Victorian 'language of flowers' is Bradley's example, because flowers are also appreciated for their own sake. Although the recipient could enjoy the colour or scent in itself, she could only get the message by identifying the particular blooms and 'translating' in accordance with the code. Used in this way, they are no longer simply a bunch of flowers:

> A symbol is a fact which stands for something else, and by this, we may say, it both loses and gains, is degraded and exalted. In its use as a symbol it forgoes individuality, and self-existence. It is not the main point that *this* rose or forget-me-not, and none other, has been chosen. We give it, or we take it, for the sake of its meaning; and that may prove true or false long after the flower has perished. The word dies as it is spoken, but the particular sound of the mere pulsation was nothing to our minds. Its existence was lost in the speech and the significance. The paper and the ink are facts unique and with definite qualities. They are the same in all points with none other in the world. But, in reading, we apprehend not paper or ink, but what they represent; and, so long as only they stand for this, their private existence is a matter of indifference. A fact taken as a symbol ceases so far to be fact. It no longer can be said to exist for its own sake, its individuality is lost in its universal meaning. It is no more a substantive, but becomes the adjective that holds of another. But, on the other hand, the change is not all loss. By merging its own quality in a wider meaning, it can

pass beyond itself and stand for others. It gains admission and influence in a world which it otherwise could not enter. The paper and ink cut the throats of men, and the sound of a breath may shake the world. (*PL,* pp. 3–4)

The particularity is no longer of interest, only the universality or meaning. Bradley certainly does not deny that an image possesses particularity, that it is a 'psychic content' whose character can be discovered by introspection. Later in his career he was to spend much time on the examination of psychological questions and to revise some conclusions of the *Principles* as a result. In 'Floating Ideas and the Imaginary' (*ETR,* pp. 28–64) he specifically criticizes what he maintains here. But at this stage he is certain that images are irrelevant to logic. This position he maintains throughout. It is the notion that ideas can 'float freely' in the mind that he attacks. For logic, images are used:

We have ideas of redness, of a foul smell, of a horse, and of death; and, as we call them up more or less distinctly, there is a kind of redness, a sort of offensiveness, some image of a horse, and some appearance of mortality, which rises before us. And should we be asked, Are roses red? Has coal gas a foul smell? Is that white beast a horse? Is it true that he is dead? we should answer, Yes, our ideas are all true, and are attributed to the reality. But the idea of redness may have been that of a lobster, or a smell that of castor-oil, the imaged horse may have been a black horse, and death perhaps a withered flower. And *these* ideas are *not* true, nor did we apply them. What we really applied was that part of their content which our minds had fixed as the general meaning. (*PL,* p. 9)

A particular image may come to mind whenever I hear a certain word, but this is irrelevant so long as it does not affect my understanding of the word. In Bradley's example the image may be of a red rose for the word 'rose.' So long as the image does not prevent me from recognizing that a white flower is also a rose, or from saying that a red poppy is red, the image has no role to play in language. This is particularly clear in the second negative case:

In denying that iron is yellow, do I say that it is not yellow like gold, or topaz, or do I say that it is not any kind of yellow? (*PL,* p. 9)

If ideas are 'copies' of reality, 'reflections' of the world, it is hard to see how they can refer to other things. The empiricist doctrine of the 'association of ideas' was intended to explain how this was possible, as well as to account for inference. Bradley is convinced the whole doctrine is nonsensical:

But the fashionable doctrine of 'association,' in which particular images are recalled by and unite with particular images, is, I think, not true of *any* stage of mind. . . . It does not exist outside our psychology. (*PL,* p. 34)

The chapter on this topic is a sustained polemic against Mill and his followers, in which he accuses them of adhering to metaphysical dogma and failing to examine the facts. Even the alternative name is inappropriate; the notion of a 'chemistry of ideas' will not fit the doctrines of the associationists, for 'In a chemical union the molecules of the substances cease to be molecules of either substance. It is therefore nonsense to say that they are associated' (*PL,* pp. 344–5). He quotes Hume's remark that 'All our distinct perceptions are distinct existences' and claims that this form of psychological atomism can never account for any mental phenomena; nor can it serve as a basis for logic. The source of the doctrine is that 'everything that exists is particular,' but

this is of course a metaphysical view, and, what is more, it is nothing but a dogma. The Philosophers of Experience have, so far as I know, never offered any proof of it; they have heard it from their fathers, and their fathers had heard it. (*PL,* p. 330)

Bradley had no objection to the empirical study of psychology; what he objected to was the confusion of psychology and philosophy. His chapter on Association (book II, part II, chapter I) concludes with a long passage on the desirability of a proper scientific study of the subject, using the method of the exact sciences, which he takes to be hypothetico-deductive. Because they are hypothetical, there is no reason for sciences to come into conflict with metaphysics, though he thinks that this is always possible. The remedy for bad metaphysics is to be found in philosophy, not in science (*PL,* pp. 340–2). For there is only one science which has no hypotheses, which uses no fictions or mythologies, and 'this science with some reason is suspected of non-existence' (*PL,* p. 342).*

Bradley asks the empiricists about the nature of a particular image or idea. If they mean a mental content which comes into the mind at a precise moment, then two images or ideas cannot be the same. At the very least, there can be no criterion for judging two such to be the self-same idea or image. In the case of some physical objects there can be differing criteria of identity: The '*Principles of Logic*' may refer to the text, identical in all copies, or to a particular copy, e.g. the one annotated for the purpose of writing this book. In the second case, the identity is 'carried' by the fact that it is the same physical object which is in question. But ideas or images are by definition not physical objects and so cannot be the same in this sense; two distinct images or ideas, and their distinctiveness consists in their appearing at different times, may be similar but in no sense can they be the same. 'There is nothing we know which can warrant the belief that a particular (mental) fact can survive its moment, or that, when it is past, it can live again' (*PL,* p. 306). This applies not only to ideas but even to feelings. If castor oil has once made me sick, that the smell of it will again make me sick is, Bradley says, certainly a fact. But the explanation of that fact must run *via* a universal (*PL*, pp. 307–8), for the feeling of sickness produced on the second occasion is similar to, but not absolutely identical with, the first one, if only because its context is different. Similarly with the castor oil which I recognize as such. What is identical is the universal involved. In most of the cases where association is invoked, the unlikeness between the two incidents is even greater:

Again, if an animal has been burnt one day at the kitchen fire, the next day it may shrink from a lighted match. But how different are the two. How much more unlike than like. Will you say then that the match cannot operate unless it first summons up, and then is confused with the image of the kitchen fire; or will you not rather say that a connection between elements, which are none of them particular, is produced in the mind by the first experience? But, if so, from the outset universals are used, and the

---

* This position is expanded in the paper 'Association and Thought' (*CE,* pp. 205–38), which he regards as an essay in psychology in the scientific sense. He is willing to make use of a principle of 'association,' though one which differs from the traditional English school in that it 'denies atomism and confines itself to facts.'

difference between the fact and the idea, the existence and the meaning, is unconsciously active in the undeveloped intelligence. (*PL,* p. 37)

Another example is of a child eating sugar. On Monday he finds a round piece is sweet. On Tuesday he concludes that a square piece will also be sweet. To do this there is no need to call up an image of Monday's piece. Even if this were done, it is unclear how it would help, for what is needed is something which is *like* the present piece. If the two images are to be judged similar, we must be dealing with universals. Identity is of no assistance (*PL,* pp. 323–9).

In essence Bradley's argument against associationism is one which has been used frequently in recent times. A bare particular, whether it be a physical object or an image, cannot be compared with another such except in respect of a (or several) particular feature(s) which need to be independently identified. It is impossible to teach someone the meaning of the word 'red' simply by showing him a set of red objects and uttering the word 'red,' or by saying 'These are all red;' the latter sentence presumes a knowledge of other universals. Unless the learner has an idea of 'colour,' he cannot grasp what feature he is to attend to. If he can grasp that, then he has already achieved what the associationists consider subsequent to this process. Bradley says that the same applies to animals, that a male dog recognizes a female as female, not as that particular dog. The universals which are used at this level may be of a low order, of a 'vague felt type,' but they must exist if we are to explain the mental functioning of animals and children. Bradley's belief in the continuity of thinking in all its manifestations is involved here; he sees no sharp break between 'feeling' and 'intellect;' but an explanation which couples children and animals seems dubious. For it seems possible to explain the 'recognition' of the danger of a lighted match as a response to a stimulus, heat, rather than depending on a universal. Pavlovian conditioning certainly exists and can be experimentally demonstrated. It may not be adequate to explain the full range even of animal behaviour but this needs to be shown. If universals are involved, it is we who provide them by our identification of the stimulus as of heat or whatever. With children, even babies, the case is different because they are going to develop into language-users. Hence their first grasp of language is explicable in the same terms as would be used of an adult's. It is possible to see it in this way, though the question remains whether it is the only way it can be seen. Even if we admit that Bradley has valid arguments against associationism, and I think it is clear that he can show that it does rest on a collection of *ad hoc* 'laws' introduced in the service of a metaphysical belief in the particularity of all that exists, it does not follow that his own account is correct.

The central point of his positive account is a distinction between the 'that' and the 'what:'

Whatever differences may separate the various kinds of psychical phenomena, they are all alike in one point. They all have content as well as existence. They are not confined to the 'that,' but each has a 'what,' since there is a complex quality and relations of quality. And, this being so, we have all that is required for the formation of universals. For an identity of content in different contexts is and must be an universal, whether we are dealing with perceptions or feelings or volitions. (*PL,* p. 309. He adds on a footnote that 'quality' covers 'quantity' at this stage.)

Certainly to recognize different psychic phenomena is to use universals; to call an event 'the same as' some previous one is to distinguish the 'that' from the 'what,' in Bradley's terms. In a later passage he argues that to discriminate particular mental events from the original flux of undiscriminated feeling is to possess universals, for here again we have picked something out, and even to pick something out *as* a particular implies the possession of a universal (*CE*, p. 216). It is not so clear whether he has any positive account of how this comes about; the associationists at least attempted to deal with this problem.

It might seem that this discussion was irrelevant to logic, that what was required was to demolish associationist doctrines, and to show that what was at issue in logic was the sign or symbol. This involves a different use of the idea or image, employing it to stand for or to mean something. Bradley did this adequately in the argument I sketched at the beginning of this chapter, so the rest could be left to psychology. He obviously thought that there is a danger that readers would take the chapter on the association of ideas and that on 'The Beginnings of Inference' as a mere deviation into psychology of no logical interest. In a note appended to the second edition of the book, he said:

And one aim of this book was hence to show that a truer logic must imply a diverse view of psychical fact. Judgment and Inference, in other words, when interpreted rightly by logic, must show their essential nature even at their psychical beginning. They must in an undeveloped form be actually there, and must be really effective at the earliest stage of mental life. This is the conclusion at which the psychological enquiries of this volume are aimed and which they endeavour throughout to enforce. (*PL,* p. 515)

He also adds one of the fuller statements on his relation to Hegel; he learnt from him that association is 'only between universals.' He is referring to *Encyclopaedia* paragraph 456, 'Thus even the association of ideas is to be treated as a subsumption of the individual under the universal, which forms their connecting link.' But to say that the doctrine was learnt from Hegel is hardly to provide a justification. Further, the insistence that judgment and inference exist from the earliest stages seems odd. For the modern account of learning logic would be that we learn it in learning words like 'all,' 'some,' etc. That most people recognize the validity of a syllogistic argument, when presented with it for the first time, is because they have already mastered the 'rules' for the use of syncategorematic words. Logic classes do not teach people to infer, they teach them to articulate and criticize inferences which they already recognize as valid.

The linguistic solution is one that Bradley does not accept, though this seems to clash with the passage I have already quoted above (p. 49) that the only ideas of interest to logic are symbols; for us the natural assumption is that ideas must be linguistic symbols. Bradley does not assume that the 'functioning of the mind' could be reduced to the 'functioning of the rules of language.' The reason would seem to be that the latter implies that there is something arbitrary about logic, that it could have been different if different linguistic rules had evolved. Bradley wants to show how logical necessity has arisen. The belief that some logical powers are present at the earliest stage does not imply that animals or children are capable of the same activities as adults. Nevertheless, he concludes the chapter with a defence of Darwinian evolution, which he thinks must apply as much to the mental (or psychic) as to the physical. This is not a derogation of man's powers, for 'in every man's history the transition has been made from the lowest to the highest' (*PL,* p. 513); if ontogeny does recapitulate phylogeny in the case of reason, then it must be possible to trace its development using either animals or children as examples, and this may illumine our abilities.

The fact that I can find within myself 'those processes and those feelings which . . . seem to explain the acts of the lowest creatures' (*PL*, p. 510), that the mental life is a continuum, does not imply that logical necessity is present at its beginning. For one of the things to be explained is such necessity. Part of the difference between Bradley and ourselves is that he thinks that we feel the force of logical necessity when we reason, that there is a sense in which we are compelled to think as we do. At the earliest stages this is not so: '*in the infancy of reason there is no necessity*' (*PL*, p. 510, Bradley's italics). It is worth quoting the explanation in full:

The nascent intelligence goes to its result, not because of the premises A and B, but because it can go forward in no other direction. And even that is incorrect. It advances, not because it can not do otherwise, but because it advances. The ideal change takes place before it and is effected by its act; but it has not reflected on the existence of that change, and still less on its ground. Thus it sees, not at all because it must see, but simply because it happens to see. (*PL*, p. 510)

At this level there can be no reason or necessity: mental change takes place, and that is all that can be said. The reason is that there is no self-consciousness involved, if indeed there is even consciousness. When the processes have become conscious, their logical nature begins to emerge. Bradley's argument is that the origin of our reasoning must lie in something which is not itself reasoning if there is to be no break in our evolution. This involves the belief that logical necessity is, as it were, a reflection of the way the mind works. At the early stage the mind may advance simply because it advances, but when it achieves reason the same process is seen as necessary.

Thus the two problems which seem merely to have been juxtaposed by Bradley, that of the origin of universals and the beginning of inference, are one and the same: 'In what is called "association" is involved the vital principle of the highest logic' (*PL*, p. 507). For to associate ideas is to infer, albeit at a low level, and to have an idea, in the full sense of the word, is to have something which is fitted to take its place in an inference. In other words the attempt to discover the 'mechanism' by which we reason is wrong, if by 'mechanism' is meant something which serves to explain, in different terms, the operation of the mind. This could be put by saying that the mechanism *is* logical, that there is no way of producing a 'theory of reasoning' of a psychological or physiological kind. This is not to deny that we might discover how the brain operates, nor even that we could produce a computer model of the process, wherein transistors and wires performed functions analogous to those carried out by nerves and synapses. The former might even permit us to come to a better understanding of the latter. But they would not give us an explanation of reason. One writer on 'artificial intelligence' says that in the long run 'we want a theory, not just of one rational process or the other, but of rationality *per se.*'[2] Bradley would have denied that such a theory would give understanding of logical thought. For just as we are not taught to infer, but to criticize and formalize inferences, so understanding of those processes involves a grasp of logic and could not be provided by extra-logical means. This is a consequence of the claim that logic is circular; the kind of understanding given by the study of it is not like that which, as often in the sciences, works by reducing a process to simpler parts which are not of the same kind as that to be explained. Herein lies, I think, the difference between logic and psychology; success in the latter would correlate our mental processes with neurological ones, would describe what was going on when we thought. And there is good reason to believe that such a description must in principle be possible. But this would not explain logical operations, nor reduce them to something different; an electronic calculator can be used to perform arithmetical operations, but to understand how it works is not to grasp addition or multiplication. Such a device does not reduce mathematics to electronics. Further, the way in which the electronic calculator produces its result might be different from the way in which the human brain operates; the same effect can be produced by different causal chains. This is not intended as an attack on psychology, nor on the use of computer models to assist in understanding of the ways in which the mind or brain work; it is merely that such understanding will not solve logical problems. Hence Bradley must claim that the mental processes of children and animals are of the same kind as those found in adults, that we understand the former only because we can grasp their explicit later form. In the mental sphere at least, the anatomy of man is the key to the anatomy of the ape.

Bradley only claims that there must be some ideas which pre-date language, and that most of the mental operations of an adult human being are due to language. Talking of an elementary form of disjunctive reasoning which some had argued could be attributed to dogs, he says:

And we should remember that the retention of an idea, which, by being denied, forms the basis for a further positive advance, is a very late acquisition of the mind. It is hard to believe that, where speech is undeveloped, this function can be present. (*PL*, p. 509)

Even if there are only a few 'ideas' which possess a 'universal' aspect before language is learned it would seem that Bradley must believe in a private language. All that empiricists needed to claim was a small 'private vocabulary' as the foundation on which subsequent elaborations were built. It is possible that there is no clash here. The empiricists started from the atomicity of sensations, the belief that each was an original existence. Wittgenstein said: 'the verbal expression of pain replaces crying and does not describe it.'[3] Bradley claimed that the fact that a particular sensation was accompanied by the same expression showed that a universal was operative, that already a distinction between the 'that' and the 'what' existed in the mind of the infant. It formed a basis for subsequent language learning. Wittgenstein's attack on private language may be valid against ordinary empiricism but it does not follow that it destroys Bradley's position as well. Without withdrawing any of the things I said in the article 'Pain and Private Language,'[4] I think Wittgenstein could have admitted this, for he postulated an 'agreement in reactions' as the basis for language, though it was shown by the existence of language rather than capable of being expressed in language. In spite of the difference of vocabulary, his notion of agreement seems like that which Bradley argued for. In each case there is a 'natural' basis for future developments. Unless there were such, it is hard to see how the process could ever have started; certainly language could not have begun by some one individual having invented it and then communicating it to others. The classical empiricists erred by thinking that something of this nature occurred for every individual. Other writers who could not accept such an account have argued that language must have been divinely inspired. Neither of these views is plausible, so unless the theory I have attributed to Bradley and Wittgenstein is adopted, the only solution left is the mysterious one that language is innate.

A final point is that there are obvious differences between talking in terms of ideas and of words or language, but that this can be over-stressed. The contemporary fashion is to equate the mental and the linguistic; this approach has undoubtedly had the effect of clearing away some of the problems which beset older theories. But the danger is that this technique only serves as a translation, that the same problems, albeit expressed in different terms, will still remain and require solution or dissolution. One of the objects of examining the works of philosophers in a different tradition is to see how the same problems plagued them; sometimes what they had to say was as, or more, interesting than contemporary accounts. Bradley said important things about logic, and hence I make no apology for discussing them in terms that occur in books and articles subsequent to his writing.

NOTES

1 *Implication and Linear Inference,* London, 1920.
2 J. A. Fodor, *The Language of Thought,* Hassocks, 1976, p. 195.
3 *Philosophical Investigations,* Oxford, 1953, para. 244.
4 *Studies in the Philosophy of Wittgenstein,* ed. Peter Winch, London, 1969, pp. 166–83.

IV
Words and Meanings

If, as I claim, the problem of meaning is central to Bradley's thought in the *Principles of Logic,* it may seem strange that the book contains no section on words. The chapter that contains most on the topic is entitled 'The Quantity of Judgments,' and is concerned primarily with that. Bradley replaced the tripartite division of logic, standard in the textbooks, into terms, propositions and inferences by a twofold division into judgment and inference. In a notice of the *Principles,* which appeared in *Mind* in 1883, he says:

The above work may be described as an attempt to answer two questions, What is Judgment, and What is Reasoning, and is a treatment of some of the topics which those questions involve.

Even this division was not as absolute as the corresponding textbook one; judgment and inference merge into one another. For Bradley the unit of meaning was the judgment, and consequently the *Principles of Logic* does not contain, as books on logic of his time commonly did, a section on words. Here he seems to be in agreement with the slogan 'Only in the context of a sentence do words have any meaning.' Some contemporary writers refer to this as 'Frege's Principle.' It is because of Frege that it comes to be accepted by many modern philosophers, but it does not follow from this that it was his discovery. Indeed, it was a commonplace among grammarians of the period. Mansel, reviewing in 1850 a book on Universal Grammar, writes:

That there ever was a period in the history of man, as Reid conjectures, when every single word represented a sentence, when the noun and the verb themselves held the same place which their several syllables hold now, as fractional and imperfect in speech as they still are in thought; this is an hypothesis which we may reasonably hesitate to admit. But logically the position is true. The sentence, we may go farther, the enunciative sentence, is the unit of speech, as the judgment is of thought; and it behoves us to remember, that the verbal analysis of the thoughts we utter, like the chemical decomposition of the air we breathe, exhibits only the forced and unnatural dissolution of parts whose vital force and efficacy exists only in combination.[1]

Similar expressions can be found in other philosophical works of the nineteenth century. More important for my purpose is the fact that it also was a commonplace of post-Kantian philosophy. Kant himself, in justifying his table of judgments, talks of the understanding as a 'faculty of judgment' and argues that concepts are 'predicates of possible judgments.'[2] Hegel had made this point even more strongly. One of the few German logicians who held the opposite view was Lotze, whose *Logic* influenced both Frege and Bradley:

This obvious reflexion has given rise to the assertion, that in logic the theory of judgment at least must precede the treatment of concepts, with which it is only an old tradition to begin the subject. I consider this to be an over-hasty assertion. . . .[3]

Frege's comment in a letter of 1882 seems to be a reply to this remark:

I do not think that the formation of concepts can precede judgment, for that would presuppose the independent existence of concepts; but I imagine the concept originating in the analysis of a judgeable content.[4]

In an unpublished paper, Frege explicitly refers to a discussion of this topic in a review of A. H. Sayce's *Introduction to the Science of Language,* published in England in 1880.[5]

Bradley himself seems to be engaged in a debate with Lotze, seeing the force of the latter's claim that the formation of a higher concept depends on lower concepts which themselves depend on the stream of ideas or impressions. This is the common empiricist argument for the necessity of a base level of 'data,' on which all the higher concepts must rest. In the case of Lotze, it is what Bosanquet characterized as the 'German reaction' to Hegel. The argument is a powerful one, though contrary to the whole direction of Bradley's thinking. Ultimately the 'idealist' contextual principle prevails with him.

It does, of course, present problems to those holders of empiricist

views who believe that our mental life is constructed out of 'atoms.'
T. H. Green began his consideration of Mill's *Logic* by attacking
him on precisely this point:

The order which Mill adopts – beginning with names, going on to nameable
things, and finally to the import of propositions – is essentially misleading.
. . . Nothing less than what can be stated in a proposition is a matter of fact
at all. Except, then, as a constituent in a matter of fact, a 'nameable thing'
has no intelligible character. It is for knowledge nothing.[6]

He says a little later:

The distinction between 'singular' and 'general' names as Mill gives it (I,ii.
§3), presupposes the propositions (1) 'this is a man,' (2) 'this is John.'
Except in relation to a proposition, the distinction is unmeaning. 'John' by
itself means nothing. 'Man' by itself means something only because it is the
symbol for a multitude of judgments in which qualities might be asserted of
'man' as subject. 'John' is significant in such judgments as 'this is John' or
'John has red hair.' The distinction of these judgments from such as 'man is
a mammal' or 'this is man' lies in the more complex determination by
attributes of the object 'John' than of the object 'man,' from which it
results that only one individual object . . . can be brought under the former
conception of attributes, while many can be brought under the latter. . . .
Apart from propositions, then, the distinction between 'general' and
'singular' names is a distinction between names that have a meaning and
those that have none. And the meaning of those that have meaning is
always resoluble into propositions. Only in propositions has a singular
name significance. . . .[7]

The basic line of argument fits well with Green's attack on empiricism in his edition of Hume. Bosanquet later expresses similar senti-
ments in his elementary logic text:

We ought not to think of propositions as built up by putting words or
names together, but of words or names as distinguished though not separ-
able elements in propositions.[8]

There is evidence, then, that the slogan 'Only in the context of a
proposition (or judgment) do words have meaning' is an Anglo-
Hegelian commonplace.

There are problems in accepting the slogan, for it seems to make
it difficult to explain how we can understand sentences we have not

come across before. It is normally assumed that we proceed by grasping the senses of the words we have previously encountered and assemble them to give sense of the whole judgment. Dummett, in his book on Frege, finds this an overwhelming objection to one way of reading the slogan. He says the principle is 'either truistic or nonsensical,'[9] and that what Frege really meant was that 'The sentence is the unit of meaning,' which he regards as an original contribution to the philosophy of language. Consequently he expresses what he takes to be the sense of the slogan as:

in the order of *explanation* the sense of a sentence is primary, but in the order of *recognition* the sense of a word is primary.[10]

The point is that to 'understand' a word, and I use scare quotes advisedly, is to see how it can function in sentences or judgments. The only utterances that can be understood in the full sense are complete ones that *say* something. It would be impossible to learn a language just from a dictionary. To use Dummett's example, to be told that the ace ranks above all other cards is not to be told anything unless one also understands how to play cards. The ace only has a significance in card games; outside them it is a piece of board with a design. This points towards another of Frege's formulations of his principle:

never to ask for the meaning of a word in isolation, but only in the context of a proposition.[11]

Within Frege's view of language there is one class of words which constitute an exception to the principle. Dummett says:

Proper names, form, indeed, a linguistic category of the most general possible kind: they constitute the only complete expressions that fall short of being sentences.[12]

Within a Fregean analysis there must be such a class to form the foundation for more complex expressions. Most post-Fregean symbolisms start from an 'elementary' proposition represented as *Fa*, where '*a*' is the name of an individual. There may be metaphysical problems about what constitutes an individual, as Russell thought there were, but the notion of analysis which this kind of logical symbolism involved seems to demand that there are such 'basic' individuals. This issue will be further discussed in chapter V; here I only want to point out the difference between Frege and Green on this issue. The latter did not see any logical difference between 'John' and 'man.' Indeed, he expressly says that 'Only in propositions has a singular name significance.'

It follows from the slogan that language learning is not a process of first acquiring a vocabulary and then subsequently using it to say something. The child learns language by hearing things said, and these are normally fully formed sentences. It is only later that it comes to realize that the same 'units' occur in many of these utterances and can be used to form new ones. In particular, there could be no primary process of 'ostensive definition' by which a single word was correlated with an object, though this is not to deny that at a later stage a word may be defined ostensively. But the need for such definition often arises because the word has formed part of a complete utterance. The philosophical importance of the issue lies in the question of the 'foundations' of language. There is a tendency to assume that there must be simple and original atoms out of which everything else arises. The Anglo-Hegelians were quite willing to deny any necessary foundation of elementary atoms. It is important, they thought, to separate what is logically simple from what is educationally so.

A further consequence of the slogan is that it is necessary to distinguish between a single word and something said by means of a 'single word.'

When we hear the cry of 'Wolf,' or 'Fire,' or 'Rain,' it is impossible to say we hear no assertion. (*PL*, p. 56)

After all, the boy who cried 'Wolf' was held to be lying when no wolf appeared. If someone 'utters a word' in normal, i.e. non-philosophical, discourse, he is taken to be asserting something or asking a question. If he denies he did either then the 'word' becomes a meaningless noise. This applies whether the 'word' is a general term or a proper name. To utter the sound 'John' and deny that I am trying to attract his attention or supply an answer to a question, etc., is as meaningless as to say 'saucepan.' The confusion between words and sentences has affected some research into animal communication:

> Monkeys make noises which appear to be genuine words, corresponding to specific objects in the external world. . . . The first three entries in the Vervet Monkey/English dictionary are:
> A series of short tonal calls, rather like a dog barking: LEOPARD.
> Low pitched staccato grunts: EAGLE.
> High pitched 'chuttering' . . .: BABOON.[13]

The evidence presented is that when the monkeys hear one of their number making such sounds, they react appropriately, climbing trees for the first, looking up and running into dense bush for the second, and scanning the ground for the third. This implies that the real meaning of the sounds is more like 'There's an *x* about.' It is hardly surprising that this should be so, for the purpose of the calls is to elicit appropriate reactions to danger. The confusion in the non-linguistically trained researchers is not important to their work; to have established something of how monkeys communicate is a worthwhile achievement. But similar confusions in philosophers may be more dangerous; the doctrine that words possess 'extension,' that 'leopard' covers the class of leopards, does have misleading consequences, some of which will be discussed below.

It is important that the Anglo-Hegelians used the term 'judgment' in preference to 'sentence.' The latter is a grammatical description; it can be agreed that something is an English sentence without the question of its meaning even arising. But to make a judgment is to say something for a reason. There is a sense in which a judgment cannot be nonsense. I may take what I hear *to be* nonsensical, but this may be because I have misunderstood or do not have appropriate knowledge. An instance of the former would be to assume that the 'bank' is that of a river, whereas the speaker was talking of a place to deposit money. The latter could perhaps be illustrated by a physicist's statement such as 'This particle travels backwards in time.' It has been claimed that such a remark is self-contradictory, but it may be that the results of the latest experiments demand to be expressed in this way. I am not here worried about the truth of the judgment, for any one may prove to be false. But its sense depends on the whole of the physical theory which led the physicist in question to say what he did. One way of putting this is to say 'it is through the sense of the whole that the parts get their content.'[14] If we accept this, then it is no longer permissible to say that the meaning of the word 'backwards' forbids its application to movement in time. This argument is in the spirit of Bradley, for he thought that judgments could not be isolated; they necessarily depend on a context, in this case the conext of physical theory at a particular time. (It is because such theory can change that this judgment may turn out in the future to be false, but that presents no problems for logic. The Greeks were wrong but not stupid to reject the heliocentric theory of Aristarchus.) But if the contextual principle is accepted, then the view that words have meanings 'in themselves' or invariably has to be rejected.

It is clear that Bradley accepted the contextual principle, and that much of what he says about judgment can only make sense on this supposition. He does not always remain true to the insight, and some of his difficulties are due to this. His acceptance is also shown by his belief that 'the grammatical form of a proposition may conceal its logical form,' which will be discussed in chapter VI. This was a commonplace of traditional logic, for all texts contained exercises of 'putting propositions into logical form,' which meant getting them into a shape suitable for premises of syllogisms. 'All is not gold that glitters,'[15] a standard example, is not an instance of an 'A' proposition, but needs to be rephrased as an 'O,' 'Some things that glitter are not gold.' But those who made much of the notion grammatical form concealing logical form, as did Bradley, Frege and Russell, had something more radical in mind. Bradley and Russell agreed that what appeared to be (was grammatically) a categorical proposition might turn out to be 'really' hypothetical. The connection between the slogan about grammatical and logical form and the belief that words cannot function in isolation is that units of grammar may well turn out not to be the 'units' of logic.

The idea that grammatical form is not necessarily a guide to logical form may be applied in a variety of ways, some more radical than others. A sentence is a grammatical entity, and it is composed of words; a proposition or a judgment is a logical entity; the question is what its component parts are. Further, sentences can be constructed out of words, and one element in grammatical instruction has often been to get pupils to make well-formed sentences out of sets of words given to them. If we take the slogan seriously, we should not think of judgments as being built up in this way. It then becomes hard to see what the constituents of a judgment are. The belief that it has constituents in the way that words compose the sentence is an example of an insufficiently radical application of the dictum about logical and grammatical form. Another way of dealing with the problem would be to say that the parts of a judgment or proposition are ideas, which are put together as are the words in a sentence. It might be thought that this would be Bradley's solution, given what he has said about the nature of 'ideas' and their quality of being 'universal.' But he does not make this move for two reasons. The first, which will be discussed later, is that he thinks it raises difficulties for the attribution of truth or falsity. The second is that he does not believe that ideas can be correlated with words in a one-to-one manner; the counting of ideas is not the same as the counting of words; indeed he is prepared to take what seems an extreme position:

It is not true that every judgment has two ideas. We may say on the contrary that all have but one. (*PL*, p. 11)

This is a radical use of the dictum that logical and grammatical form do not coincide.

Bradley argues that it has been assumed too quickly that words are signs of ideas, and that the latter can be counted in the same way as the former. But no arguments have been put forward for this position, nor could there be, because there is no independent way of counting ideas as meanings. It is not even clear that there could be a way of counting psychical events; even if there were, it would not help with the logical question. If we judge that a wolf is eating a lamb:

We have a relation here suggested or asserted between wolf and lamb, but that relation is . . . not a *factual* connection between events in my head. What is meant is no psychical conjunction of images. (*PL*, p. 12)

The judgment is about an event in the world, not about what is going on in my mind or in my head, though, as was pointed out in the last chapter, something must have been going on in both places. The important thing, as far as the judgment is concerned, is the event, and this is something which exists in reality. To say that the judgment must contain two ideas, that of the wolf and that of the lamb, still leaves us with a possible third idea, the relation which joins them. This issue will have to be postponed until the discussion of Internal Relations in chapter VII. But, Bradley asks, why say that the idea of the wolf is one, for it is obvious that it must be complex, for we could say a number of things about wolves or about this particular wolf? If we try to carry this analysis as far as ideas which cannot be analysed, those so simple that they have no internal complexity, we shall find ourselves left with no idea at all (*PL,* p. 12). The only alternative is to say that 'whatever is fixed by the mind, however simple or complex, is but one idea' (*PL,* p. 13). Although it makes sense to talk of joining words together to make sentences, it is odd to say the same of ideas which have no criterion of identity except what the idea is 'of.' And, as any object can be regarded as complex, can be analysed, this does not give a criterion in any strict sense. However, the 'one idea' which is a judgment is not therefore simple; it is complex. His central point is that we should not assume that the number of ideas is the same as the number of words. Further, to assume that there are several ideas conjoined to make a judgment leaves the question of what makes the judgment into a unity. It is a unity, and this implies that it has internal complexity. For Bradley, 'one idea' is different from the 'simple idea' of the empiricists.

To say anything about wolves implies having an idea of 'wolf,' but this is a way of referring to a certain competence, not a way of counting the contents of the mind. Bradley later admitted (*ETR,* p. 29n) that he used 'various more or less objectionable expressions' in the account of ideas in this book, but that he 'could not understand how a careful reader of the volume could be deceived.' It is true that he does not always follow a clear line, and is often led to fall back on views inconsistent with his main doctrine. Instead of talking of someone 'having an idea of "wolf",' it might be thought better to say that he had the 'concept "wolf".' To our eyes it is strange that the word 'concept' does not figure in the *Principles of Logic,* nor occur in the indexes of Bradley's other works. Yet he must have been familiar with the term and his avoidance of it be deliberate. G. E. Moore, in an article which he never reprinted,[16] says that the word 'idea' is so ambiguous that he will use 'concept' for what Bradley calls a 'universal meaning.' Moore came to strange conclusions in this article; perhaps they constitute that 'idealist prison' referred to by Russell:

It seems necessary, then, to regard the world as formed of concepts. These are the only objects of knowledge.[17]

He goes on:

Our result then is as follows: That a judgment is necessarily a necessary combination of concepts, equally necessary whether it is true or false. That it must be either true or false, but that its truth or falsity cannot depend on its relation to anything else whatever, reality, for instance, or the world in space or time.[18]

It is hard to see what Moore's 'concepts' are, though certain combinations of them are propositions which possess the character of truth or falsity. This view is similar to that of Russell at the same period; that some propositions had the property of truth and others of falsity, just as some flowers were red and some yellow. It is unclear how to discover which are which, unless by 'intuition.' I suspect that Moore, in this article, was in a halfway stage between Idealism and his later views. Certainly he goes beyond Bradley, but in a way which seems to cut the link between thought and reality altogether, though Russell took the article as an attack on Idealism.[19]

Concepts seem to be 'mental' entities and to be correlated in some way with words, for the proposition is a combination of concepts as the sentence is of words. But they are not mental in the sense in which they are the property of an individual; indeed, it is hard to see, on Moore's views, how we come into the possession of concepts. Bradley certainly wished to deny any correlation between the number of words and the number of entities, whatever they might be, which compose judgments. What he wanted to say about 'ideas' as used in judgments was that they had no characteristics beyond pointing to or 'meaning' their objects. They may have other characteristics, indeed must have them, but these are irrelevant to their symbolic function. In this respect they are analogous to the words used in making a judgment; these are patterns which can be analysed as sound, though are not so analysed when understood. 'What I said' may be correctly reported in indirect speech without any of my words being employed. There is a tendency to think that words or ideas exist in one realm, reality in another, and that truth consists of a correspondence between the two. Such an unsophisticated notion often arises from thinking of pictures which can be directly compared with their originals. But ideas cannot be independently inspected, or rather there is nothing to inspect. A judgment is 'transparent' in the sense that we look through it at reality. In judging, the mind is (must be) operative, but it is the world that we are thinking about. In what was intended as an elementary text, Bosanquet put the point in this way:

We are not to think of (i) Ideas, and (ii) Things which they represent; the ideas, taken as parts of a world, *are* the things.[20]

T. S. Eliot attributed a similar view to Bradley:

A reference to an identity . . . *is* the identity, in the manner in which a word *is* that which it denotes.[21]

Eliot is discussing *Appearance and Reality,* not the *Principles.* It appears that both he and Bosanquet are expressing a form of 'linguistic idealism,' a view that words *are* reality. This, as will be seen more clearly in chapter VI, is not what is meant. The point is rather that there is no independent way of reaching 'things' in the world outside, at least so far as logic is concerned. (I insert this qualification because Bradley later came to a somewhat different view.) Bosanquet, in the passage just quoted, already differs from Bradley; he assumes that there is 'my real world' which is distinguishable from *the* real world. Bradley at this stage thinks of truth as dependent on the existence of a single reality. The problem is that access to it can only be *via* ideas or words. Moore thinks Bradley slides over this point:

Later he used 'idea' not of the symbol, but of the symbolized. He slurs over the transition with the phrase 'But it is better to say the idea *is* the meaning.' The question surely is not which is 'better to say,' but which is true.[22]

But his conclusion seems to be more 'idealist:'

I assume Mr. Bradley's proof that the concept [Bradley's 'Idea'] is necessary to truth and falsehood. I endeavour to show, what I must own appears to me perfectly obvious, that the concept can consistently be described neither as an existent, nor as part of an existent, since it is presupposed in the conception of an existent. It is similarly impossible that truth should depend on a relation to existents or to an existent. . . .[23]

He is faced with the problem that the traditional views of the relation between words, or ideas, and the world raise apparently insuperable philosophic difficulties, yet the attempt to present a view which does not fall into those difficulties seems to end in paradox.

One way out might be by use of a distinction between 'saying' and 'showing,' but this is hardly clearer. At the present stage of my exposition it is difficult to say more than that ideas are 'transparent,' though I would add that the attempt to put into words the basic fact of symbolism on which the use of words itself depends is liable to give rise to difficulties. This, and the next three chapters, might be said to be an attempt to explain three lines from the beginning of the first chapter of Bradley's *Principles:*

The relations between the ideas are themselves ideal. They are not the psychical relations of mental facts. They do not exist between the symbols, but hold in the symbolized. (*PL*, p. 11)

Many misunderstandings come from failing to appreciate what he said here. The use of the word 'idea' in this context may be the source, for it is easy to confuse the psychical entity with the meaning. Even talk of symbols may mislead, and some of that carelessness of expression that Bradley refers to occurs in his use of that word. The fox is a symbol of cunning. This seems to imply that it is because foxes are cunning that 'the fox' can serve as a symbol. And this leads us to think that the ground of the relation of symbolism is some likeness between the symbol and what it symbolizes, which pushes us back to representationalism. It is hard to express the relation between an idea and reality without falling into error; to say one is the other sounds paradoxical, but for some of the time Bradley seems to assert this. However, he did not always stick firmly to this view:

An idea is symbolic, and in every symbol we separate what it *means* from that which it stands for. A sign indicates or points to something other than itself; and it does this by conveying, artificially or naturally, those attributes of the thing by which we recognize it. A word, we may say, never quite means what it stands for or stands for what it means. . . . The idea and the reality are presumed to be different. (*PL,* p. 168)

Although not strictly relevant here, it is worth adding the continuation of this passage for the light it throws on Bradley's metaphysics:

It is perhaps an ideal we secretly cherish, that words should mean what they stand for and stand for what they mean. And in metaphysics we should be forced to consider seriously the claims of this ideal. But for logical purposes it is better to ignore it. (ibid.)

The distinction is between intension and extension, terms which he prefers to Mill's 'connotation' and 'denotation.' The intension is the 'meaning' of the term, its extension the individuals to which it applies; the distinction is made in traditional logic. What is not clear is whether Bradley has any right to avail himself of it, given the views he holds. He introduces his discussion by saying: 'If in considering an idea you attend to its content, you have its intension or comprehension' (*PL,* p. 168). The question is what, on his terms, is the 'content' of an idea? He has already (*PL,* p. 3, quoted above, p. 49) distinguished between the existence and content of an idea, between the 'that' and the 'what,' but said that the meaning was a third element. In this sense, the content cannot be the meaning. Hence it would seem that meaning has a distinction within it. But it ought not to be possible to 'attend to its content' except in the sense of attending to the thing or things which it means, which would be to attend to the extension in the traditional sense of the word. Further, it is hard to see how this view can be reconciled with his talk of the 'concrete universal' and his attack on the 'abstract particular' and 'abstract universal' (cf. *PL,* pp. 188–9, and chapter V below). Also the opening pages of book I, chapter VI, which talk of words, seem inconsistent with some of what he later says about the extension and intension of judgments. This is not surprising, for if words do not have any real sense except in judgments, it will be hard to say anything of importance about their meaning in isolation. It seems, in short, if here Bradley has merely taken over a traditional view without adequately examining how far it fits with the rest of his doctrine.

The traditional view that words possess both intension and extension has a certain plausibility. 'Triangle' means 'a three-sided figure' and we can find in the world many triangles, or talk about features which belong to all triangles, thus forming the class of triangles. Keynes explains the equivalent terms, 'connotation' and 'denotation,' in the following way:

Every concrete general name is the name of a class, real or imaginary: by its *connotation* we mean the attributes on account of which any individual is placed in the class or called by the name; by its *denotation* we mean the individuals which possess these attributes, and which are therefore placed in the class and called by the name.[24]

The difficulty is, however, that it implies the word has a meaning in itself, and this makes it hard to see how it functions in co-operation with other words. The utterance 'I met a man with red hair yesterday' uses the word 'man,' but it does not refer to the class of men nor to the attributes which are used to classify him as a man; it refers to a particular individual. Similarly, in 'All men are mortal,' it is the whole proposition which makes the reference to the class, not the single word. The word 'man' is not the name of a class, though it can be used to refer to a class. Part of the trouble is the use of the term 'name,' though it should be remembered that at this period it did not carry quite the sense it now tends to do in philosophic discussions. The central fault of the doctrine is that it makes it difficult to account for the significance of judgments. In this respect the Fregean distinction between sense and reference, where these two terms are analogous to, though not identical with, the pair connotation/denotation or intension/extension, is obviously an improvement. I will have more to say about the Fregean distinction in chapter V.

Here I am concerned with the traditional terminology. This accounts for the discourse by placing all the emphasis on individual words; the point of stressing the judgment as the unit of sense is that it gets rid of this problem. If the old view is maintained, words become a barrier between thought and reality, because the fact that they possess both connotation and denotation makes it hard to see how we can express what we do express. The same occurs when 'ideas' are given semi-independent status as mental representatives; indeed, we might look on the doctrine of connotation and denotation as a transfer of older views about ideas to linguistic entities. Bradley seems committed to arguing that the mistake depends on putting the task of judgments on to the individual 'units' of judgments. Words, or Bradleian 'ideas,' are not representatives; judgments reach right up to reality.

Bradley, as I have said, seems in some places still to accept the old distinction; for example he prefaces his discussion of the inverse relation between extension and intension by saying:

If we take extension to mean that number of real individuals of which the meaning is true, then it is ludicrously false that an increase of the extension is a decrease in the meaning. (*PL*, p. 171)

His *argumentum ad hominem* here is the new facts learnt by the logician who 'impelled by the practical syllogism, begets a child.' But when he turns, in the same chapter, to deal with judgments taken in extension, he is scathing of the attempt to give a class interpretation of such propositions as 'Dogs are mammals.' This does not assert that one class is included in another, but what it is to be a dog. The class of dogs must either exist in my head or outside it (*PL*, p. 175); it is clear that there is no physical collection of all dogs:

The idea that 'mammals' is the name of a flock of mammal-images, herded together in my mental field, and that among these I can see the little pack of dogs, and all the cats sitting together, and the rats and the rabbits, as well as the elephants, all marked with curious references and cross-references to heads 'quadruped' and 'carnivorous' and 'placental' and Heaven knows what else – I do not think that this looks like the fact. (*PL*, p. 175)*

Bradley concludes 'The inclusion within the class has no meaning, if the class *is* the mere individuals themselves' (*PL*, p. 176), for to say that 'The dogs are included in the mammals' is either to make a false statement about a physical fact or to say that dogs are mammals. The use of a word to refer to a number of objects is no more problematic in ordinary language than reference to a single thing: there are many linguistic devices for doing this. The matter only becomes difficult if it is assumed that reference is basically to an

---

* Bradley's criticisms of the difficulties with the class of dogs bears many similarities to a paper of Max Black's, 'The Elusiveness of Sets,' *Caveats and Critiques*, London and Ithaca, 1975, pp. 85–108.

individual, via that 'logically simple' device the proper name and hence plural reference is something sophisticated for which more elaborate methods are needed. Neither should it be assumed that because a logical device enables us to systematize a number of inferences it therefore represents the way in which the mind functions. That we can analyse inferences by means of Venn diagrams which 'represent' classes by circles intersecting or including each other does not entail that this is the way we think. If the reading of judgments in extension turns out to be nonsensical, then so must any idea of extension of individual words; in the traditional view the former is a result of the latter.

The empiricists believed 'everything that exists is particular;' universals presented problems. Hence, they claimed, discourse about the world must be founded on reference to particulars, that basic to language were 'proper names' which were linked to particular objects in a manner that was uncomplicated in comparison with the way in which general words were related to the world. These proper names must stand for individuals, though they do not possess a meaning in the proper sense; they 'denote' but do not 'connote.' This doctrine has both logical and epistemological elements, as can be seen by its elaboration in Russell's 'Logical Atomism.' Bradley's attack is also both logical and epistemological. The former is represented by his belief that ideas, as meanings, are universal. He denies that 'merely individual ideas are the furniture of the primitive mind' (*PL,* p. 35), which presumably would be better phrased 'there are no ideas of individuals in the primitive mind.' This point has already been discussed in chapter III, but Bradley argues in addition that it is an error to assume that because what is seen *is* individual, it is therefore seen *as* individual. To be able to recognize an unique individual is to be able to make comparisons, and therefore a sophisticated achievement. Children tend to use the first proper names they are taught as the name for a class of individuals; if the pet dog is called 'Rover,' all dogs may be referred to as 'Rovers:'

And when young children call all men father, it is the merest distortion of fact to suppose that they perceive their father as individual, and then, perceiving other individuals, confuse a distinction they have previously made. (*PL,* p. 35)

In other words the use of proper names is a late development; it may be that they are logically the simplest elements, but there is no reason to suppose that the genetic and the logical coincide.

Mill argued that a proper name must be an 'unmeaning mark;' Bradley claims that if a mark really were unmeaning it would not even be a word, could not appear in the language or be understood. Even a noise when quoted becomes more than a mere noise:

'Why did you make that noise *Theophilus* when you saw that man? *Theophilus* is not a pleasant sound.' We have here no signification and no meaning, nor have we any longer a word. (*PL*, p. 170)

But we do have a distinction, Bradley continues, for the very fact that I can use a noise like the one you made to refer to the latter implies a universal. 'Theophilus,' as I say it, is intended to be the same as your utterance, and in this way refers to your utterance. I could have merely asked why you made 'that particular noise' when you did. The fact that I can, in some sense, repeat it or write it down, shows that something more is involved. It could be said that 'Theophilus' is the name of the noise you made, but this is to make virtually the same point as Bradley. My (or your) utterance is something unique, because it is unlikely that the timbre and expression of our voices as patterns of sounds are identical; a voice-print would indicate differences between them. But these differences are normally ignored, and must be ignored if we are to understand one another. The situation here is like the use of ideas in the mind as meanings. Ideas are particular psychic events, but in using them their particularity is ignored. Noises are not words, but there is no particular feature of a noise which makes it into a word except its being used as a word. And this feature is not something which can be explained, for any explanation must presuppose it.

If Mill's doctrine were true, Bradley argues, it would be hard to understand what is meant by such judgments as 'John is asleep' (*PL*, p. 59). He will not accept the 'heroic remedy' that the name itself is the subject of the sentence. He suggests that part of the trouble is due to a confusion about 'unmeaning mark;' it is true that the proper name is not conferred in most cases for a reason, but once given it acquires a meaning:

If it did not to some extent get to *mean* the thing, it could never get to *stand* for it at all. (*PL*, p. 60)

Here he seems to be applying the same notions of intension and extension to proper names:

And can one say that a proper name, if you are aware of its designation, brings *no* ideas with it, or that these ideas are a mere chance conjunction? . . . You may have no idea of what 'William' connotes, but if so you can hardly know what it stands for. (*PL*, p. 60)

This is similar to a point made by Russell:

The names that we commonly use, like 'Socrates,' are really abbreviations for descriptions; not only that, but what they describe are not particulars but complicated systems of classes or series.[25]

Russell subsequently went on to find the true proper name in such words as 'this,' which merely indicated a present sense-datum at the time it appeared, a 'mark' which had reference but no meaning.

Proper names are, for Bradley, radically different from 'this:'

For, unless the person were recognised as distinct, he would hardly get a name of his own, and his recognition depends on his remaining the same throughout change of context. We could not recognise anything unless it possessed an attribute, or attributes, which from time to time we are able to identify. The individual remains the same amid that change of appearance which we predicate as its quality. (*PL*, p. 61)

This would seem to assimilate proper names to other words and to the conventional explanation of their meanings in terms of intension and extension. Bradley appears to do this, for he has argued just before the discussion of proper names that

The idea, which stands as the grammatical subject, is certainly more than an indefinite reference, more even than a sign of indication. (*PL*, p. 58)

His example is the sentence 'This bird is yellow,' and the claim is that just as 'This bird' does not merely indicate, but also says something about what is referred to – my hearer can say 'No, it's not a bird' – so does the proper name. It can be applied wrongly. Consequently Bradley transforms the question about the nature of the proper name into one about the nature of the individual, into what it is that remains the same throughout change, has a stable identity. It is at this point that he introduces the notion of the 'concrete universal,' which is often thought to be a hallmark of Idealist thought, and which received a great deal of attention from both advocates and critics. It will be best to deal with it in a separate chapter.

NOTES

1 *Letters, Lectures and Reviews,* ed. H. W. Chandler, London, 1873, p. 23.
2 *Critique of Pure Reason,* trans. N. Kemp Smith, London, 1929, A69=B94.
3 *Logic,* trans. Bernard Bosanquet, Oxford, 1888, p. 12. The original was published in 1874.
4 *Wissenschaftlicher Briefwechsel,* ed. G. Gabriel *et al.,* Hamburg, 1976, quoted H. D. Sluga, *Frege,* London, 1980, p. 92.
5 *Posthumous Writings,* trans. P. Long and R. White, Oxford, 1979, p. 17.
6 *Works of T. H. Green,* ed. R. L. Nettleship, vol. II, London, 1890, p. 196.
7 Ibid., pp. 202–3.
8 *The Essentials of Logic,* London, 1895, p. 87.
9 *Frege,* London, 1973, p. 3.
10 Ibid., p. 4.
11 *The Foundations of Arithmetic,* trans. J. L. Austin, Oxford, 1950, p.x.
12 *Frege,* p. 57.
13 *The Sunday Times,* 16 November 1980, p. 14.
14 Cora Diamond, 'What Nonsense might be,' *Philosophy,* January 1981, p. 19.
15 This is cited by J. N. Keynes from an Oxford Examination Paper in *Formal Logic,* London, 1887, p. 96.
16 'The Nature of Judgment,' *Mind,* 1899, p. 177.
17 Ibid., p. 182.
18 Ibid., p. 192.
19 *My Philosophical Development,* London, 1975, p. 42.
20 *The Essentials of Logic,* p. 12.
21 *Knowledge and Experience in the Philosophy of F. H. Bradley,* London, 1964, p. 143.
22 *Mind,* 1899, p. 176.
23 Ibid., p. 181.
24 *Formal Logic,* p. 21.
25 *Logic and Knowledge,* ed. R. C. Marsh, London, 1956, pp. 200–1.

V

The Concrete Universal

The term 'concrete universal' was used by Bradley in *Ethical Studies*, and given a somewhat different interpretation in the *Principles of Logic*. It does not figure explicitly in *Appearance and Reality*, whose index contains no references even to 'universals.' It seems that Bradley no longer made use of the phrase after writing the *Principles of Logic*, but Kemp Smith referred to Bradley's transition from the ordinary to the concrete universal being 'abrupt' and gave a reference to *Appearance and Reality* to confirm his point.[1] The major development of the notion was by Bosanquet, whose views formed the basis for subsequent discussion. One problem in discussing this topic is the difficulty of discovering exactly what was meant by the phrase; it is by no means clear that there was consistent doctrine, or that Bradley ever really accepted Bosanquet's developments, however much he may have given verbal assent to them. It is generally agreed by commentators that the doctrine had a Hegelian origin, though it is also suggested that its formulation was influenced by Kant's distinction between Understanding and Reason. Kemp Smith says that it is one

which has tended to perpetuate in idealist thinkers the belief in a twofold employment of the intelligence, one appropriate to the uses of ordinary life and of the positive sciences in dealing with appearances, and another better suited to yield insight of a metaphysical character.[2]

Though it is true that much of what is regarded as Hegelian in Idealist thinking was Kantian, I can find no evidence that Bradley thought of the concrete universal as something peculiarly of interest to metaphysics. Indeed, its virtual absence from the pages of *Appearance and Reality* would seem to tell against this interpretation. Certainly in his *Principles* it is introduced to solve logical problems.

In a symposium entitled 'Is the "Concrete Universal" the true type of universality?' one of the symposiasts, H. Wildon Carr, interpreted it as follows:

The 'concrete universal' I take to mean the theory of those who, following the Hegelian principle, the real is the rational, hold that it is possible to give a consistent account of experience, subjective and objective, internal and external, without resorting to the notion of an extra-mental object of knowledge, existing independently, confronting the mind and exercising upon it an influence to which it is purely passive and receptive.[3]

I do not quote this passage to explain what the concrete universal was thought to be; indeed, one of the startling features of much of the later debate over the subject is the extent to which it takes place in terms of an apparently settled theory, the basis of which is hard to discover. After all, the whole question began with a consideration of 'universals' in a quite ordinary sense, i.e. problems about what sort of an entity was 'red' in such sentences as 'The book is red.' The problem is often represented as that of the One and the Many. It is necessary here, however, to try to disentangle what Bosanquet and his followers were talking about to clear the way for a close look at Bradley's views. Both started from the same formula, itself a commonplace in the discussion of universality, 'Identity in Difference,' but they did not handle this obscure phrase in the same manner. To a large extent this is the result of a difference in interest between the two philosophers. Bosanquet was more concerned with political philosophy and, perhaps as a consequence, biology formed his model for science. Michael Foster remarks in his examination of the concrete universal:

The understanding of Bosanquet's *Logic* becomes suddenly illuminated by the recognition that it is derived almost exclusively from reflection upon the 'comparative' sciences (Botany, Zoology, Anthropology) and its conclusions then applied uncritically to the whole of knowledge.[4]

Bosanquet's work is best represented by such books as *The Philosophical Theory of The State* and *The Principle of Individuality and Value*, evidence of its social and political orientation. One of his themes is that the state is 'more real' than its citizens, who exist as private individuals only because they are citizens. Associations are prior, in some sense, to those who belong to them. Even a group that would not seem to be central to the lives of its members, the Aristotelian Society, becomes an entity with metaphysical attributes:

But in as far as our membership plays any part in our consciousness, so far this real identity actually and in sober earnest forms part of our being as the individuals that we are, and our solidarity as a Society is only another aspect of a real identity which is recognised in a different form by each several member of the Society, according to his individual relations to it.[5]

As a part of this way of thinking, aesthetic judgments become assimilated to logical ones:

The rhythm that completes a rhythm, the sound that with other sounds satisfies the educated ear, the colour that is demanded by a colour-scheme, are I take it as necessary and as rational as the conclusion of a syllogism.[6]

To modern ears, the whole discussion sounds metaphysical and unrelated to what are now seen as philosophical issues. Hence it is desirable to give a brief defence of Bosanquet. One problem is that his vocabulary seems so remote from what we are used to, though it should be remembered that the same philosophical problem can be discussed in very different terminologies, and there is no reason to suspect that one is inherently superior to the others. His article 'On the True Conception of Another World,' mentioned in chapter I, is perhaps the best exposition of the down-to-earth character of Hegelian Idealism that can be found, and many contemporary thinkers have, all unawares, made points like his. He claims that the object of talk about 'another world' is 'to enforce a distinction which falls *within* the world which we know, and not *between* the world we know and another which we do not know.'[7] Again, mind and body, he insists, are not two entities connected in a mysterious way; the mind is the body and human action would be incomprehensible if it were not. Mind–brain identity would not seem ridiculous to him, though the way he developed the idea might surprise some of its modern adherents. In short it is necessary to penetrate below the form in which the arguments are put to the content, and not to assume too quickly that anything not presented in the language of the analytical tradition is automatically the result of 'metaphysics.' Close reading of Bosanquet reveals that he, like Bradley at the period of the *Principles of Logic*, is more realistic, nearer to 'ordinary language' than seems at first sight to be the case. The picture of the Anglo-Hegelians given by Russell and Moore should not be taken as a true one. After all, they were interested in putting forward their own views of philosophy, and emphasizing differences with their predecessors.

Bradley is not interested in the same things as Bosanquet; he did not develop the argument of *Ethical Studies*, nor was he much concerned with the nature of the state as a political entity. Unlike Bosanquet he had no active concern in measures of reform. It is a logical issue which led him to speak of the concrete universal, and when he came to write on metaphysics it is clear that he had doubts as to whether such an entity could exist. There is something paradoxical in talking of a 'concrete universal' and in such remarks as 'The true universal is the individual.' For universality is normally taken to be an example of abstractness, and, although an individual may be characterized by many universals, the notion of a universal is the antithesis of that of an individual. The classic issue was that there seemed no problem about the existence of individual things, but it was hard to see how universals could exist in the same sense. And if they existed in a different manner, or in a different realm, then it was difficult to see how they could be known. Such questions have been the staple of philosophic discussion since the time of Plato. Hence to couple the terms 'individual' and 'universal' seems either a confusion or the result of using one or both in senses radically different from the normal.

The problem arose from the logical issue of whether proper names are 'unmeaning marks,' as Mill had maintained. Bradley argues that they must have meaning, which would seem to lead to the conclusion that a proper name should be classed with other universals; that there was no logical difference between 'John' and 'dog.' Indeed, this was traditional logical doctrine, for as far as its function in the syllogism was concerned, a proposition containing a proper name was taken as equivalent to a 'universal proposition.' J. N. Keynes says in his *Formal Logic:*

Singular propositions may usually be regarded as forming a sub-class of universals, since in every singular proposition the affirmation or denial is of the *whole* of the subject.*

Bradley comments on this doctrine:

It is sufficient for the technical use of the syllogism, and it is perhaps in itself not so foolish as it seems to be. (*PL,* p. 186)

In the passage quoted above (pp. 77), he seems to transform the issue into an epistemological one, to a question of how it is possible to apply a proper name correctly or to re-identify the bearer of the name. This view is then extended to apply to things which do not have proper names in the ordinary sense, so that objects also become concrete universals. What looks odd here is that 'universal' has become removed from the word or 'idea' and transferred to the object named by the word. The passage quoted above continues: 'Its proper name is the sign of a universal, of an ideal content which actually *is* in the real world' (*PL*, p. 61). We should not say '"John" is a concrete universal,' but 'John is a concrete universal,' i.e. that man over there is one, and it is hard to make sense of such a statement.

Besides universal and singular, traditional logic accepted a third class of propositions, namely particular, beginning with 'Some' or its cognates, and this usage seems to have been a source of confusion. One writer attributes the use of the word in two senses to both Berkeley and Mill:

[a particular] may mean some particular thing pointed to, where no reference is made to its membership of a class or, at any rate, where no stress is

---

* *Formal Logic,* London, 1887, p. 58. Leibniz claimed that a singular proposition is both particular and universal: 'Should we say that a singular proposition is equivalent to a particular and to a universal proposition, Yes we should. . . . for 'Some Apostle Peter' and 'Every Apostle Peter' coincide, since the term is singular' (G. H. Parkinson, ed. and trans., *Leibniz's Logical Papers,* Oxford, 1966, p. 115). This enabled him to solve certain logical problems. Fred Sommers argues that Leibniz's proposal can be built into a viable alternative to the 'classical' Fregean logic, and that this system might be a better one for certain extra-logical purposes (see 'Leibniz's Program for the Development of Logic, in *Essays in Memory of Imre Lakatos,* ed. R. S. Cohen, P. K. Feyerabend and M. W. Wartofsky, Dordrecht, 1976, pp. 589–615). Although there are many affinities between Leibniz and Bradley, it is unlikely that he could have seen the passage Sommers cites. I quote it, and refer to Sommers' paper, only in order to make the point that the purely logical success of the Fregean system should not lead us to ignore or dismiss other ways of dealing with the problem of singular propositions.

laid upon its class characteristics. Or it may mean some particular member of a class whose class characteristics are obvious enough to justify us in treating it as a typical member, that is as *any* member, of its class.[8]

Bradley, in his discussion of the concrete universal, seems to do the same thing. For he introduces it in the chapter on 'The Quantity of Judgments' so the reader is inclined to think the subject is propositions, and this is reinforced by the distinction between 'particular' and 'individual.' But when he makes a distinction between both 'concrete particular' and 'concrete universal' and 'abstract particular' and 'abstract universal,' we seem to be in the realm of objects which can be pointed to (*PL*, p. 188). When he states four propositions that he accepts:

    (i)   Nothing that is real is universal,
   (ii)   All that is real is universal,
  (iii)   Nothing that is real is particular,
  (iv)   Most that is real is particular,

(*PL*, p. 187), the reader is liable to be simply bemused or to conclude that the reconciliation of these antithetical statements is either a piece of dialectical legerdemain or the simple result of using words in different senses, as Bradley himself admits at this point (*PL*, p. 188). Proposition (i) is a traditional view, namely that universals are mental creations. It would seem that (iv) should have been expressed as 'All that is real is particular' so as to make it correspond to (i) and bring us back to a standard empiricist doctrine.

    Bradley's argument rests on a distinction between 'particular' and 'individual.' The discussion of (iii) seems to take 'particular' in the sense of something merely given, of which some quality is predicated, for he says of it:

The particular is atomic. It excludes all difference. It is itself and nothing beyond itself . . . . The true particular in respect of quality is shut up in one quality; (*PL*, p. 187)

The 'sense-datum' which has (or is) a simple quality would seem to be what Bradley had in mind:

And this holds again with psychical atoms. For, as observed, they have internal multiplicity, duration in time, quality and degree; and as anything else they could not be observed. An atom which was really particular, which was not divisible at least in idea, could not possibly be fact. It is one aspect of fact torn away from the rest, and is nothing in itself and apart from the act which tears it away. (*PL,* pp. 188–9)

The contrast is with an individual, for when a quality is attributed to that it is as one of a set of possible qualities; the individual is something which persists through time and is the subject of change:

We are accustomed to speak of, and believe in, realities which exist in more than one moment of time or portion of space. Any such reality would be an identity which appears and remains the same under differences; and it therefore would be a real universal.* (*PL,* p. 45)

The argument would seem to involve simple trickery. Traditionally the universal was regarded as 'one in many' because, e.g., redness was the same in all its instances. This is what made it universal, for it could appear in different places and at different times and remain the same. It was an 'identity which occurred in different things,' whereas Bradley's 'identity in difference' is not something which is perceived to be the same in many places, but something which must be the same if we are to use proper names as we do. In another book he suggests that the concrete universal is 'perhaps really, though not avowedly, admitted by Mr. Russell under the name of "unity"' (*ETR,* p. 297). (The unity of the self is here the issue.) In the *Principles* he explicitly says of a man: 'He is universal because he is one throughout all his different attributes' *PL,* p. 188). To use the word 'universal' to refer to 'unity' in this sense seems an example of using a word in a new sense, and hence to be misleading.

At its introduction in *Ethical Studies,* the concrete universal played a different role; its presence there is, I think, connected with the more Hegelian tone of that work. Bradley relates it to the distinction between the true and spurious infinite; the latter is the infinite of mathematics, the endless repetition of identical units. The former is that which is 'unbounded,' i.e. not limited by anything other than itself, for example Spinoza's *'Deus sive natura'* or the

---

* Bradley adds a footnote: 'The following reflection may interest the reader. If space and time are continuous, and if all appearances must occupy some time or space and it is not hard to support both these *theses* – we can at once proceed to the conclusion, no mere particular exists. Every phenomenon will exist in more times or spaces than one; and against that diversity will itself be an universal' (*PL,* p. 45).

Absolute itself. In the *Principles* the true infinite is not mentioned as such, though there are a number of references to the spurious variety. As he developed his own views, Bradley relied less on Hegelian modes of expression and on Hegelian arguments. He explicitly states that he is no Hegelian in the preface to the *Principles* (*PL*, p.x). But at the stage when he wrote 'My Station and its Duties,' he is much more imbued with Hegelian ideas, and the concrete universal is taken as characterizing the view expressed by the title of the chapter, 'My Station and its Duties.' 'My Station' is given by the 'real moral organism' (*ES*, p. 187) which is the state, and by this means the inner and the outer are reconciled:

We see thus that, when morals are looked at as a whole, the will of the inside, so far as it is moral, *is* the will of the outside, and the two are one and cannot be torn apart without *ipso facto* destroying the unity in which morality consists. (*ES*, p. 180)

The moral self is thus not limited by anything outside it, for the inner and outer are identified; it is thus 'infinite' in the true sense, and what it wills is the 'concrete universal.' This passage reveals that the concrete universal is not at this stage thought of as an existing entity; its concreteness derives from the specification in detail of someone's duties by his station, its universality from the fact that the state is an 'organic whole' (*ES*, p. 176). It is because the two are intimately linked that we can call their union the concrete universal:

The two problems of the best man and the best state are two sides, two distinguishable aspects of the one problem, how to realize in human nature the perfect unity of homogeneity and specification, (*ES*, p. 188)

Bradley seldom referred to the state in his later works; Bosanquet continued to use the notion of an 'organic whole' in his discussion of the concrete universal.

Thus the concrete universal in *Ethical Studies* was an ideal, a recipe for attaining the maximum of identity in difference; in the *Principles* it becomes a characterization of an identity in difference which is actually encountered, part of the explanation of how thought relates to the world. Bradley's use of such a phrase as 'identity in difference' to describe the self or any other object that persists through time sounds odd to us. Bradley is aware of this:

> It sounds terrible to say that Identity is an ideal synthesis of differences, and that this identity is a real fact. The words are strange to the common mind, but it has always tacitly accepted their meaning. We believe that a body has changed its place, but at the end of the movement the change that is past is no fact of sense. We abstract the body from its present position and, treating this abstraction as a continuous identity, we predicate of it the changing differences. But do we doubt that motion is a real fact? (*PL*, p. 293)

What is not clear is why he should have used the word 'universal' to characterize it, for many writers had talked of identities in difference but had thought them to be particulars. His argument would seem to be as follows; abstract universals (and the abstract particulars of empiricism) cannot exist in reality; they are mental constructs, exist only in our minds. Therefore there is nothing which corresponds to them in the world; he says of one of them: 'It is nothing but an adjective, an internal distinction which we try to take as a substantial fact' (*PL*, p. 188). For logical inference what is needed is a real identity, one which does exist in the world, otherwise our thinking becomes the manipulation of symbols and there is no reason why what we infer should be true of the things we are ostensibly talking about. Oddly enough, Bradley's arguments here seem to lead him into agreeing with Mill, though verbally rather than in substance. Both are concerned with what Mill called the 'Logic of Truth' against the traditional, or formal, logic, which Mill calls the 'Logic of Consistency' and obviously regards as inferior to the former. It is hard to see how Bradley could quarrel with the following remarks:

> If thought be anything more than a sportive exercise of the mind, its purpose is to enable us to know what can be known respecting the facts of the universe: its judgments and conclusions express, or are intended to express, some of those facts: and the connexion which Formal Logic, by its analysis of the reasoning process, points out between one proposition and another, exists only because there is a connexion between one objective truth and another, which makes it possible for us to know objective truths which have never been observed, in virtue of others which have. This possibility is an eternal mystery and stumbling-block to Formal Logic.[9]

The classic difficulty with such an attack on formal logic is that it ignores the fact that we often want to know the relation between two sentences, neither of which is, at that time, asserted. We do this, perhaps, in order to decide which of them we can go on to assert. Also we make use of the principle of contradiction to criticize a piece of discourse without ourselves assenting to either of the sentences which we claim are incompatible. From Socrates onwards the logic of consistency has been used in argument as the means of discovering falsehood. This implies that logical relations hold between sentences. Bradley is well aware that he has to deny these common beliefs if he is to give the account of logic that he wishes to. It is for this reason that he makes the subject-matter of logic judgments and not sentences. In this he would appear to have the company of Strawson in the latter's attack on the theory of descriptions.[10] Such a view has plausibility because people do not normally utter sentences unless they intend to assert them. There are deviant cases, such as the logic lecture room, in which many of the sentences uttered are not expected to be taken as true by the hearers, but because these areas are 'marked off' in an obvious way, no real problems arise. However, if you have asserted 'p,' you have no right immediately to assert 'not-p.' No one can ever assert 'p and-p.' In other words, we do use the Principle of Contradiction. Bradley thinks Hegel did not deny the principle, though some of his followers may have. He himself had no intention of doing so; indeed, the argument of *Appearance and Reality* rests largely on its application.

It is possible to find a basis for the principle in language; to assert and to deny at the same time is to say nothing. I think Bradley's move is to claim that it is not a matter of rules, but of judgments, i.e. the reason why you cannot both affirm and deny 'p' is that you cannot both think 'p' and 'not p' or 'A is b' and 'A is not b.' This cannot be because language forbids one, for thought is prior to language; the reason why we accept the linguistic ban is because we cannot think in this way. That this must be the right answer is shown by the fact that we can utter apparently contradictory sentences: 'Is it raining?' 'It is and it isn't.' But we then interpret such a sentence in a non-contradictory manner. This seems to point to the fact that the principles of logic do not depend on language alone. For rather different reasons Mill comes to a similar conclusion in the passage just quoted. This led him to the belief that inference must be from particulars to particulars, for these were the only things that could exist in reality. Universals must be 'mental creations' and so could not form the basis for a logic of truth. Bradley retained the more traditional view that inference depended on universals, but felt that these had to be 'real' universals, i.e. ones that did exist in reality. What are normally thought of as such could only function in merely formal inferences, those which gave rise to a logic of consistency. Hence there must be special kinds of universals, namely 'concrete' ones.

This is one strand which drives Bradley to use this form of words. The other, as I have indicated, is connected with the use of proper names, though in fact it has a wider application. But Bradley's starting point was thinking about them, and the question of what it was that formed the basis of personal identity. In *Ethical Studies* there occurs the famous attack on the view of the self as a mere string of experiences, summed up by 'Mr. Bain collects that the mind is a collection. Has he ever thought who collects Mr. Bain?' (*ES* , p. 39n). In the *Principles* he says: 'The oneness or identity of a man, we know, is not found when we search the series of mental phenomena' (*PL*, p. 188). Earlier, talking of individuals, he had stressed the point about identity:

And this implies that it has real identity. Its proper name is the sign of a universal, of an ideal content which actually *is* in the real world. . . . What concerns us here is that the practice (of giving proper names) transcends presented reality. In 'John is asleep', the ultimate subject can not be the real as it is now given; for 'John' implies a continuous existence, not got by mere analysis. (*PL*, p. 61)

In his book *Identity and Spatio-temporal Continuity*, David Wiggins makes use of the term 'concrete universal' in the context of a possible problem about identity. If the two halves of a person's brain were to be transplanted into separate bodies, and each part were to retain all the prior memories and skills of the individual so treated, then there is a sense in which both the new individuals would be the same person, at least until they had had a number of different experiences. Hence if the original person were called Brown, Brown I and Brown II, as the two could be called for convenience, would both be instances of Brown, and the possession of instances implies that 'Brown' has become a universal. Wiggins explicitly uses the term 'concrete universal' and also the term 'clone-universal' in talking of these cases.[11] He is clearly pointing to something important, for there is a biological sense in which all members of a clone, e.g. all specimens of Cox's Orange Pippin trees, are not just similar to one another but in biological respects identical. They are essentially the same even though individuated by spatial positions and certain 'accidental' features like size and shape. Hence 'Cox's Orange Pippin' can be considered to be a proper name, even though it incorporates descriptive features, the type of apple, its colour and the name of its originator. The original tree was named in something analogous to a christening ceremony. More important for this discussion is the fact that even though there were another sort of apple which shared many features of this variety of Cox, it would not be a Cox's Orange Pippin unless it came of the same stock. Similarity is not enough, as it is with manufactured articles, for the application of the name; strict identity is required.

This point could be put in Bradleian form by saying that to call an apple 'Cox's Orange Pippin' analysis of its qualities is not sufficient, a 'continuous existence' from the original parent is needed. A particular apple tree is a Cox's Orange Pippin because of its descent from an individual tree; it is biologically or genetically identical with its 'ancestor.' This is not to deny that we may identify a particular tree as a Cox by means of its qualities. But, whatever the similarity between two trees, if one is not descended from the original Cox, it is not entitled to that name. These remarks perhaps help to bring out Bradley's point. The human individual 'John' is not like a clone in the sense that there could normally be many 'instances' of him co-existing. But he is like it in the sense that there can be radical changes in all or some of his characteristics without his name being changed. Given the law of this country there is no reason why even so drastic a change as that of sex would necessarily lead to a change of name. His essential features are 'being the same individual,' and this is independent of his apparent features. We apply the same name because he *is* the same person, not because he is *like* the original bearer of the name. 'John' is the name of something which is in itself universal, not a mere symbol of reality but something which, as it were, reaches right out to it.

The problems which arise in this area are partly due to a confusion between logical and epistemological issues, between the question of the meaning of a proper name and our ability correctly to apply a proper name. Bradley, it seems clear, is committed to making a firm distinction between the two, though immediately before the last quotation he says:

For, unless the person were recognized as distinct, he would hardly get a name of his own, and his recognition depends on his remaining the same throughout change of context. We could not recognize anything unless it possessed an attribute, or attributes, which from time to time we are able to identify. The individual remains the same amid that change of appearances which we predicate as its quality. (*PL*, p. 61)

However, the fact that our method of recognizing a person is by means of a constant attribute does not imply that the meaning of the proper name we use is the attribute in question. The meaning of the name is (or the name is) the individual. This view differs from that which Dummett attributes to Frege; if Leo Peter understands by 'Dr Gustav Lauben' the doctor who lives in a certain place, while Herbert Garner knows his unique place and time of birth but not where he lives now, the senses they attach to the name must be different and the two men

do not speak the same language, since, although they do in fact refer to the same man by means of this name, they do not know that they do so.[12]

Such a case can certainly occur, and in extreme forms can given rise to the phenomenon of the same object possessing two names, as 'The Morning Star' and 'the Evening Star,' or the case of the mountain called both 'Afla' and 'Ateb' as a result of two explorers independently discovering it.[13] And it is these possibilities which are the roots of the Fregean doctrine of 'sense and reference.' In such cases the sense is the criterion an individual has for identifying the bearer of the name, whilst the reference is the bearer itself. There is no doubt that when someone learns that the Morning Star is the Evening Star, or that both are the planet Venus, he has learnt a new fact about the world and this will be incorporated in his use of one or both of the words in future.

The increase in his knowledge of course affects the position of the person who learns the new fact; it does not alter the meaning of the name. If it were held to alter the meaning of the name itself, it would seem to result in the establishment of a number of 'private meanings' to the name, as Frege seems to have thought. But if this occurred, the name would no longer be the name of an individual. It would rather be a sign for a particular person to recognize that individual. Bradley, as I understand him, wants to assert that the name is something which belongs inalienably to an individual, in other words that the meaning of a proper name is its referent.

This is what is meant by saying that 'John is a concrete universal,' i.e. a combination of various qualities which persists through time. We may only know a small part of those qualities, and may even be mistaken about some of them; if 'Mount Q' is identified by its being the highest mountain in its range, the discovery that a higher peak exists does not lead to a change in name, but to a change in what is said about it. On the other hand a mistake about the identification of a natural kind leads to its being referred to by a different name; if I had constantly referred to my gold ring in the past, the discovery that it is really pinchbeck will lead me to talk differently of it. There are intermediate cases, where the name of a natural kind has been incorporated into a proper name; e.g. the Black Prince's Ruby in the Crown Jewels is now believed by most gemmologists to be not a ruby but a spinel, a quite different kind of stone. But they still use the name 'Black Prince's Ruby,' thereby showing that the phrase is a proper name. Roughly, if the same name is retained in spite of mistake about its bearer being discovered, the name in question is a proper one. 'My gold ring' was not a proper name because I would no longer refer to it as such when I had discovered its real composition. The point is, however, rather more complex; I mentioned above (p. 83) that Bradley also extended his talk of the 'concrete universal' to some objects. Dummett makes what is in substance the same point when he says:

It has, for instance, frequently been remarked that the identification of chemical substances may resemble that of geographical objects in that a range of distinct criteria may be used in practice without it being possible for us to single out any one of them as that which anyone who understands the sense of the word must be aware of. The point can equally be made for animal and plant species, for diseases, and the like.[14]

A classic case would be the retention of the name 'chlorine' in spite of the discovery that it consisted of a mixture of two isotopes, though it should not be forgotten that biologists are constantly changing the names of species as new relationships or facts are discovered. An existing species may be split into two, or two species lumped together into a single one.

Such changes in nomenclature are well known and it would be both tedious and unnecessary to detail them. Here the question is whether such alterations are of interest to logic. In spite of Frege's view, this does not seem to be so. Dummett argues that there must be some route that the individual uses for reaching the referent from the expression. In the case of a proper name 'some criterion he has for recognizing the object as being or not being the bearer of the name.'[15] As so often, the use of the word 'criterion' helps to confuse an issue. Even if there is some means which enables me to recognize John, this is certainly not a criterion of his being John in any of the many senses in which that ambiguous term is used. He is still John even if I fail to recognize him. Dummett argues that it makes no sense to suppose that the user attaches the reference directly to the expression and therefore the link must pass via the 'sense.' But the problem for logic, it seems to me, is how 'John' means that individual, in other words how reference is achieved, and this is the problem Bradley is endeavouring to solve. His answer, which I have tried to express in terms of 'transparency,' may amount to saying that 'John' just does mean that individual and no further explanation is possible.

It also implies that what is necessary for learning language is just to grasp this. Helen Keller, in her autobiography, describes the revelation of learning her first word. She already could make some of her wants known, but she suddenly realized that the movement of her teacher's fingers, which I will for convenience transcribe as 'water,' stood for the stuff itself, not for her desire for it. 'Water' could still be used to express a desire for water, but it did this because it was the name of water. The correct use of the name shows that a connection has been made. This is all that is required for the word to have a meaning.

Hence I am puzzled by a remark of Dummett's:

In order to determine whether or not a sentence is true, it is enough to know the reference ot the various constituent expressions; but, in order to know what information it conveys, we must know their sense.[16]

It seems odd to say that I can discover that a sentence is true without its having conveyed any information to me; if I can verify it, then we would normally think I had extracted the information that it contained. Nor does Dummett's explanation make the point any clearer; he seems to claim that the notion of sense is required for two things, for justification or verification and for the systematization of language. The point is connected with Frege's discussion of the sense and reference of sentences. Here all that needs to be said is that this point does not show that the notion of sense is needed for dealing with proper names and their analogues. The traditional doctrine of non-connotative words was not entirely silly as far as proper names were concerned. We do not christen somebody 'John' because of features that he possesses, whereas we do call something a triangle because it has three sides. In the latter case there are further problems, which I have discussed from a more epistemological point of view in 'Games and Family Resemblances.'[17] Mill was mistaken when he called the proper name an 'unmeaning mark;' it has a meaning, namely its bearer. The epistemological question of how anyone knows when to apply a particular name is outside the concern of logic, as is that of what is learned when it is discovered that the Morning Star and the Evening Star are the same planet. Given our methods of naming, it is hardly surprising that one object might be given different names by some mistake. But this would seem to be a feature of the pragmatics of language, not of its syntax or semantics.

It is only because the logical theory of Frege follows, albeit distantly, the tradition of 'substance' and gives a special role to proper names, that a problem arises about the statement that 'The Morning Star is the Evening Star.' One use to which the doctrine of the concrete universal might be put is to say that there is no bar against a proper name occurring in the predicate position, for as it is a universal, no logical problems are raised by this. There is a difference between learning that the Morning Star is round and learning that it is the Evening Star, but it does not follow that this is a logical difference. Aristotle distinguished a quality from a substance by pointing out that the former has contraries, whereas the latter does not, and this criterion would seem to mark an irreducible logical difference between 'The Morning Star is round,' which has, among others, the contrary 'The Morning Star is square,' and 'The Morning Star is the Evening Star' which has a contradictory but no contrary, it being assumed that the contradictory is 'The Morning Star is not the Evening Star.' As we do not have names of the same form for many heavenly bodies, perhaps a better example would be 'The Morning Star is Venus.' which has contraries such as 'The Morning Star is Uranus,' 'The Morning Star is Mercury,' etc. (I am assuming that 'the Morning Star' is being taken as a name in all these examples.) It is, of course, true that in most cases a proper name occurs in the subject position, and often where it does not a minor revision will put it there without altering the sense of what is said. And there are very good reasons why this should be so, but they seem to spring from the nature of human discourse, from the fact that we are interested in people and other objects to which we give proper names. But I do not think this fact is itself enough to establish a categorial distinction between names (or their bearers) and qualities. Ramsey argued[18] that logic did not prove that it was necessary to make a distinction between universals and particulars; he even refers to 'that great muddle the theory of universals.'[19] He is quite willing to admit the possibility that material objects are 'true Aristotelian adjectives.'[20] There is no space to go into the details of the argument, which aims to show that so-called individuals and qualities are symmetrically related so that no purpose is served in distinguishing them. Except, I would add, in the case where one already has a metaphysical theory which demands such a distinction. Bradley, it is clear, does not regard individuals as substances in the Aristotelian sense. Indeed, part of the role of the term 'concrete universal' seems to be to make this very point. It might be said that it follows from Bradley's suggestion that the correct form of any judgment is 'Reality is such that S is P' that there can be no significant logical difference between the two constituents of the judgment. Hence there is no reason not to talk of both as 'universals.' It would follow that there is no reason for an analysis of identity statements that differed from any other type. (Fred Sommers argues for a similar position, though on rather different grounds.)[21]

Thus the concrete universal is, in the *Principles of Logic*, a logical device, not a metaphysical discovery, the finding by analysis of a strange entity whose existence had previously been unsuspected. The coincidence of two lines of thought forced Bradley into talking in these terms. Bosanquet's notion of the concrete universal is more like that of *Ethical Studies*, and this explains the difference between their accounts of it. Subsequent discussion has concentrated on Bosanquet's version, not Bradley's, and the fact that the doctrine could have a logical basis was forgotten or ignored. Indeed, Bradley had metaphysical doubts about the possibility of such a thing; the passage omitted from the quotation from *PL*, p. 61 above reads 'This assumption, and the practice of giving proper names, may no doubt be indefensible.' In the later discussion he realizes that talking of the concrete universal in the way he did may have wider metaphysical implications. Casting back to the discussion of the true and false infinite, he says: 'An individual which is finite or relative turns out in the end to be no individual; individual and infinite are inseparable characters.' (*PL*, p. 190). But 'infinite' here seems to be used in its more traditional sense, for Bradley argues that we are forced by the argument to postulate only one real individual, the Absolute. In the *Principles of Logic* there is a certain ambiguity about Bradley's attitude to metaphysics, an ambiguity which is resolved when he comes to write the terminal essays and notes to the book, because in the interval he has produced *Appearance and Reality*. However, the role of logic in that work should not be forgotten; it is by no means a piece of 'constructive metaphysics.' Perhaps the best description of his attitude there is that given by Richard Wollheim, who talks of Bradley being

more like a man forced backwards, step by step, down a strange labyrinth, in self-defence, until at last finding himself in the comparative safety of some murky cave he rests among the shadows.[22]

Wollheim makes it clear that it is logic that pushes Bradley down this path; it is his 'willingness to follow the argument wherever it leads' that produces those conclusions which sound so odd to our ears, not the desire to exhibit a vision of the world which came to him prior to his writing. And it is this which leads him to close his three major books with sceptical conclusions. As far as this section of the *Principles* is concerned, Bradley has no doubts:

Metaphysics, it is clear, would have to take up these questions, and in any case to revise the account which is given in this chapter. But that revision must be left to metaphysics; and for the purposes of logic we may keep to the distinctions already laid down. (*PL*, p. 190)

In 'The Final Essence of Reasoning' Bradley again mentions the 'concrete universal:'

. . . a fundamental error. And it arose from our use of the abstract universal. That can not be real, and in consequence our thoughts were all built on unreality and ended in falsehood. But in the concrete universal, which has guided our steps, and which has appeared as the identity of analysis and synthesis, we have returned to truth and made our peace with reality. (*PL*, pp. 486–7)

He goes on, in the next paragraph:

If for metaphysics what is individual is real and what is real is individual, for logic too the rational is individual and individuality is truth. (*PL*, p. 487)

I shall have more to say about the identity of analysis and synthesis in the discussion of inference in chapter X below; here the important point for logic is that Bradley thinks that in practice, as distinct from metaphysically, every inquiry demands 'the gaining all the facts and the getting them consistent' (*PL*, p. 487), which involves employing the 'concrete universal.' Thus we can look on the term as a means of stressing the concreteness of real logic as against the false abstraction of the logic of the Schools. There may be no real and 'concrete' stopping place short of the absolute if we raise ultimate, or metaphysical, questions, which is why there is no mention of the concrete universal in the text of *Appearance and Reality*, but for logic and for the practical purposes of everyday life, it has a role to play.

NOTES

1 N. Kemp Smith, 'The Nature of Universals,' *Mind*, 1927, p. 156.
2 Ibid., p. 141.
3 *Proceedings of the Aristotelian Society*, vol. 20, 1919–20, pp. 140–1.
4 *Mind*, 1931, p. 13.
5 'The Philosophical Importance of a True Theory of Identity, *Essays and Addresses*, London, 1889, p. 173.
6 *The Principle of Individuality and Value*, London, 1912, p. 62.
7 *Essays and Addresses*, p. 94.
8 R. P. Anschutz, *The Philosophy of J. S. Mill*, Oxford, 1953, p. 137.
9 *Examination of Sir William Hamilton's Philosophy*, London, 1872, p. 477.
10 *Introduction to Logical Theory*, London, 1952, p.184ff.
11 *Identity and Spatio-temporal Continuity*, Oxford, 1967, pp. 53–5 and p. 64.
12 *Frege*, London 1973, p. 584.
13 Ibid., p. 97.
14 Ibid., p. 100.

15 Ibid., p. 102.
16 Ibid., p. 104.
17 *Philosophy*, 1967, pp. 210–25.
18 'Universals,' *The Foundations of Mathematics*, London, 1950, pp. 112–37.
19 Ibid., p. 134.
20 Ibid., p. 112.
21 'Do we need Identity?', *Journal of Philosophy*, vol. 66, 1969, pp. 499–504.
22 *F. H. Bradley*, London, 1959, p. 18

VI

Judgment

The problem of the nature of judgment is clearly central to Bradley's discussion of logic, and many different interpretations of it have been given. Most writers on the subject, however, have taken his account of judgment to be a stage on the way to the metaphysics of *Appearance and Reality*, and hence have tried to produce a (relatively) consistent doctrine by considering what he says about it in all his writings. Here my concern is with the first edition of the *Principles of Logic* only, though in a later chapter I will consider the modifications that he introduced into the second edition. Hence my interest is somewhat different from that of others who have written about him, and I shall not discuss what they have said.* I have already pointed out (pp. 65–6) the importance of Bradley's use of 'judgment' in contrast to the now more usual 'sentence,' as well as his stress on the importance of truth in logic (p. 87). It is time to bring these two things together, for the problem that obsesses Bradley is how judgments can be true or false, how they can be related to 'reality.' I have used scare quotes round 'reality' because the mention of that word in connection with Bradley is liable to make the reader think that a metaphysical doctrine is in question. But what he means by this use here is what we all mean when we talk of what someone said being true; that his words refer to something beyond themselves and it is this that makes them true. The problem is to specify exactly what this means. It looks as if it were unproblematic, but Bradley has little difficulty in showing that many of the views that have been advanced in this area fail to show how

---

*However, I have been greatly helped in the writing of this chapter by an as yet unpublished article by Guy Stock entitled 'Bradley's Theory of Judgment.' I am broadly in agreement with what he says there, and am grateful for the opportunity to consult it. It has made many points clearer to me.

such a thing is possible. He himself has a hard struggle to reach a satisfactory conclusion:

There is a natural presumption that truth, to be true, must be true of reality. And this result, that comes as soon as we reflect, will be the goal we shall attain in this chapter. But we shall reach it with a struggle, distressed by subtleties, and perhaps in some points disillusioned and shaken. (*PL,* p. 42)

It will turn out that some forms of judgment that are normally thought of as unproblematic are not so easy to grasp. He even goes so far as to maintain that all of one class of judgments are false (*PL,* p. 93). There are what he calls 'analytic judgments of sense,' i.e. assertions about what is now perceived or felt, such as 'I have toothache,' 'There is a wolf.' This would seem an excess of metaphysical zeal. The purpose of this chapter is to show that the problem is a logical one, and Bradley's claims are not simply silly from the point of view of logic itself.

The starting point is that judgment is linked with the distinction between truth and falsehood (*PL*, p. 29) and it is probably connected with the existence of language (*PL*, p. 31). The qualification is inserted because Bradley does not deny that there may be something rather like judgment which occurs lower on the evolutionary scale. This point is not a part of the argument, but an instance of his stress on the way in which the 'higher' mental functions must have evolved from lower ones; there are no breaks in the transition from animal to man. What is clear is that once words and thoughts 'are seen to be symbols, . . . this insight it is which in the strict sense constitutes judgment' (*PL*, p. 33). A mind which was merely conscious would not be in a position to judge; only when it can think and realize that its thoughts are not necessarily a reflection of the external world, that mistakes and lies are possible, does judgment proper come into being:

And speech in its perversion to lies and deceit makes the dullest comprehend that words and ideas can be and be real, and can yet be illusion and wholly unreal in relation to facts. (*PL*, p. 33)

Judgment proper can only occur when the ideas of truth and falsity have been grasped.

Truth and falsity imply a reference to something beyond the

judgment, that which renders the judgment true or false. Hence Bradley can give the following definition of judgment:

Judgment proper is the act which refers an ideal content (recognized as such) to a reality beyond the act. This sounds perhaps harder than it is.

The ideal content is the logical idea, the meaning as just defined. It is recognized as such, when we know that, by itself, it is not a fact but a wandering adjective. In the act of assertion we transfer this adjective to, and unite it with, a real substantive. And we perceive at the same time, that the relation thus set up is neither made by the act, nor merely holds within it or by right of it, but is real both independent of it and beyond it. (*PL*, p. 10)

I have already discussed the point that there is but one idea in judgment; hence there is for Bradley no problem about the copula. In other words it is not an element within the judgment which differentiates it from a mere idea, it is the reference to a 'reality' which lies outside the mind:

in every judgment there is a subject of which the ideal content is asserted. But this subject of course can not belong to the content or fall within it, for, in that case, it would be the idea attributed to itself. (*PL*, p. 13)

It is for this reason that a tautology is not a judgment (cf. *PL*, p. 141) but a judgment that has 'been gutted and finally vanished' (*PL*, p. 26). The reasons are much the same as those expressed by Wittgenstein:

In a tautology the conditions of agreement with the world – the representational relations – cancel one another, so that it does not stand in any representational relation to reality.[1]

'Reality' seems to have the same role in this remark of Wittgenstein's as it does in Bradley's thought at this time. But there is a difference; the former says 'The existence and non-existence of states of affairs is reality.[3] This implies that reality is already divided into 'states of affairs' which are distinguishable prior to language. However, in commenting on this remark, James Bogen says:

If reality is the prototype to which a proposition is compared for truth, we must distinguish between the connection between the proposition and reality on the one hand, and the proposition and what it asserts to be a fact on the other. Reality stands to the proposition as a mapped region stands to a map, while a putative fact stands to the proposition as a possible arrangement of towns shown on the map stands to the map.[3]

For Bradley, reality cannot be considered as already 'divided up' in any way. However, for both thinkers it is a 'reference to reality' which makes objectivity possible, makes it possible for our thoughts or our words to be true or false. The problem is as to what can be said about it beyond individual true judgments. Clearly for Bradley talk of judgments 'picturing reality' would not help, for the 'picture' consists of words:

> But reality is not a connection of adjectives, nor can it be so represented. Its essence is to be substantial and individual. But can we reach self-existence and individual character by manipulating adjectives and putting universals together? If not, the fact is not given *directly* in any truth whatsoever. (*PL*, p. 46)

Words or ideas are universals, reality one and individual; in addition, they imply plurality. The same point could be made, Bradley thinks, by taking judgments other than the simple affirmative categorical, such as negative or hypothetical. These can be true but need not 'correspond to' anything; indeed, it is hard to imagine what a negative or hypothetical fact would be. Yet such judgments are just as capable of truth and falsity as any other type.

'Truth must be true of reality' (*PL*, p. 42). Further, we feel compelled to judge as we do; it is not a matter of just ascribing a predicate to a subject; we feel that the predicate already belongs to it, and we are merely recognizing the fact in making the judgment. The relations 'do not exist between the symbols, but hold in the symbolized' (*PL*, p. 11). Bradley tends to use the form 'S – P' to represent a judgment, though he also employs 'A is B' or 'A is b.' He comments on the first of these:

> This form I found of course in use, and I employed it in this volume where that seemed convenient. I neither did nor do attach importance to its use. (*PL*, p. 117)

To us, brought up on the idea of precision of symbolism, this may seem a somewhat cavalier attitude, but there is a point to the apparent arbitrariness. Traditional logic had given priority to the subject–predicate form; indeed, it was often referred to as 'logical form.' The first move was to put judgments which were not represented in this way into that form so they could be used in the traditional syllogism. Bradley emphasizes that many judgments are not properly taken as attributing a predicate to a subject. This is obvious in the case of one-word judgments, such as 'Wolf' or 'Fire,' which can certainly be true or false (*PL*, p. 56) and in judgments of existence, such as 'The four-cornered circle does not exist,' or 'There are no ghosts' (*PL*, p. 42).

In the *Principles of Logic* Bradley argues about the logical form of judgments at two different levels, though both depend on the belief that the grammatical form is not a guide to the logical form. This belief follows from the argument that judgment does not consist of 'putting ideas together,' that most judgments consist of only one idea. Grammatically, it seems that every judgment has a subject which can easily be determined, though the possibility of verbal transformations shows that this may not always be so simple (cf. *PL*, p. 22). It is easy to say that the subject of 'All the books on this desk are mine' is the set of books referred to, but not so easy to determine the subject of 'All men are mortal,' for here there is no existing class of 'all men.' The traditional way of talking may assimilate rather different things, as is shown by the method of verification for the two cases just mentioned. Such examples show the need for a close look at what is asserted; Bradley spends much effort in detailed examination of the various grammatical forms in which truth-claims are expressed. Before dealing with this, it is necessary to look at the wider claim, covering all judgments, that reality is the true subject of every one, that the correct logical form is 'Reality is such that S – P.' The formulation 'Reality is such that S – P' specifies what was said in the definition of judgment quoted above (p. 101).

Reality is the real subject, even when the judgment turns out to be false, for the point of making it was that it was felt or believed to be true. In the case of a lie, it is intended that the hearer or reader will so take it, though the originator knows that it is false. Metaphysics may lead us to reject certain putative judgments, such as 'God is a spirit' or 'The soul is a substance,' but logic must include them (*PL*, p. 49). For they equally claim truth. Thus 'Reality is such that S – P' says that judgments claim truth; this is what makes them into judgments. It does not say anything about reality in a metaphysical sense, does not tell us what the 'ultimate nature of things' is. Within logic that reality exists only means that judgments can be true or false. There may be another mode of access to reality in metaphysics; for logic there can be no independent access; we cannot 'station ourselves with propositions somewhere outside logic, that is to say outside the world'[4] in order to make a comparison. Just as in the *Tractatus Logico-Philosophicus* the talk of 'reality' was not a piece of metaphysics, so in the *Principles of Logic* it is not either, whatever Bradley may later have come to think.

Consequently the use of 'reality' in the singular is not a prejudgment of the question of monism. It might, at first sight, seem that we would need to talk of 'realities.' For we are inclined to say that 'The wrath of the Homeric gods is fearful' is 'true in Homer' where the 'in' seems to represent a separate or different reality from that of everyday life. Bradley remarks in this context 'Mathematical truths at least hold good inside mathematics. But where are mathematics?' (*PL* p. 43n) The spatial metaphor we are inclined to use indicates a problem rather than solves it. There is not a world of mathematics or of Homeric characters lying beyond the 'real' one. It is a fact, like any other fact, that the *Iliad* describes how the gods behaved, and to verify the judgment about their wrath reference to that poem is necessary:

surely a poem, surely any imagination, surely dreams and delusions, and surely much more our words and our names are all of them facts of a certain kind. (*PL*, p. 42)

Bradley refers to them as 'existences of different orders;' we should not expect to meet a Homeric god, but we can verify the statement by reading the *Iliad*, which is a real text. If there were separate realities it would be hard to understand what verification meant; 'The wrath of Homeric gods is fearful' could not be true in Homer and false somewhere else if the words 'true' and 'false' are to retain their normal meaning.

It is partly because readers approach Bradley with the belief that he is a metaphysician that they are liable to take any use of the term 'reality' as indicating a metaphysical theory. For the doctrine that reality is the subject of all judgments can appear as almost a truism, particularly if it is put into the form 'judgments are about facts.' Many would be willing to assent to that. But, when expressed in this way, there is a problem about the identification of facts, a problem which parallels that of identifying ideas which was discussed above. For even if we agree that the world (or reality) is the totality of facts, it does not seem to appear to us neatly divided into separate facts. And how can we count facts? If q follows from p, is the fact that q identical to the fact that p, or different? It soon appears that there is no way of distinguishing facts except via judgments about them, so that the form of words "'The cat is on the mat" corresponds to the fact that the cat is on the mat' could equally be abbreviated to "'The cat is on the mat" corresponds to the fact' or to 'corresponds to the facts.' Frege makes this point explicitly:

We can imagine a language in which the proposition, 'Archimedes perished at the conquest of Syracuse.', would be expressed in the following way: 'The violent death of Archimedes at the conquest of Syracuse is a fact.' Even here, if one wishes, he can distinguish between subject and predicate; but the subject contains the whole content, and the predicate serves only to present this as a judgement. *Such a language would have only a single predicate for all judgements; namely, 'is a fact'.* We see here that we cannot speak of subject and predicate in the usual sense. *Our 'conceptual notation' is such a language and the symbol* ⊢ *is its common predicate for all judgements.*[5]

Frege's '⊢' is normally thought of as an 'assertion sign,' the device which turns a sentence into a judgment. This quotation seems to indicate that rather more is involved, for the act of judging consists in attaching a sentence conceived as a single subject to an unalterable predicate 'is a fact.'

Donald Davidson, perhaps ironically, makes almost the same point:

Since aside from matters of correspondence no way of distinguishing facts has been proposed, and this test fails to uncover a single difference, we may read the result of our argument as showing that there is exactly one fact. Descriptions like 'the fact that there are stupas in Nepal', if they describe at all, describe the same thing: The Great Fact. No point remains in disting-uishing among various names of The Great Fact when written after 'corres-ponds to'; we may as well settle for the single phrase 'corresponds to The Great Fact'. This unalterable predicate carries with it a redundant whiff of ontology, but beyond this there is apparently no telling it apart from 'is true'.[6]

Davidson suggests that talk of 'the Great Fact' need not imply an ontological commitment; my suggestion is that the same applies to 'Reality is such that. . . .' There may even be advantages in putting the content of the proposition or sentence in the predicate position, for it indicates that what is asserted is asserted *of* reality; we normally think of the subject as what the proposition is about. On the other hand, the predicate position is less likely to arouse thoughts of ontology. Neither need there be any worry about the use of 'corresponds to' by Davidson. Bradley is commonly believed to have held a 'coherence theory of truth.' It is clear that in the *Principles* he did not; he asserts 'There are no degrees of truth and falsity' (*PL*, p. 197). Belief in the existence of such degrees is normally a mark of a holder of a coherence doctrine. This need not imply that he believed in a 'correspondence theory' of truth. If such a theory is what he means by a 'copy-theory' he specifically denies that he did hold such in the *Principles*; in a later footnote referring to that work he says:

It did not occur to me that I should be taken there or anywhere else to be advocating a copy-theory of truth. (*ETR*, p. 109n)

In any case, it is not clear that a 'theory of truth,' in the sense in which correspondence and coherence are alternative candidates, is needed by Bradley. His point is that what is required by logic is to establish the logical form of judgments, and this is 'Reality is such that S – P.' Both true and false judgments have the same form, and it is not in general the task of logic to establish whether a particular judgment is true or false. Logic can say that of two contradictory judgments one at least must be false; inference can produce new truths from ones already accepted. It is not in the same business as the special sciences, which may well be concerned with details of verification of particular types of judgment. To say this is to say that reality or truth are for logic undefined and indefinable notions. Metaphysics may tell something about the 'nature of reality,' but logic does not. It is significant that when Bradley did establish a positive account of reality, after the publication of the *Principles*, he 'corrected' many of the things he had earlier said about logic. At the time of the *Principles* he neither did nor could make any general statements about reality beyond those ordinary judgments that we all make and which are judged to be true.

What has just been said might seem to contradict the earlier point (pp. 87–8) that Bradley was concerned with the 'logic of truth' as against the 'logic of consistency,' but this distinction can be taken in two ways. It may mean that logic is concerned with the ways in which truth is discovered, in other words that there is no real difference between logic and epistemology. This, I think, is the sense that Bosanquet gave to the notion. Curiously a view similar to this survived into post-war Oxford, where it was fashionable to talk of 'the logic of religion or 'the logic of art' etc. when what was meant was the way in which truth-claims in these areas were assessed. The 'logic of religion' could be studied by an unbeliever, for he could examine the ways in which religious people argued for their view. There were as many 'logics' as there were separate universes of discourse. There is a similarity between this way of talking and the Wittgenstinian notion of a 'language-game,' though it has been suggested in the latter case that only participants in the game are capable of understanding it fully. Bosanquet would have welcomed the talk of 'logics,' for he was inclined to set up different 'universes,' Bradley would have rejected it at the time of the *Principles*, for there was only one 'reality' of which true judgments were true. However, the 'logic of truth' may also mean something rather different, as it did for Bradley, namely that logic was concerned with more than consistency, for the important thing about judgments was their reference to reality. Real logic would have to take this into account, for to understand a judgment was to understand it as predicating something of reality, and the central question of logic was how this could be. Thus Bradley's version was radically different from that of J. S. Mill, who took the 'logic of truth' to mean that logic was a discussion of how truths were to be established, in other words as being concerned mainly with induction or the principles of scientific inference.

To have reached the conclusion that the logical form of all judgments is 'reality is such that S – P' is not to have solved all problems, for it certainly seems that judgments can refer to 'reality' in a variety of ways, make different kinds of truth-claims. There is a substantial difference between 'This is white' and 'If anything is a metal, then it conducts electricity.' Traditionally the differences in grammatical form provided a guide to such differences in logical form; in the case of the pair just given to the distinction between categorical and hypothetical (or conditional) judgments. Much of the substance of chapter II of the *Principles*, and almost all of its difficulties, are concerned with these issues. In the course of dealing with them, Bradley produces a sustained attack on empiricism, though it has not been always clear to his commentators what he was doing. Here again they have taken startling statements like 'analytic judgments of sense are all false' (*PL*, p. 93), Bradley is referring to those of the form 'This is white,' as evidence of a metaphysical theory at work, and consequently have not seen what the argument actually was. The attack on empiricism is not extraneous to the main argument; it is a part of the logical enquiry itself.

One important empiricist principle is that reports of sense-experience have logical priority; they are regarded as the 'foundations' on which all other types of judgment are based, and it is on them that the certainty of those types rest. Bradley, at the end of chapter II, claims to have established precisely the opposite position. The highest grade of judgments, the most true, are hypotheticals. 'Analytic judgments of sense' are only 'low and rudimentary' judgments (*PL*, p. 104), though even they involve universality; a genuinely 'particular judgment' would not deserve the name. These are striking claims; in the remainder of this chapter I will follow Bradley's arguments for them.

The first stage, like many others in Bradley's work, is discussed twice (*PL*, pp. 47–8, 82–90). The burden of the argument is familiar; restricted universal judgments, such as 'All the people in the room are wearing shoes,' are particular and categorical, for they are really conjunctions of individual judgments, 'A is in the room and wearing shoes. . . .' An unrestricted universal, such as 'All animals are mortal' cannot be represented as a conjunction, for it refers to animals as yet unborn and would still be true even if all life had disappeared. The correct way of representing it is 'If anything is an animal, then it is mortal.'

The abstract universal, 'A is B,' means no more than 'given A, in that case B,' or 'if A, then B.' In short, such judgments are always hypothetical and can never be categorical. And the proper terms by which to introduce them are 'given,' or 'if,' or 'whenever,' or 'where,' or 'any,' or 'whatever.' We should beware of 'all.'

For the use of 'all,' . . . is most misleading and dangerous. It encourages that tendency to understand the universal in the sense of a collection, which has led to so many mistaken consequences. (*PL*, p. 82)

Bradley adds a footnote in the second edition in which he acknowledges that he had been somewhat cavalier in his treatment of restricted universals, for he had ignored the fact that they at least need the addition of, in the example cited, 'and these are all the people in the room.' Nevertheless, this does not alter the positive claim; it is interesting to note that it was accepted by Russell in 'On Denoting,' in the course of which he says that the hypothetical nature of universal judgments has 'been ably argued in Mr. Bradley's *Logic* Book I, Chap. II.'[7] Indeed, the positive claim would not now be regarded as particularly controversial.

However, it is normally made on the basis that other sorts of judgments are categorical; Bradley accepts that this can be

valid at a certain level of thought; and, for the purposes of logical enquiry, individual judgments, both synthetic and analytic, may conveniently be taken as categorical, and in this sense contrasted with universal judgments. (*PL*, p. 101)

However, he goes on to say 'It is not enough to know that we have a ground of distinction. We must ask if it is a *true* ground.' We must not be misled by grammatical differences into thinking that we have found formal ones. It could be claimed that Bradley has no clear notion of 'logical form,' for if he did he could not make statements like that just quoted. Certainly his notion is not that of contemporary logicians, who tend to equate it with the canonical forms of the Fregean calculus; their reasons for so doing are presumably not dissimilar from those of the neo-Aristotelian logicians, who also made much of the idea of canonical logical form. Its use permits a great simplification of the variety of expressions in natural languages, for it is possible to show perspicuously the relations between formalized sentences, and on to these the aberrant sentences of everyday life can be mapped. In the words of Donald Davidson:

Philosophers have long been at the hard work of applying theory to ordinary language by the device of matching sentences in the vernacular with sentences for which they have a theory. Frege's massive contribution was to show how 'all', 'some', 'every', 'each', 'none', and associated pronouns, in some of their uses, could be tamed; for the first time, it was possible to dream of a formal semantics for a signficant part of a natural language.[8]

There is a sense in which Bradley's procedure is not too remote from this, though the absence of a systematic symbolism may conceal the fact. However, his pluralism, the fact the he can say that at one level of analysis such and such is the case, whereas at another level the situation is quite other, marks a signficant difference.

For after saying that unrestricted universals are to be counted as hypotheticals, he goes on to argue that the remaining categoricals are also to be seen as hypothetical, and as less well grounded. Bradley divides non-universal judgments into three classes:

1. Analytic judgments of sense, which involve assertions about what I now feel or perceive. His examples are 'I have toothache,' 'There is a wolf,' 'That bough is broken.'
2. Synthetic judgments of sense 'which state either some fact of time or space, or again some quality of the matter given, which I do not here and now directly perceive. "This road leads to London," "Yesterday it rained," "Tomorrow there will be full moon"' (*PL*, p. 49). He adds a footnote to say that this use of 'analytic' and 'synthetic' must not be confused with Kant's, adding cryptically 'Every possible judgment, we will see hereafter, is both analytic and synthetic.'
3. This class 'have to do with a reality which is never a sensible event in time. "God is a spirit," "The soul is a substance." We may think what we like of the validity of these judgments, and may or may not decline to recognize them in metaphysics. But in logic they certainly must have a place' (*PL*, p. 49). He says less about the third class than about the other two.

The problem with both types of sensory judgments is that they do not indicate a unique event, for the words used are general. I may have toothache now, but so do others, and they can say the same thing. Similar problems arise with the other examples, for, e.g. many roads lead to London. These judgments purport to give the unique results of a perceptual contact with the world, but they fail to do so. Nor will the addition of further indicators help, for however many we add, we are still faced with a judgment that could be uttered in more than one context. Because they fail to reach the claimed unique event, Bradley describes them as 'false' (*PL*, p. 50). To say this seems silly, though I must stress that there is no easy way out; Bradley means what he says. One move which might be made would be an 'indexing' by space or time. This would not be possible for the first class, analytic judgments of sense, for to add space and time would be to transform them into the second class. In any case, Bradley thinks that it is erroneous to regard space and time as 'principles of individuation' (*PL*, p. 63). Within a given series we can achieve uniqueness, for the parts of a series are mutually exclusive, by definition. But Bradley asks:

How can you, so long as you are not willing to transcend ideas, determine or in any way characterize your series, so as to get its difference from every possible series within your description? (*PL*, p. 64)

What is needed to solve the problem is an 'Archimedean point' which serves to anchor the series in reality. This cannot be given by another word or idea, because it is still another thing of the same kind. The only device which would do this is a Russellian 'logically proper name' which does serve to fill the gap between language and the world, or thought and reality. Bradley's claim is that no such entity could exist. Marx is scornful of a similar attempt:

This great problem, in so far as it at all entered the minds of our ideologists, was bound, of course, to result finally in one of those knight-errants setting out in search of a word which, as a word, formed the transition in question, which, as a word, ceases to be simply a word, and which points, in a mysterious super-linguistic manner, the way out from language to the actual object it denotes; which, in short, plays among words the same role as the Redeeming God–Man plays among people in Christian fantasy.[9]

There is no way to crawl out from 'under the net' and touch reality directly.

It could be objected that this is not a practical problem, that indexicals function within a context which does give an anchorage to a series that we actually use, e.g. the normal time series. 'I have toothache' is only ambiguous because it is taken in isolation from the context of utterance. Bradley makes a move which is not too remote from this. Returning to the point that judgment is the reference of an ideal content to the real which appears, he says:

It is not by its quality as a temporal event or phenomenon of space, that the given is unique. It is unique, not because it has a certain character, but because it *is given*. It is by the reference of our series to the real, as it appears directly within this point of contact, or indirectly in the element continuous with this point, that these series become exclusive. (*PL*, p. 64)

The use of an indexical expresses uniqueness, but it is the uniqueness of the particular experience which is the issue, not its position in time or space. For the latter are constructed in thought, not directly given. 'This' is the term he discusses, though 'I', 'me' and 'mine' are much the same (*PL*, p. 69n). Indexicals are peculiar: 'The idea of "this," unlike most ideas, can not be used as a symbol in judgment' (*PL*, p. 67). 'This' is not a word like any other, because there is no contrast between its meaning and its reference. It does not tell us anything about the presented reality but simply marks its presence. In Bradley's words:

Between the fact and the idea of the 'this' in judgment, there can be no practical difference. The idea of this [Bradley omits quotes here] would be falsely used unless what it marks were actually presented. (*PL*, p. 68)

It seems thus to be a word which fulfils the metaphysical ideal of 'meaning what it stands for and standing for what it means' (cf. *PL*, p. 68). The same point could be made by saying that it is impossible to misapply 'this.' This seems very like Russell's claim that 'this' and 'that' are the only examples of 'logically proper names.' What he actually said is not quite what he is normally believed to have said about them:

We say 'This is white'. If you agree that 'This is white', meaning the 'this' that you see, you are using 'this' as a proper name. But if you try to apprehend the proposition that I am expressing when I say 'This is white', you cannot do it. If you mean this piece of chalk as a physical object, then you are not using a proper name. It is only when you use 'this' quite strictly, to stand for an actual object of sense, that it is really a proper name.[10]

For both thinkers 'this' stands for that which is given; it does not attribute qualities or characteristics to it. To use another vocabulary, it has reference but no sense. If it did have sense it would, for Russell, no longer be a logically proper name, for it could turn out that a mistake had been made; it is always logically possible that a physical object has been mistakenly identified. Bradley says that when 'this' is coupled to a noun, as in 'This bird is yellow,' it is no longer functioning in the same way as in analytic judgments of sense, for the speaker could be mistaken in thinking that it was a bird that was yellow, even if he were right about the colour (cf. p. 77 above). It begins to seem as if he is using the word in the way condemned by Marx in the passage quoted above, as a means of bridging a gap which he declares cannot be filled. He thinks that it functions differently from other words, that much is clear. Russell is touched by Marx's attack, for he thought of the logically proper name as a 'foundation' for other discourse; Bradley does not, as will be made clear shortly. As far as this question is concerned, it seems to me that Bradley is denying not just the possibility of a guaranteed reference but also the possibility of a *theory* of reference, an account of how language or ideas hook on to reality.

That being so, it would seem that there should be no special problem about the truth of judgments employing such terms. Bradley summarizes this part of his discussion:

We escape from ideas, and from mere universals, by a reference to the real which appears in perception . . . And analytic judgments, it may seem, are thus secured to us. (*PL*, pp. 69 –70)

It would also follow that they are categorical. However, when he returns to this type of judgment in the second part of chapter II, he again asserts that they are all false (*PL*, p. 93). The grounds for this are that what is actually given is a whole complex, but what is asserted is only a fragment. He admits that it sounds 'preposterous and ridiculous' to say 'There is a wolf' is false because it is given in a context containing numerous features which are unmentioned in the judgment (*PL*, p. 94), though he thinks this oddness is a result of inherited empiricist prejudice. For, if the presented whole is, as it must be, complex, the judgment only asserts a fragment of that complex, assuming that this makes no difference to what is asserted. We have no reason to assume that analysis does not involve falsification (cf. *PL*, p. 97).

It can be objected that it is one thing to admit that there is a risk of falsification in analysis, another to declare all its results false. However, I think Bradley's reasons are somewhat different; they have to do with the nature of our perceptual contact with reality. Earlier he had said:

It is one thing to seek reality *in* that series; it is quite another thing to try to find it *as* the series. (*PL*, p. 71)

This refers to the series of phenomena, that which appears to us in perception. The judgment 'There is a wolf' is only in contact with reality through a perceptual link. The judgment asserts the existence of an enduring entity, the wolf. Bradley's argument at this point is difficult to follow, but he appears to claim that we cannot, on the basis of perceptual experience, justifiably assert that there is an enduring entity or Aristotelian substance which is what we are referring to. Reality is in itself undifferentiated, whatever may be the character of what appears to us. He concludes by saying:

And when asked what is ultimate, and can stand as an individual, you can answer nothing.
    The real can not be identical with the content that appears in presentation. It for ever transcends it, and gives us title to make search elsewhere. (*PL*, p. 71)

This is another way of expressing the claim that hypotheticals are better grounded than are categoricals; connections of qualities may be discoverable by sense, substances cannot. This is not a question of scepticism about perception, of the fact that we might make a mistake because the 'senses are liable to deceive.' What is given in sense is not adequate for the claims that are made by the analytic judgment of sense. This is a logical, not an epistemological, point, and hence does not cast doubt on the truth of a particular judgment, such as the one I now make about some feature of my environment by using an indexical expression. However, such a judgment cannot serve as a foundation for knowledge in the way empiricism always envisages.
    In a long metaphor (*PL*, p. 100) Bradley likens truth to a chain, and says of it:

A last fact, a final link, is not merely a thing which we cannot know, but a thing which could not possibly be real. Our chain by its nature can not have a support. Its essence excludes a fastening at the end. We do not merely fear that it hangs in the air, but we know it must do so. And when the end is unsupported, all the rest is unsupported. Hence our conditioned truth is only conditional. (*PL,* p. 100)

There is no word or idea, no 'logically proper name' which could constitute a final link to reality; nothing which serves as a 'fastening.' Words or ideas may reach right out to reality, but they do not constitute it and hence are, in a sense, necessarily separated from it.

So judgments cannot be categorical but only conditional or hypothetical. 'If anything is a metal, then it conducts electricity' is a
better form, for it explicitly does not attempt to refer to a percep-
tually given element:

> In hypothetical judgments there is a sense in which the real is given; for
> we feel its presence in the connection of the elements, and we ascribe the
> ground to the real as its quality. Hypothetical judgments in the end must
> rest on direct presentation, though from that presentation we do not take
> the elements and receive them as fact. It is merely their synthesis which
> holds good of the real, and it is in our perception of the ground of that
> synthesis that we come into present contact with reality. (*PL*, P. 103)

Hence they are as it were more true than those judgments which
purported to be categorical, which can only be ranked on the 'lowest
round' of the 'ladder of truth' (*PL*, p. 104). All judgments approxi-
mate to scientific ones; even 'There is a wolf' is not a pure particular
affirmation, for if it were it would be of no use. At the very least it
asserts the consequences that follow from the presence of a wolf,
e.g. danger to flocks, etc. There would be no point in asserting a
judgment which did not have implications beyond itself. 'If it were
really particular and wholly confined to the case it appears in, it
might as well never have existed, for it could not be used' (*PL*, p.
106). It is not just the fact that if there is a conflict between sensory
evidence and a well-established scientific principle, then the sensory
evidence will in most cases be rejected, though this can serve to
confirm Bradley's claim. It is rather that if we examine closely the
way in which judgments are related to reality, then we will be forced
to admit that they could not be linked in the way in which empiricism assumes they are, for no word could do the job that would be
required. It is not that what appears to us is not reality, for it is, but
its appearance is not reality, but only a fragment of it. Reality is the
totality of what exists, and that could not appear. It is important to
see what this distinction between appearance and reality amounts
to. I must again remind the reader that it is a logical point that we
are concerned with, that the distinction between appearance and
reality falls within what is given. He expresses this obscurely in
saying:

Are the presented phenomenon, and series of phenomena, actual realities?
And, we have seen, they are not so. The given in sense, if we could seize it

in judgment, would still disappoint us. It is not self-existent and is therefore unreal, and the reality transcends it, first in the infinite process of phenomena, and then altogether. The real, which (as we say) appears in perception, is neither a phenomenon nor a series of phenomena. (*PL*, p. 101)

It is not a series of phenomena; this represents Bradley's rejection of classical empiricism. For a series is not *given*, it is something that we have to construct:

If we mean by phenomena the things we perceive, or the facts or appearances that are given to us, then the whole of England below our horizon (to say nothing at all of America or Asia), and every event that is past or future are *not* phenomena. They are not perceived facts. They exist in our minds as mere ideas, as the meaning of symbols. A phenomenon, I repeat, that is past or future is a sheer self-contradiction. (*PL*, p. 74)

This is not to deny the reality of America or of the past; 'America was discovered in 1492' is true of reality, or, in his formulation, 'Reality is such that America was discovered in 1492.' Such a truth could not, logically, be given to sense. It is an 'ideal construction' or form of words true of reality, but its truth is not 'given.'

Similarly, the real is not a phenomenon, though a phenomenon may be real; the judgment is not simply convertible. A phenomenon is what is given in perception, and to that extent is real. But for most of the judgments based on perception, what is said of reality goes beyond what is presented. There may be inferences involved; 'This bird is yellow' goes beyond what is given. It is not that it might suddenly turn into something else, but that what the judgment asserts could not be presented at an instant. This could be put by saying that Bradley is not denying the existence or reality of sense-data, but that we can say anything of great interest about them. Even in the case of 'I have toothache' it is because the pain is expected to continue, and to continue to affect the bearer, that the judgment is made. Only in rare and peculiar cases do people make judgments about their immediate sense-data; reality may be such that red is here now, but that does not tell us much about reality. What is mentioned in the judgment is thus 'a mere appearance.' Our normal interest is in why or how this particular red appears at this moment, e.g. as a sign that the reaction is beginning to take place. Similarly, 'that white dot on the hill is John's house' may be true, but John does not live in a dot. There need be nothing 'metaphysical' about a distinction between appearance and reality.

The summary he gives of the results reached in the first two chapters may appear somewhat at odds with the general conclusion, for it seems to give back some of what has been taken away:

All judgments are categorical, for they all do affirm about the reality, and assert the existence of a quality in that. Again, all are hypothetical, for not one of them can ascribe to real existence its elements as such. All are individual, since the real which supports that quality which forms the ground of synthesis, is itself substantial. Again, all are universal, since the synthesis they affirm holds out of and beyond the particular appearance. They are every one abstract, for they disregard context, they leave out the environment of the sensible context, and they substantiate adjectives. And yet all are concrete for they none of them are true of anything else than that individual reality which appears in the sensuous wealth of presentation. (*PL*, p. 106)

In fact the summary does not give anything back, for the points should be taken in the light of the whole argument. What it does do is to emphasize that logical form is unrelated to grammatical form, that the underlying logical form of all judgments is 'Reality is such that S – P.' This could be expressed by saying that, for Bradley, logical form is the relation between ideas or words and reality. Judgments can be true of reality, words can apply to the world, but the way in which this can occur is very different from what traditional logicians have thought. There is a further point to be made. There are likenesses between his treatment of judgment and Hegel's. Both privilege hypothetical judgments above categorical. But their reasons are different, and might be expressed by saying that Hegel's seem in the main epistemological; he is concerned with the degree of knowledge expressed in the judgment. Bradley, as I have tried to show, uses a different battery of arguments, mainly connected with the relation between words and the world.

NOTES

1 *Tractatus Logico-Philosophicus*, 4.462.
2 Ibid., 2.06.
3 *Wittgenstein's Philosophy of Language*, London, 1972, p. 25.
4 *Tractatus Logico-Philosophicus*, 4.12.

5 *Conceptual Notation*, tr. T. W. Bynum, Oxford, 1972, p. 113.
6 'True to the Facts,' *Journal of Philosophy*, vol. 66, 1969, p. 753.
7 *Logic and Knowledge*, ed. R. C. Marsh, London, 1956, p. 43.
8 *Synthese,* vol. 17, 1967, p. 315.
9 *The German Ideology*, London, 1965, p. 495.
10 'The Philosophy of Logical Atomism,' *Logic and Knowledge*, p. 201.

VII

Internal Relations

It is generally accepted that Bradley believed that all relations were internal. To many recent philosophers this has been enough to show that he was either confused or silly, even though they have not been clear what the belief actually was. The following passage from the appendix to *Appearance and Reality* can be taken as a classic statement of the doctrine:

And if you could have a perfect relational knowledge of the world, you could go on from the nature of red-hairedness to these other characters which qualify it, and you could from the nature of red-hairedness reconstruct all the red-haired men. In such perfect knowledge you could start internally from any one character in the Universe, and you could from that pass to the rest. . . . For example, a red-haired man who knew himself utterly would and must, starting from within, go on to know every one else who had red hair, and he would not know himself until he knew them. But, as things are, he does not know how or why he himself has red hair, nor how and why a different man is also the same in that point, and therefore, because he does not know the ground, the how and why, of his relation to other men, it remains for him relatively external, contingent, and fortuitous. But there is really no mere externality except in his ignorance. (*AR*, pp. 520–1)

Few have paused to wonder why the stress was on relations and not on properties, for the example of the red-haired man would seem more naturally to be taken as an instance of the latter. Certainly much of the discussion of the topic has not distinguished between these two. Relations are not seen nowadays as particularly problematic in philosophy; properties are one-place predicates, relations two-place or many-place predicates; both are susceptible of the same treatment. The formal difficulties in handling relations, the fact that they can be transitive, intransitive or non-transitive, symmetrical, asymmetrical or non-symmetrical, seem of little philosophic interest, of no more concern than the fact that the old syllogistic logic could only represent the obviously valid argument 'A = B, B = C, therefore A = C' as committing the fallacy of four terms. Hence it is surprising that Russell could write in 1924:

The question of relations is one of the most important that arise in philosophy, as most other issues turn on it: monism and pluralism: the question whether anything is true except the whole of truth, or wholly real except the whole of reality: idealism and realism, in some of their forms; perhaps the whole existence of philosophy as a subject distinct from science and possessing a method of its own.[1]

However, there seems to have been little written about the controversy that Russell thought so important. Moore published a paper on the topic in 1917,[2] and in 1935 Ryle and Ayer debated the question at a Joint Session,[3] evidence that at least the committee thought it a worthwhile subject. The two symposiasts, however, found the doctrine of internal relations absurd. They did not take the obvious step demanded by philosophic charity and ask whether they had misunderstood a view which seemed to them patently ridiculous. The same applies to more recent commentators on Bradley; Wollheim explains 'internal relations' thus:

In the first place, some of a term's relations are *internal*: by this is meant that the term in question necessarily stands in these relations, or that, if it did not stand in these relations, it would not be what it is or would be other than what it is. So for instance, a husband necessarily stands in the relation of being married to someone: if he were not married to someone, he would be other than what he is. Hence the relation 'being married to someone' is internal to him. Similarly the relation of being disloyal to one's country is internal to a traitor, that of being indifferent to culture is internal to a philistine, that of being printed before 1500 is internal to an incunabulum.[4]

Pears, writing on Russell, says much the same:

A relation is internal if the proposition attributing it to an individual is true *a priori*. For instance the married state is a relation between two individuals, and the proposition that a particular husband is married, or a particular wife is married, is true *a priori*, because it is guaranteed by definition. So in these two cases we have an internal relation.[5]

Thus both these philosophers reduce 'internal relations' to simple analytic truths. Neither of them raises the question of why Bradley, if he wished to maintain all true propositions to be analytic, did not make use of the Kantian terminology, which was certainly known to him (cf. *PL* p. 49n). Neither did they ask why, if analyticity were the issue, both Bradley and Russell talked of relations in this context, rather than of properties. In this they seem to be following the tradition of Moore, Ryle and Ayer.

Strangely enough, in spite of these dismissals of the terminology, some contemporary writers have taken to using the word 'internal' when what is at issue is a conceptual connection; for example Peter Winch employs 'internal' or its synonym 'intrinsic' frequently in *The Idea of a Social Science*. He says in a section entitled 'The Internality of Social Relations:'

An event's character as an act of obedience is *intrinsic* to it in a way which is not true of an event's character as a clap of thunder;[6]

There certainly is a conceptual connection between a command being given and its being obeyed. If someone does what he was in fact ordered to, though unaware of the order, his act was not one of obedience. This would be generally agreed, as would the reason, namely that it is due to the meaning of the words 'command' and 'obedience,' not to the particular command that was given. We are still at the level of analytic truths; there is no important difference between Winch's example and Wollheim's. That Winch thinks that internal relations involve generality is made even more clear by his taking conventions as examples of them.[7] Even though I do not want to follow Bradley's doctrines in his later works here, it is perhaps significant that the example from *Appearance and Reality* was of a particular red-haired man. Certainly in the *Principles of Logic* 'internal relations' hold between particulars, not between concepts. However, Winch does also use an example which at first sight seems different. He is talking of a scene from the film *Shane:*

And what I want to insist on is that, just as in a conversation the point of a remark (or of a pause) depends on its internal relation to what has gone before, so in the scene from the film the interchange of glances derives its full meaning from its internal relation to the situation in which it occurs: the loneliness, the threat of danger, the sharing of a common life in difficult circumstances, the satisfaction in physical effort, and so on.[8]

Unfortunately this example will not give true particularity; hence it does not differ from the earlier examples. If we observed an actual glance between two men digging out a tree root, there would be room for discussion of its meaning or even for doubt as to whether it had a meaning. In the film this doubt cannot arise, because the significance of the glance has been emphasized by the way the camera lingers on it, changes in the incidental music, etc. No doubt the director told the actors to give the glance the meaning that Winch attributes to it as they rehearsed the scene. But I doubt that their actual expressions could convey all that Winch rightly says it means in the film. For that we need the rest of the story. The loneliness, the threat of danger, and so on are only revealed by the whole of the film, which shows the relationship between Shane and the crofter developing. If Shane had later eloped with the latter's wife, then we would have to interpret the glance differently; it would no longer be the same.

The fact that what happens subsequently in the film alters, or can alter, our interpretation is relevant here, for it shows that the connections are both to what has happened and to what will happen. This is part of what is meant by calling the film a work of art. In such a work, the connections that exist between the different parts are more like conceptual relations than like those that exist in real life between individuals. The structure of the whole is designed to force a certain interpretation on us and in this resembles a proof in logic or mathematics rather than a description of a series of events in the world. I am not denying that the author or director intended the completed whole to look like a simple description, like the chronicle of a series of real events, I am concerned with its logical status. For an actual series of events does not force an interpretation; it is normally open to several and part of the difficulty is to discover the correct one. But the notion of a correct interpretation is different in the case of a piece of history and of a story. In the latter there is in principle one that is 'authoritative,' that of the author himself. In the former there is no final interpretation possible. New facts may come to light which compel us to change the way we interpret the event. In a story the 'facts' are given us complete; it does not make sense to try to discover things which the author did not tell us. Hence even if certain connections in the story are like logical ones, it does not follow that analogous connections in life are of the same sort. If the term 'internal relation' is defined as that which holds between such items as the glance and its background in the passage quoted from Winch, then it is a very different relation from the one with which I am concerned, or the one which Bradley dealt with in his *Principles*.

The argument here is that the relations that Winch calls 'internal' hold between universals, those of Bradley between particulars. Shane is not a particular or 'Shane' is not a proper name – there is no such person. Nor will it do to say that he is an imaginary individual, for to be that is not to be a particular either. I am claiming that a story, as distinct from a chronicle or a piece of history, is in essence not concerned with particulars – although it is nominally about individuals. There are no individuals in a novel. Hence it is more like a philosophic argument than a piece of history. If internal relations hold between particulars, and all Bradley's examples suggest this, then his topic is radically different from that of Winch. It seems that a similar stress on particulars as the bearers of internal relations was in Wittgenstein's mind when he wrote:

A property is internal if it is unthinkable that its object should not possess it.
(This shade of blue and that one stand, *eo ipso*, in the internal relation of lighter to darker. It is unthinkable that *these* two objects should not stand in this relation.[9]

This remark is a puzzling one, and will perhaps become clearer when Bradley's views have been explained. Here I cite it to bring out the difference I am trying to indicate. If an author says that A was wearing a darker suit than B it does not make sense to challenge this, except in the trivial case where he says the opposite a few pages later. Wittgenstein is not thinking of such a case but one where two actual shades of blue are presented or pointed to.

Thus it is necessary to reject various interpretations of 'internal relation' that have recently been offered. For a more positive consideration of the topic it might be best to begin with the fact that relational propositions differ from ordinary predications. We may feel untroubled about the meanings of the words used in 'The book is red,' but in 'The book is on the table' we face a problem about what 'on' stands for. This might be brought out by a question about how many 'elements' there are in the two propositions. Some would say both contained three, taking the copula in the first as an element; others would say the first contained two, the second three or even four. Wittgenstein thought the second only had two elements:

Instead of, 'The complex sign "*aRb*" says that *a* stands to *b* in the relation *R*,' we ought to put, 'That "*a*" stands to "*b*" in a certain relation says that *aRb*.'[10]

I take it that Wittgenstein meant that we are forced by our language to include 'on' as an 'element,' though in a more perspicuous notation it might be possible to eliminate it by a device that 'pictures' reality better, e.g.

'The book
the table.'

Here there would be no temptation to think of 'on' as a term or element. (The new method of representation could be compared with musical notation.) The situation only consists of a book and a table. It would be different if the book were attached to the table with a piece of string, for then the string would need to be mentioned in any proposition that described the situation. Here there exists a contrast which is not too distant from that between internal and external relations. Roughly it could be said that a relation that would have to be represented in a perspicuous language would be an external one. That the details of Wittgenstein's remarks are connected with his 'picture theory' of language does not vitiate the point I am making, for the argument can be presented without substantive reference to that theory.

Russell, in his earlier period, certainly thought of relations as 'terms,' which he said meant the same as 'unit, individual and entity.'[11] Later he was still concerned with the issue:

For my part, I think it as certain as anything can be that there are relational facts such as 'A is earlier than B.' But does it follow that there is an object of which the name is 'earlier'? It is very difficult to make out what can be meant by such a question and still more difficult to see how an answer can be found.[12]

Thus, at least for Russell, the question of the 'reality of relations' was a question about the existence of entities, not just the logical point as to whether relational propositions could be reduced to subject-predicate ones, though that was also an element in the total problem. Here I do not wish to go into the details of the controversy between Bradley and Russell, which would involve a great deal of space to explain the shifts in the latter's views. It is clear, however, that if 'earlier' is an existent or entity, then there is a problem about its link to the other elements of the proposition. Russell would here seem vulnerable to an argument he tried to use against Bradley, but which Bradley had himself used to show that a relation could not be an entity in its own right, namely that if R could exist by itself, it would need a relation R' to attach it to a in the proposition 'aRb'. If R' also could exist by itself, it would need a further relation R'' and so on. (*AR*, pp. 27–8). Much the same would apply in the case of subject–predicate propositions if the copula is regarded as the element which links the two terms together, in other words if it is taken to function as a relation. Bradley argued that:

if the copula is a connection which couples a pair of ideas, it falls outside judgment; and, if on the other hand it is the sign of judgment, then it does not couple. (*PL*, p. 21)

Part of his reason for saying this is he believes that a question has the same content as an assertion. That the problem about copulation can also be seen as involving relations helps to show why Russell thought the issue so central.

One way out of the difficulty is to say that relations are special sorts of entities, which just have the property of linking other entities. This could be put formally by saying that a relation is a two-place function, properly written $()R()$, just as a predicate can be represented by a one-place function, $F()$. Relations, like predicates, could then be described in Fregean terms as 'unsaturated' to indicate that they demand completion by a pair of terms which can stand on their own, such as proper names; in Frege's words:

For not all parts of a thought can be complete; at least one must be 'unsaturated' or predicative; otherwise they would not hold together.[13]

This passage occurs in an explicit discussion of relations. The notions of 'completeness' and 'unsaturation' are, as he makes clear, only metaphorical. It is not because they are such that they are unsatisfactory, but because they fail to explain what they purport to.

Certainly if we translate 'Socrates is mortal' or 'John loves Mary' into *F(a)* and *(a)R(b)* and then omit the constants *'a'* and *'b'* we get forms which contain a blank and which then appear to demand completion in a way that the constants themselves do not. In ordinary language 'is mortal' also appears to demand completion. Geach accuses Dummett of making another mistake at this point:

. . . the thought that John hit Mary has three component parts: the sense of 'John', the sense of 'hit', the sense of 'Mary'. He does not tell us how these cohere into a whole, and into the right whole at that, rather than into the thought that Mary hit John.[14]

There are two problems here, the first about the coherence of Frege's views, the second about the way in which a proposition forms a unity, which Geach mentions. If we accept Frege's (and Bradley's) view that a word only has *meaning* in the context of a sentence, it is hard to see why any distinction should be made between different sorts of words. In the case of predicates it can be argued that their correct form should be 'is mortal,' 'is red' etc., but this does not make a great deal of difference. In any case, 'hit' or 'loves' are single words. But it is hard to see why, if all words are, as it were, incomplete until they are set into a sentential context, one group should be singled out for special attention as 'unsaturated.' The problem that this notion was introduced to solve is, of course, that of the unity of a judgment or assertion; only if there was some linkage would the parts hold together. The suggestion that one part of the sentence is unsaturated is meant to account for the unity. Dummett even talks of 'the process whereby an atomic sentence is put together out of its parts.'[15] But it is not because '— is mortal' demands completion by some such expression as 'Socrates' that we say 'Socrates is mortal,' but because Socrates *is* mortal. Similarly, 'That flash of lightning was followed by a very loud clap of thunder' is said because it was, not because 'was followed by' demands some such completion. In a sense the whole of the doctrine of 'internal relations' is contained in this remark. What Bradley was primarily concerned about, at least as far as the *Principles of Logic* dealt with the issue, was the question of what made a judgment into a unity.

One possible answer is that some kind of 'logical cement' holds the parts (or terms) together. Many traditional logicians took the copula to be this special ingredient which transformed a string of words into a piece of meaningful discourse. It was because the copula, and only the copula, performed this function that all propositions had to be reducible to subject–predicate form. To argue for the possibility of other forms, such as relational ones, was to claim that there were other things that could join words together. The Fregean talk of 'unsaturated elements' can be seen as another effort to find this 'logical cement.' Certainly as far as sentences are concerned, it is true that verbs have the function of transforming lists of words into properly formed grammatical units which can stand by themselves; in general I cannot make myself understood by uttering a string of words. But, and this seems to be the nub of Bradley's views, neither can I make sense just by uttering any sentence, even though that sentence happens to be true. It is here that Bradley's use of the term 'judgment' in preference to 'proposition' or 'sentence' becomes significant; what philosophical logic is concerned with is not merely well-formed formulae but what can form part of intelligible discourse; for such intelligibility more is needed than consonance with grammatical and logical rules. Part of what is denied by the thesis of internal relations is the extensionality of logic, the view that all complex propositions are truth-functions of simple or atomic ones. This is perhaps shown by what is, to our eyes, the very curious treatment of disjunction by Bradley in book I, chapter IV. (See chapter VIII.)

Thus the issue of the internality or externality of relations, as far as Bradley was concerned at this period of his life, is one which at other times has been represented by questions about the copula or about the 'unsaturatedness' of certain terms. Although there are some unclarities in the passage, this at least would seem to be clear in the following:

In their ordinary acceptation the traditional subject, predicate and copula are mere superstitions. The ideal matter which is affirmed in the judgment, no doubt possesses internal relations, and in *most* cases (not all) the matter may be arranged as subject and attribute. But this content, we have seen, is the same both in the assertion and out of it . . . . So that it is impossible that this internal relation can itself *be* the judgment; it can at best be no more than a condition of judging. (*PL*, p. 21)

It is not explicitly 'relational' propositions that Bradley is talking about, but any possible proposition. This point is perhaps brought out more clearly by a later passage in which he is explicitly arguing with Russell:

Let us take Mr. Russell's instance of 'between'. 'Between' requires a multiplicity of terms, and 'between', it is said, is a relation, and so much may seem obvious. But, I reply, to my mind it is not true that 'between' is a relation, and the opposite of this I even venture to regard as evident. 'Between' is certainly a feature which appears in a relational arrangement. But the arrangement is not itself a relation, and still less could it be the relation of 'between'. What is 'between' is one piece of the related whole, and it could never be that whole itself. (*ETR*, p. 306)

(Bradley refers in a footnote to Russell's *Problems of Philosophy* and to chapter XXV of the *Principles of Mathematics*.) The relations with which he is concerned are those that make a judgment into a unity; elsewhere he expresses this by saying that a judgment consists of one idea, not several (cf. chapter IV, pp. 67–8). For the purpose of analysis it may be necessary to distinguish different 'ideas' within a unity, but we must not therefore assume that these ideas are independent existences. Russell, Bradley could claim, falls into this trap by his talk of 'terms' and his statement that:

The notion that a term can be modified arises from neglect to observe the eternal self-identity of all terms and all logical concepts, which alone form the constituents of propositions.[16]

The central core of Bradley's view is best expressed in the following passage:

the relations between the ideas are themselves ideal. They are not the psychical relations of mental facts. They do not exist between symbols, but hold in the symbolized. They are part of the meaning and not of the existence. And the whole in which they subsist is ideal, and so one idea. (*PL*, p. 11)

Given the way in which, as I have argued, Bradley's terminology can be expressed in forms more familiar to present-day readers, it is possible to 'translate' this passage into:

The relations between symbols are themselves symbolic. They are not the physical relations between marks on paper. They do not exist between the symbols but hold in the symbolized. They are part of the meaning of the symbols and not features of their existence as matters of fact. And the whole in which they subsist is symbolic, and so is one symbol.

If it is accepted that a word only has meaning in the context of a proposition, then it seems to follow that the whole proposition is in some sense a single symbol, that, as Bradley argues, a judgment is a unity. There is a sense in which the doctrine of internal relations can be seen as a denial of relations, as in the passage quoted above about 'between.' There are no self-subsistent entities which need to be connected together by some device such as a copula or relation, but only parts which are artificially isolated for the purpose of understanding. In this sense the 'doctrine of internal relations' is not a special metaphysical thesis for which Bradley was offering arguments in the *Principles of Logic*, but only another formulation of the central doctrine of the book. It is for this reason that he seldom refers to it explicitly there.

The first two sentences of my 'translation' are easily dealt with; as I have pointed out before, symbols are physical objects and as such have physical relations. To have grasped the essence of symbolism is to have understood that these relations are not the important thing. And the same applies to 'ideas;' the logician is not engaged in any sort of psychological investigation. Hence the connections which we are interested in are those that hold in the real world. To take the example which Bradley uses on the next page, the perception of a wolf eating a lamb. We express this by saying 'The wolf eats the lamb,' of which Bradley says:

We have a relation here suggested or asserted between wolf and lamb, but that relation is (if I may use the word) not a *factual* connection between events in my head. What is meant is no psychical conjunction of images. (*PL*, p. 12)

What we express by the judgment is that an actual wolf actually ate a lamb, that an event occurred in the real world. The means by which we express this necessarily involves the use of some 'material,' ideas or symbols, but that is not what we are talking about. Here it is possible to begin to see Bradley's meaning. He is not here suggesting that there is any necessity involved in the wolf eating the lamb, but that the proposition, if true, describes an actual event. The fact that it is asserted is the claim that it is true. The judgment or proposition 'reaches right out to reality.' Thus '"The wolf eats the lamb" expresses an internal relation' does not mean that it could have been deduced that this would happen (nor that the lamb is now inside the wolf). It is not about the world at all, but about the way in which we talk about the world. One way of expressing this would be to say that internal relations are shown by the use of language, but that they cannot be expressed *in* language. This is not the way Bradley here puts it, but it helps to bring out the kind of claim he is making.

To use the example of the book and the table again, when I say that the one is on the other, this is because of what I have seen, but I did not see something called 'on' which connected the two objects. Nonetheless it is true that the book is on the table, and the relation between the two is 'internal' in the sense that it is something which is the result of our methods of symbolization, not an extra object existing in addition to the two (real) objects, the book and the table. An 'external relation' would be a physical connection, like the piece of string which tied one thing to another and which would have to be mentioned in any description of the state of affairs. Wittgenstein talks of the confusion between 'internal relations and relations proper (external relations), which is very widespread among philosophers' and adds:

It is impossible, however, to assert by means of propositions that such internal properties and relations exist: rather, they make themselves manifest in the propositions that represent the relevant states of affairs and are concerned with the relevant objects.[17]

Bradley makes much the same point when he says:

In this ideal content there are groups and joinings of qualities and relations, such as answer to nouns and verbs and prepositions. But these various elements, though you are right to distinguish them, have no validity outside the whole content. (*PL*, p. 12)

Internal relations are products of our symbolism, not features of the real world. But they do not represent *de dicto* necessity; there is all the difference in the world between 'The wolf eats the lamb' and 'A bachelor is an unmarried man,' for the latter is about symbols, the former about an event in the world. But it is not legitimate either to argue that the former must represent *de re* necessity, for if my argument is correct Bradley is not claiming any sort of necessity for 'internal relations' at this period. Indeed, it is hard to see how he could so long as he remains at the level of logic. Bradley frequently emphasizes that the *Principles of Logic* does not deal with metaphysical questions but leaves them for treatment in a different place, though I must add that the notes and appendices to the *Principles* do involve metaphysical discussion; it is for this reason that I do not make much use of them at this stage.

Thus the doctrine of internal relations is the consequence of the view that a judgment contains only one idea and hence that the separate 'ideas' or words which we normally think of as making up or composing a judgment are not fully independent entities, only products of analysis. In the linguistic mode this is equivalent to saying that words only have meaning in the context of a proposition. To understand a word is to be able to make sense of sentences in which it appears. The contextual principle leads to the view that any word is dependent on others, and hence is only the word it is in relation to other words. Its existence as a word depends on its relation to other words, and so these relations are 'internal,' make the word the word it is. It also follows that there is no particular item in the sentence which has the role of making it into a unity, no such thing as a copula or 'unsaturated item,' for every part is equally dependent on every other. It seems clear that it is impossible to hold both to the contextual principle, a word only has meaning in the context of a proposition, and to a belief in the copula or the unsaturated nature of predicates, and insofar as Frege did hold both these views he must be considered wrong. The contextual principle can be glossed as maintaining that all words are unsaturated, because they all depend on internal relations to other words to do their job.

It may legitimately be objected that my analysis of the doctrine of internal relations has rendered it plausible at the cost of removing from it all that Russell and his followers found objectionable and which led them to uphold the doctrine of external relations. They were opposing a set of metaphysical views, in particular those of *Appearance and Reality*, in which a rather different doctrine of internal relations played a vital role. Consequently it is necessary to look briefly at how Bradley managed to get a set of substantive, and very odd, philosophical theses out of what I claim is merely a logical doctrine. But before turning to that question it is worth pointing out that Russell did have serious problems with the unity of the proposition. Wittgenstein argued that a correct explanation of the form of the proposition must show that 'it is impossible for a judgment to be a piece of nonsense.'[18] If any word can be juxtaposed with any other word, then nonsense is liable to result. But if words are independent entities, each existing in its own right, then there is nothing to stop this being done. If the theory that all relations are external is construed in this manner, there is nothing to be said against nonsense judgments.

What turns the issue from one of logic to one of metaphysics is a confusion between sense and truth. 'John is bigger than Joan' and 'Joan is bigger than John' are well-formed sentences, but clearly both cannot be true at once. The normal way of deciding between them is to look at John and Joan in order to see which applies; in other words to rely on a correspondence between the judgment and the world. The error comes in carelessness over the way in which this is expressed. Russell, in his criticism of the doctrine of internal relations, put it thus:

. . . there is the fact that, if two terms have a certain relation, they cannot but have it, and if they did not have it they would be different; which seems to show that there is something in the terms themselves which leads to their being related as they are.[19]

Here the word 'terms,' as so often, serves to confuse the issue. For it it not clear if it refers to 'John' and 'Joan' or to John and Joan. If two human beings have a certain relation then it is true that they would be different if they did not have it. John's height is something which he actually has, and if he had a different height he would be different from what he is, and it might turn out that 'John is bigger than Joan' is no longer true. This seems to be something which no one would wish to challenge. In other words, if we take 'terms' as referring to the individuals in question, the 'doctrine' turns out to be a harmless truism. On the other hand, if we take 'term' to refer to 'John' we seem to be in a different position, for he was not given that name because he had a particular height. The confusion might be said to arise because there is a failure to distinguish between the fact that, if I am looking at the two standing side by side, I cannot but say that John is taller than Joan and the idea that it is necessary that John is taller than Joan. The latter is the position that Bradley gets into in the passage I quoted at the beginning of this chapter, where he suggests that starting from any one piece of knowledge it would be possible to reach all others by a chain of deduction.

It is not difficult to see how he gets to this position from a view of judgment which is perfectly respectable. A judgment is a unity, and to abstract a part from the judgment is to falsify that part, for it is only what it is in the context of the judgment. The fatal move is to say that it follows that the reality which is the true subject of the judgment is therefore also a unity, and extract one part from that is to falsify it. All judgments have the form 'Reality is such that S is P' for Bradley, but, I have argued in the previous chapter, this did not imply a separation between the two things; judgments 'reach right up to reality.' The 'elements' which compose the judgment are internally related. But in *Appearance and Reality* he seems to come to believe that reality itself must be 'internally related.' This view is forced upon him by his adoption of a coherence theory of truth in the latter work, a doctrine which itself is connected with his attempt to make language and reality coincide. For, he claims, any judgment we utter is partial, abstracts from the full situation it is meant to describe. We say 'The book is on the table,' but it must be in a particular position on the table for which co-ordinates could be given. And it is there because I put it there half an hour ago, no doubt for particular reasons. The table is where it is because . . . The account could be extended indefinitely. At the present moment there is a large number of different 'books on tables;' only if the full account were (*per impossibile*) to be given would it be clear that the judgment referred to this particular book, only then could it be really true. The way of ensuring that general words can 'latch on' to reality is to go on specifying until absolute particularity is reached. A passage from the appendix to *Appearance and Reality* shows this:

For a thing may remain unaltered if you identify it with a certain character, while taken otherwise the thing is suffering change. If, that is, you take a billiard-ball and a man in abstraction from place, they will of course – as far as this is maintained – be indifferent to changes of place. But on the other hand neither of them, if regarded so, is a thing which actually exists; each is a more or less valid abstraction. But take them as existing things and take them without mutilation, and you must regard them as determined by their places and qualified by the whole material system into which they enter. (*AR*, p. 517)

'Abstraction' is here the enemy, and the only way to guarantee the reference to this actual billiard-ball is to bring in all the circumstances, even though they would be infinite. Hence only the whole truth can properly be said to be true. This is why the red-haired man, in the passage quoted at the beginning of the chapter, could only grasp his red-hairedness if he knew everything about it. Even at this stage, however, it is clear that the doctrine of internal relations is concerned with particulars, not with universals. Indeed, it seems as if it is because universals fail in the task of firmly anchoring what we say to the reality about which we are talking that a device for reaching particularity is needed. To this end in *Appearance and Reality* Bradley adapts what he has earlier said about the unity of judgments, giving it a metaphysical air which it did not have in the *Principles of Logic*, Hence he now thinks that there can only be a single unity, which is the totality of things; anything less is not really a unity at all. I think it is clear that this later view is a falling away from the interesting and probably correct analysis of the nature of judgment and language which he gives in the *Principles*.

It is also clear that Russell and subsequent philosophers failed completely to understand what Bradley had been trying to do when he originally introduced the notion. This was partly because they took it to belong primarily to metaphysics, which they were committed to attacking, instead of to logic. I have tried to show that without an understanding of its logical background, the notion of 'internal relations' does not make sense. Further, because it was believed that the Fregean route was the right one for logic, there was no incentive to study Bradley's logical work in detail. Finally, I think it would be better if any contemporary use of the term should either be taken in Bradley's sense or be abandoned altogether. If it is necessary to talk of connections between concepts which are not simply analytic, then they could be called 'conceptual connections' *tout court.*

NOTES

1 'Logical Atomism' in *Logic and Knowledge*, ed. R. C. Marsh, London, 1956, p. 333.
2 'External and Internal Relations' in *Proceedings of the Aristotelian Society*, 1919–20. Reprinted in *Philosophical Studies*, London, 1922.
3 *Supplementary Proceedings of the Aristotelian Society*, vol. XIV, 1935.

4 *F. H. Bradley*, Penguin, 1959, pp. 104–5.
5 *Bertrand Russell and the British Tradition in Philosophy*, Fontana, 1967, p. 162.
6 *The Idea of a Social Science*, London, 1958, p. 125.
7 Ibid., p. 131.
8 Ibid., p. 130.
9 *Tractatus Logico-Philosophicus*, 4.123
10 Ibid., 3.1432.
11 *Principles of Mathematics*, Cambridge, 1903, p. 43
12 *My Philosophical Development*, London, 1975, p. 128.
13 *Philosophical Writings of Gottlob Frege*, Oxford, 1952, p. 54.
14 *Mind*, 1976, p. 444.
15 *Frege,* p. 23.
16 *Principles of Mathematics*, p. 448.
17 *Tractatus Logico-Philosophicus*, 4.122.
18 Ibid., 5.5422.
19 *Philosophical Essays*, London, 1910, pp. 143–4.

VIII

Forms of Judgment

Hegel, as we have seen, arranged judgments hierarchically; Bradley does not follow his practice in this respect, though his claim that the categorical judgments of ordinary speech are more properly treated as hypotheticals is a version of Hegel's view. But he does devote a chapter to negation and a shorter one to disjunction; he also considers other forms, such as modality, in a separate chapter. This topic forms a bridge to the next book, that on inference, and warrants some discussion on its own account, as do the chapters on negation and disjunction.

There is a problem about negative judgments, though in modern accounts it is more often put by asking about the relation between a positive proposition or sentence and the corresponding negative one. Ayer, in an article entitled 'Negation,'[1] commences by pointing out that although there is general agreement in saying that there is a distinction between affirmative and negative statements, it is not easy to give a satisfactory account of it.[2] He instances the equivalence of the two statements 'Everest is the highest mountain in the world' and 'There is no mountain in the world higher than Everest;' by the normal criterion one of these would count as affirmative, the other as negative. This can hardly be satisfactory, as they seem to mean the same thing.[3] Of course, he continues, there is a sense in which they have different forms, but he does not think this is an adequate way of distinguishing them. He next says:

But when philosophers contrast affirmative with negative statements, the distinction with which they are concerned applies not to the grammatical form of different sentences but to the different ways in which they are used.[4]

Bradley begins his considerations by stating that negation stands at a different level from affirmation (*PL*, p. 114). It is higher, in the sense that it is more reflective; to make an affirmative judgment, he seems to think, it is enough to look at what is presented. If I look at a tree, the word 'green' is at once seen to be applicable. Hence I can immediately say 'That tree is green.' In the case of an adjective that does not apply, such as 'yellow,' I have to ask myself the question 'Is this yellow?' before I can utter the negative judgment, 'That tree is not yellow.' Negation is more reflective than is affirmation:

What negation must begin with is the attempt on reality, the baffled approach of a qualification. And in the consciousness of this attempt is implied not only the suggestion that is made, but the subject to which that suggestion is offered. Thus in the scale of reflection negation stands higher than mere affirmation. It is in one sense more ideal, and it comes into existence at a later stage of the development of the soul.
(*PL*, p. 115)

Ayer quotes the first sentence of this passage[5] and denies that it would enable us to distinguish between positive and negative statements:

From the fact that someone asserts that it is not raining one is not entitled to infer that he has ever supposed, or that anyone has ever suggested, that it is, any more than from the fact that someone asserts that it is raining one is entitled to infer that he has ever supposed, or that anyone has ever suggested, that it is not.[6]

The comparison of these two quotations brings out part of the difference that is made to logic using 'judgment' rather than any other term. It could be claimed that Ayer was right to say that there is no great logical difference between positive and negative sentences, though not, I think, for the reason he gives. Normally no one asserts either that it is or that it is not raining without some reason, and this often is a previous remark by the person he is talking to or a suggestion that is known to both of them, such as the morning weather forecast stating that it would rain in the afternoon in that area, or that it would not. But the reason is that there must be a point to the remark in the particular context; the first section of the quotation from Ayer seems to indicate that no context is required, and this must be wrong. We do not utter statements at random, even if they happen to be true. Nevertheless, it does seem that he has made out his claim that neither is on a different level from the other. It could be that Bradley had misled himself by using a specious example; we normally expect trees to be green, whereas of the English weather rain or its absence are equally likely (and equally interesting). Which judgment is, as it were, prior in the case of the weather depends on our interests at the time; a gardener is sad that it is not raining, a cricketer delighted. If it has been pouring all day 'It is not raining' may have a very positive feel to it.

Bradley, however, claims that every negation must have a positive ground (*PL*, p. 117); this is because we cannot meet with the absence of something. We can only encounter things, and these must be positive:

A is not B because A is such that, if it were B, it would cease to be itself. Its quality would be altered if it accepted B; and it is by virtue of this quality, which B would destroy, that A maintains itself and rejects the suggestion. In other words, its quality *x* and B are discrepant. And we cannot deny B without affirming in A the pre-existence of this discrepant quality.

But in the negative judgment *x* is not made explicit. We do not say what there is in A which makes B incompatible. (*PL*, p. 117)

Sartre, on the other hand, claims that I can look round the café and see the absence of my friend Pierre; I do not make this judgment on the basis of finding that every space is occupied by something or someone which excludes Pierre from it; I simply fail to see Pierre.[7] What excludes Pierre from the café is his presence somewhere else, but this is a fact of which I am unaware, otherwise I would not be looking for him in the café. Nor is it the case that this judgment about Pierre's absence is any higher than one about his presence. For I look round the café with the question 'Is Pierre here?' whatever will be the result of my search; it is because I do not know what to expect that the question is appropriate. Sartre starts his survey of negation from questioning; I approach the café with a definite query in mind, 'Is Pierre here?' This, he thinks, is typical of any approach to the real world. A question is normally capable of being answered by 'yes' or 'no,' so to that extent it is neutral; for him there could be no difference between asserting that a tree was not yellow or that it was green. Both would be answers to a prior question. He differs from Ayer, in that he wants to argue that the possibility of making negative assertions reveals something important about the nature of human beings, though in the last resort it is the possibility of saying anything, positive or negative, which is significant for his philosophical views.

However, there does seem something right about the objections of Ayer and Sartre, and in this connection it is interesting that Bradley admits in a note to this chapter that it 'contains some serious errors' (*PL*, p. 125). He refers the reader to Bosanquet's account in *Knowledge and Reality* and in his *Logic*. However, Bosanquet, in the former book, says:

I do not think that I differ from Mr. Bradley in my view of the actual character which we must ascribe to the negative judgment as such. . . . I must, therefore, admit the essence of sect. 13 of Book I, ch. 3, the chapter on the Negative Judgment, a chapter, I may say in passing, which appears to me to be a masterpiece of logical analysis and suggestive criticism.[8]

This admission, which appears directly to contradict what Bradley has said in his revision of his book, concerns the question of the relation between negation and affirmation. Bosanquet, in the omitted passage in the quotation above, criticizes Sigwart's doctrine that negation necessarily presupposes actual affirmation, 'though it does presuppose the idea or suggestion of an affirmative relation.' It is this view which he claims to be that of Bradley. As I have already hinted Bradley seems to go further than this, but perhaps the conclusion to paragraph 12 is pointing in the direction that Bosanquet suggests:

The positive quality of the ultimate reality may remain occult or be made explicit, but this, and nothing else, lies always at the base of a negative judgment. (*PL*, p. 120)

That this must be the case follows from his view that the real subject of all judgments is 'reality.' In the case of the example he has been using, 'Chimaeras are non-existent,' this is clear, because there are no chimaeras to be the subject of the judgment. Nevertheless, there must be a reason why we exclude them from the realm of existing things. The exclusion is not just a matter of failing to encounter chimaeras 'in the world.' Even to 'notice the absence' of Pierre has a positive ground, beyond that of failing to see him; all the chairs are either occupied by someone else or are empty. These are positive grounds, Bradley claims.

The fact that negative judgments have positive grounds implies a difference between positive and negative judgments, which renders the latter 'more reflective' than the former. This view differs both from our normal attitude to negation and from that of most contemporary logicians. We normally define 'not *p*' as that proposition which is true when *p* is false and false when *p* is true. And the fact that a double negation is equivalent to an affirmation seems to confirm this. For the repetition of the sign for negation an even number of times does not alter the sense of the proposition so dealt with. If Bradley's claim were true, there ought to be a difference introduced by each extra negation. He is working with the notions of affirmation and denial, rather than that of a simple sign of negation, but if we accept the equivalence of *p* and not not *p*, then there would seem to be grounds for rejecting what he says.

Bradley in fact devotes a section of chapter V to the issue of double negation, and begins it with an assertion that double negation is equivalent to affirmation (*PL*, p. 158):

> The real reason why denial of denial is affirmation, is merely this. In all denial we must have the assertion of a positive ground; and the positive ground of the second denial can be nothing but the predicate denied by the first. I can not say 'It is false that A is not *b*,' unless I already possess the positive knowledge that *A is b*. And the reason of my incapacity is that no *other* knowledge is a sufficient ground. (*PL*, p. 159)

The view is quite other from that expressed in the *Tractatus*: 'Every proposition has only one negative, because there is only one proposition that is wholly outside it.'[9] Here the image is that of a proposition dividing reality into two areas; the affirmative proposition, as it were, deals with the interior of the island, the negation refers to all that lies outside the coastline. Hence it is obvious that the negation of a negation must be equivalent to the original affirmation; we are back on the island again! For Wittgenstein, as for most other modern logicians, negation is an operation applied to propositions. Formally, Bradley agrees with Wittgenstein. However, there obviously is a difference, which Bradley would express by saying that he was concerned with the conditions under which one could actually make such a denial, and this was something that a logician ought to be concerned with. His example (*PL*, pp. 159–60) is 'Ultimate reality is not knowable.' He claims that the only possible way to deny this is to show that it can be known, and to do this involves the use of some positive ground. This is the only way we could be in a position to deny the original judgment.

One way of expressing the difference between Bradley and modern formal logicians would be to say that he is concerned with the conditions for making judgments, whereas they are concerned with the analysis of a piece of prose that is, as it were, presented to them. They are telling us that if we come across a proposition that can be expressed 'not not *p*,' then we are justified in taking it as equivalent to '*p*.' Bradley, on the other hand, argues that if you can say 'not not *p*' it can only be because 'not *p*' has been asserted and you know that '*p*.' It might be claimed that Bradley here imports epistemological issues into logic, but this would be to misunderstand what he is saying. He is not at all interested in the question of *how* I know that *p*, but only in the fact that I do know it. This must be the case if I am sensibly to deny or to assert anything at all. His discussion, in other words, is of what is necessary to make a judgment, and this is tantamount to a discussion of the conditions of assertability, which are surely a matter for logic under any definition of the subject. I must repeat that, unlike Bosanquet, Bradley does separate logical from epistemological issues.

This point in fact gives a key to his discussions of other logical 'principles,' Identity, Contradiction and Excluded Middle, in chapter V. The principle of identity cannot, he thinks, just involve the assertion that A is A, for 'We never at any time wish to use tautologies (*PL*, p. 141). And, as is commonly recognized, those propositions which appear to be tautologies, such as 'I am myself,' are not, as they are used, tautologous. There is, however, a real 'Axiom of Identity' which is necessary for inference. Bradley expresses it as: '*What is true in one context is true in another*' (*PL*, p. 143). This amounts to claiming that a judgment does not change its truth when circumstances change, i.e. that context does not affect truth and falsity. So the result of the axiom in Bradley's form is that 'S is P is true everywhere and always' (*PL*, p. 144). But this raises metaphysical questions, and at the same time gives a reason for his denial that such standard English sentences as 'I now have toothache' are genuine judgments. For the truth of 'I have toothache' is dependent on its context:

I say that 'I have toothache today.' It is gone tomorrow. Has my former judgment become therefore false? The popular view would loudly proclaim that it is still true, for I *had* a toothache, and the judgment now holds good of the past. But what that comes to is simply this. The judgment is true because answering to fact. The fact alters so that it does not answer; and yet the judgment is still called true, because of something that does not exist. Can anything be more inconsistent and absurd? If the change of circumstance and change of day is not a fresh context which falsifies *this* truth, why should any change of context falsify *any* truth? (*PL*, pp. 143–4)

Presumably Bradley is not quarrelling with the possibility of altering the tense of the judgment, so that it now reads 'I had a toothache yesterday' though the same problem will also occur with this tomorrow. The only solution would be to produce 'tenseless' judgments, of the form 'FHB had toothache at noon on such a date' which would be timelessly true or false.

But it does not seem that this way out is one that he would have taken, for otherwise he would not say that the question raises metaphysical issues. He talks of 'abstracting from the differences of space and time' as 'changing the subject,' i.e. the subject of the judgment. If we take the fundamental form of judgment to be 'Reality is such that S is P,' then there would seem to be no logical objection to reformulating the judgment about present toothache into a timeless version and coupling it into this formula. For Bradley this would involve a radical departure from the original; it would no longer be an 'analytic judgment of sense.' There are other features of 'I have toothache' which also render it problematic as a judgment; it is too like an immediate cry of pain, a direct response to a situation, to qualify for the somewhat exalted title. It could be said that I do not really *make* this remark as a judgment, or that it does not really constitute one. What is clear is that not any form of words that constitutes a grammatical English sentence will suffice to count as a judgment for Bradley; logical and grammatical form do not coincide.

Likewise, the Principle of Contradiction should run, Bradley claims, 'Denial and affirmation of the self-same judgment is wholly inadmissible' (*PL*, p. 147). He says that in this form it is the other side of the Law of Identity. He stresses that there is nothing psychological about the Principle; it does not concern the possibility or impossibility of mentally affirming and denying at the same time. It asserts that you cannot both affirm and deny the same judgment and speak truly. With that he would be willing to leave the topic because the claims of the principle are so minimal. He expresses this picturesquely:

> Its claims, if we consider them, are so absurdly feeble, it is itself so weak and perfectly inoffensive that it cannot quarrel, for it has not a tooth with which to bite anyone. (*PL*, p. 151)

But, he says, the law has 'had the misfortune to be denied from a certain theory of the nature of things' (*PL*, p. 147). He adds in a footnote that he uses the word 'from' advisedly, which implies that he is doubtful if Hegel himself actually can be taken as denying the law of contradiction, though there is no doubt that many so-called Hegelians have wished to do so. As I hope became clear in chapter II, in his formal discussion of logic there is no doubt that Hegel himself did not deny the law. Bradley has a short way with those who claim that things in the real world are composed of contradictory elements. If certain elements are conjoined, then that very fact is evidence that they are not disparate or discrepant. That they co-exist shows that they cannot be real contraries, because it is the definition of contraries that they exclude one another. Of course it is possible that elements which, taken in abstraction, are contrary and hence mutually exclusive may not be so under certain conditions. An alexandrite can be defined as a stone which is red and green, not all over, but all through. But it is necessary to add that it appears green in daylight and red in artificial light, and there is no logical contradiction between these two situations. Hence he concludes that the question of whether we can think dialectically and of the extent to which dialectic exists 'in the real world' have nothing to do with the principle of contradiction. It is a factual question, precisely because as soon as apparent opposites do co-exist, the axiom obviously no longer applies. At this stage he does refer to our ability to think 'in the way recommended by Hegel' (*PL*, p. 151), which is an interesting change from the beginning of the discussion. Neither does he add a footnote to soften the force of the charge. In fact, I am doubtful if Hegel ever recommends such a procedure, though here the issue is not important. What is important is the fact that Bradley adheres to a firm logical line, that it is impossible for true contraries to be conjoined in the same object, and in so far as 'dialectical philosophy' claims that it is not only possible but also true of objects in the world in general, it must be considered false. Bradley later (*PL*, p. 159) refers to a 'cardinal mistake of Hegel,' and quotes somewhat selectively from Bain's *The Emotions and the Will** to show that there is a danger of the empiricists falling into the same trap as did Hegel. It is not entirely

---

* London, 1859. The full quotation runs as follows: 'We generalize all cases of particular coexistence into the abstract attribute; and all individual successions into succession in the abstract; but, without the shock of difference felt when we pass from an instance of the one to an instance of the other, we should have no cognition of either; and our cognition, as it stands, is explained as mutual negation of two properties. Each has a positive existence because of the presence of the other as its negative, like heat and cold, light and dark' (*The Emotions and the Will*, p. 638n).

clear what he means here, nor to what error he is referring, but it seems to be a matter of relativity. It does not appear that Bain is asserting a full relativity of knowledge; certainly the examples he gives are of terms that must be relative to each other on any view, such as light and dark. His point is that if the world as we experienced it were uniformly light, we would not think of it as so; this hardly seems a dangerous doctrine. Nevertheless, it is possible to conclude from the passages about Hegel in this chapter that Bradley is careful to distance himself from 'Hegelianism,' even if it is not obvious to which philosophers he is actually referring. It can hardly be the 'Anglo-Hegelians.'

The final principle to be discussed is the Law of Excluded Middle. Bradley thinks it doubtful if it should be called an axiom, for it is really an instance of disjunction, which he has already discussed in chapter IV. In spite of devoting a whole chapter to the topic, he does not give this type of judgment the special importance that Hegel and Bosanquet did. It could be claimed that the reason they did so was primarily epistemological, i.e. because of the role such judgments play in science. Bradley is concerned only with their logical status. He insists that 'or' is always exclusive, and that any cases where it looks to be inclusive can be explained away quite easily. He says: 'I confess I should despair of human language, if such distinctions as separate "and" from "or" could be broken down' (*PL*, p. 134). The apparent examples of an inclusive 'or' come from loose uses of language:

It is an excellent thing in all these questions to refer to the common usages of language, but we must remember that in those usages, besides what one calls 'unconscious logic,' there also may lurk mere looseness and careless-ness. (*PL*, p. 135)

He concludes that, although a disjunctive judgment may be partially analysed into a set of hypotheticals, it has its own character, and is not reducible to any other type. 'Its assertion again, if not quite categorical, is certainly not quite hypothetical. It involves both these elements' (*PL*, p. 137).

Perhaps more interesting is his brief discussion of Mill's state-ment, that 'Between the true and the false there is a third possi-bility, the Unmeaning.'[10] This is a view which has played an impor-

tant role in twentieth-century English philosophy. In a classic statement, Ryle said:

For he [Russell] now wielded a distinction, which Mill had seen but left inert,
the distinction between sentences which are either true or false, on the one
hand, and on the other sentences which, although proper in vocabulary and
syntax, are nonetheless nonsensical, meaningless or absurd; and therefore
neither true nor false. To assert them and to deny them are to assert and
deny nothing. For reasons of a sort which are the proper concern of logic,
certain sorts of concatenations or words and phrases into sentences produce
things which cannot significantly be said. . . . What matters for us, and what
made a big difference to subsequent philosophy, is the fact that at long last
the notion of meaning was realized to be, at least in certain crucial contexts,
the obverse of the notion of the nonsensical – what can be said, truly or
falsely, is at last contrasted with what cannot significantly be said. The
notion of meaning had been, at long last, partly detached from the notion of
naming and reattached to the notion of saying. . . . To know what an
expression means involves knowing what can (logically) be said with it and
what cannot (logically) be said with it. It involves knowing a set of bans, fiats
and obligations, or, in a word, it is to know the rules for the employment of
that expression.[11] [This was written in 1957. It is interesting that he does not
here mention Bradley, though in the introduction to the *Revolution in
Philosophy* of 1956 he couples Bradley with Frege in this respect.]

Bradley rejects this suggestion entirely:

But surely, on the one hand, it is clear that a proposition which has no
meaning is no proposition; and surely again, on the other hand, it is clear
that, if it does mean anything, it is either true or false. (*PL*, p. 155)

The argument between these two views is obviously an important
one, so I make no apology for reopening the discussion of nonsense
which occurred in chapter IV above. Ryle's claim might be said to be
that 'Simple logic itself forbids certain ostensibly denoting expressions to denote,' as he says shortly before the quotation just given. But
this is itself to extend the area covered by 'simple logic.' For part of
the problem is that there is no obvious difference in form between 'A
triangle is not a quadrilateral' and 'Virtue is not a fire shovel,' yet one
is clearly true, while the other makes no sense. Ryle, of course, is
talking in terms of sentences, i.e. grammatically well-formed sequ-
ences of English words. In the construction of such sentences rules
are obviously involved; part of a training in English consists in learn-

ing to put words together in correct ways. A schoolmaster might accept 'Virtue is not a fire shovel,' whilst rejecting 'Virtue are not a fire shovel.' But there are no rules of the sort that could be cited in a grammar lesson that forbid the use of the expression 'fire shovel' in combination with the expression 'virtue.' In fact, I remember someone at a conference producing a meaningful use of that very sentence which most of us, at first sight, accept to be meaningless. He talked of someone using his virtue 'to heap coals of fire on another's head,' and hence claimed that the sentence 'Virtue is not a fire shovel' could be used to condemn such an action. The problem is that it is often possible to produce a situation in which an apparently nonsensical combination of words is given a meaning. Many sentences occurring in works of philosophy have this character, particularly when they are taken out of context. We constantly do judge certain sentences to be nonsensical, but it is not so easy to specify what it is that makes them so. One suggestion, due to Arthur Pap, is that nonsense results from the non-linguistic relations between the designata of the constituent terms of a sentence.[12] Cora Diamond expresses the point thus:

The idea is that if you say 'Caesar is a prime number' and you mean 'Caesar' as a person's name and you mean the last four words in exactly the sense they have in '53 is a prime number' then the reason what you say is nonsense is that *the person* Caesar *having the property* you said 53 had – *that* is impossible, *that* makes no sense.[13]

Diamond argues that there is an alternative view of nonsense given by Frege and Wittgenstein, one which denies that there is such a thing as 'positive nonsense.' For the way in which, e.g. Ryle expresses the matter implies that it is the sense of the sentence which is senseless. It is because we can in some way understand it that we see that it is nonsensical. In this the kind of example I am discussing is quite different from gobbledegook like 'Cat the are hypotenuse three.' If we adopt Pap's suggestion for the kind of cases that Ryle has in mind, then we are committed to finding them nonsense as a result of half-making sense of them. Wittgenstein said:

When a sentence is called senseless it is not, as it were its sense that is senseless. But a combination of words is being excluded from the language, withdrawn from circulation.[14]

This remark is closely connected with a passage from the *Tractatus*:

> Frege says that any legitimately constructed proposition must have a sense. And I say that any possible proposition is legitimately constructed, and, if it has no sense, that can only be because we have failed to give a *meaning* to some of its constituents.
>
> (Even if we think that we have done so.)
>
> Thus the reason why 'Socrates is identical' says nothing is that we have *not* given any *adjectival* meaning to the word 'identical.' For when it appears as a sign for identity, it symbolizes in an entirely different way – the signifying relation is a different one – therefore the symbols also are entirely different in the two cases: the two symbols have only the sign in common, and that is an accident.[15]

It is difficult to see quite what is meant in this passage by 'giving a meaning' to the constituents of a sentence. It almost looks as if this were some 'mental' operation, but that, of course, would be quite contrary to the whole tenor of Wittgenstein's thought. I think it is possible to make sense of the notion by going back to a Bradleian mode of expression. He would have argued that it is impossible to *judge* any of these nonsensical sentences. There are no circumstances in which anyone would want to say that Caesar was a prime number. If he were to say this and to mean it, then it would be possible to discover the context in which the remark was made and this would be to discover its sense, i.e. make it possible to decide whether what had been said was true or false. Here, as elsewhere, the apparent logical difficulty arises from taking sentences in isolation. Sense, or meaning, depends on the context, and 'giving an expression a meaning' is precisely to construct an appropriate context for it, as was done with the sentence 'Virtue is not a fire shovel.' But this, as I have already said, easily drives us into the position in which the only truth is the whole. Only by looking at a wider context can we determine whether we are faced with a string of words imitating a judgment or a genuine judgment. But, whatever the metaphysical difficulties, I think Bradley was right to reject Mill's trichotomy of 'true, false or meaningless.' Judgments can only be true or false, and thus the law of excluded middle holds of them. Indeed, if it did not, all discourse would become impossible.

Bradley begins his discussion of modality by saying that it 'is not an alluring theme' (*PL*, p. 197). Nevertheless, it must be dealt with because the area has been the source of many confusions. A large part of the chapter is taken up with a discussion of probability. What he has to say is interesting, but would seem to be acceptable and not greatly to differ from modern views on the topic. However, what he has to say about modality in general is of importace, both for the development' of his views and for its intrinsic interest. He starts by saying that modality is supposed to affect the 'formal character' of an assertion, without regard to what is asserted. He denies this, on the grounds that 'There are no degrees of truth and falsehood' (*PL*, p. 197). All judgments are assertoric and so modality must affect their content, not the style of affirmation, though care is necessary not to confuse 'logical modality' with the

endless ways of modifying a judgment so as to make a fresh judgment. You may take the idea of a judgment S – P and express any attitude of your mind towards it. You may say 'I make it,' or 'wish to make it,' or 'fear to make it,' or 'can not make it,' or 'am inclined to make it,' or 'am forced to make it.' All these are simply assertions about my condition of mind. They have a psychological not a logical bearing, and may at once be dismissed. (*PL*, pp. 197–8)

For logic modality must affect judgments 'from the side of truth and falsehood. The ideal content must be referred to or else denied of reality. . . . What therefore must in some way be modified is the content itself' (*PL*, p. 198). There are three varieties of modality, the actual, the possible and the necessary. As regards the first, Bradley states that there is no difference between the actual, the real, the assertoric and the categorical. All are equally to be contrasted with the possible and the necessary. They have already been dealt with in the first two chapters. He states that the 'possible and the necessary have no real existence' (*PL*, pp. 198–9). By this he means that they are particular forms of the hypothetical judgment, though it is not altogether clear how what he says here is to be related to his remarks quoted on p. 144 above. Modal judgments are hypotheticals:

And these are nothing but phases of the hypothetical. What may be and what must be involve a supposition. Neither is declared to be actual fact: they both are inferred on the strength of a condition, and subject to a condition.(*PL*, p. 199)

He means that all necessity is hypothetical, at least as far as logic is concerned. 'A thing is necessary if it is not taken simply in and by itself, but by virtue of something else and because of something else' (*PL*, p. 199). In other words, for logic 'necessity' attaches only to logical consequences; it does not characterize an actual state of affairs. He uses two arguments to establish this. First, necessity is only a matter of an 'ideal connection.' It is the result of some kind of argument, not of a relation existing in the world. This topic is discussed at greater length in the books on Inference. Second, he claims that ordinary usage supports his view, quoting the hypothetical 'If two were three then four must be six,' which presents us with a sentence that is necessary and clearly false. There is no difference in the validity of the argument whether the premises are true or false. If the premises are facts, then the result is also a fact, but it is not necessary fact:

> For logic the necessary must remain the hypothetical. Facts for logic must be facts that *are* and that never *must be*. The real connection which seems the counterpart of our logical sequence, is in itself not necessary. It is necessary for us, when in ideal experiment we retrace the process of actual fact. But, at least in logic, we must not assume that our ideal relation is the bond of existence. (*PL*, p. 206)

Thus for Bradley all necessity is *de dicto*, and never *de re*, at least as far as logic is concerned. There are a number of places where he suggests reservations about this view when metaphysics is in question, and that he changes his view later is obvious from one of the opening sentences of the chapter, 'There are no degrees of truth and falsehood' (*PL*, p. 197). In a footnote added to the second edition, he states that this needs correction, and refers his readers to the discussion in *Appearance and Reality* and *Essays on Truth and Reality* (*PL*, p. 236).

Similarly, possibility is a matter of our thinking, not of the nature of things:

> And when we pass from the necessary to the possible, our conclusion remains. The possible, as such, exists nowhere at all but in the heads of men. The real is not possible unless for a moment you think of it as unreal. When the possible becomes real it ceases at once to become a mere possibility. For metaphysics I will not deny that the possible *might* bear another meaning. But for logic, wherever a fact appears, a possibility vanishes. It is not merely that the possible is confined within the limits of human thinking. It can not exist outside the domain of human doubt and human ignorance. (*PL*, p. 206)

He extends this to cover such phrases as 'potential energy,' which he links with notions of 'capacities' and 'faculties.' He denies that the potential is anything real, and describes it as 'This deplorable piece of effete metaphysics' (*PL* p. 209), when it is taken to represent something real. It is again merely the consequence of a hypothetical judgment in which the condition is not actualized. Even conditions cannot be said to exist:

A condition is an element in a hypothetical judgment and, outside that judgment, it is no condition. If you say, 'A exists and *is* an actual condition of B,' you are speaking inaccurately. What real bond corresponds to your phrase? B *is* not in existence, and if the other conditions do not appear, it will not exist. And yet you say, 'A *is* one of its conditions.' If you wish to be accurate you should say, 'A is something which, if taken from existence and placed within an ideal construction, mentally gives rise to B.' All beyond is unwarranted. (*PL*, p. 210)

He uses this to criticize Mill's definition of matter as 'the permanent possibility of sensation.' More interestingly for logic, he says that this conclusion shows the equivalence of 'Some S is P' and 'S may be P,' which he takes as justifying his earlier remark that the particular judgment is really a form of the hypothetical.

As I said earlier, this chapter marks the transition from discussion of judgment to that of inference, at least in an overt manner. Bradley says 'Silently before in the second Chapter, and now almost explicitly we have made the transition from judgment to inference. In both the latter kinds of modality we reason openly' (*PL*, p. 236). He continues:

The possible is that which we argue would follow from certain premises, part of which is taken as true. The necessary is that which we infer must follow, if its grounds are premised. It was in this sense that possibility is one kind of necessity. In both alike we deal with conclusions, reasoned results from given *data*. In logic we find that a necessary truth is really an inference, and an inference is nothing but a necessary truth. This is the secret which we hardly have kept, and with the discovery of which we may pass at once to our Second Book.

Here we can see the justification of Bradley's earlier remark that there is no absolute difference between judgment and inference, that they pass into each other. The wording is to be noted; he says that a necessary truth *is* an inference, not that it is the result of one, as might have been expected. In other words, a necessary truth cannot stand alone; to be understood it needs the conditions which make it necessary. Similarly, a judgment about probability requires the evidence on which it is based to make sense. Neither is complete in itself. This would seem to be an extension of the 'contextual principle' to cover more than just an individual judgment; we are getting towards the situation where the unit of sense is a piece of discourse which may well be of a considerable length. This can be seen if we consider the arguments that may be involved in a statement of the probability of an event. There are grounds for saying that the 'contextual principle' does naturally lead to such extensions; it is not difficult to finish up with a metaphysical system like that of *Appearance and Reality*.

NOTES

1 'Negation', *Philosophical Essays*, London, 1954, pp. 36–65.
2 Ibid., p. 36.
3 Ibid., pp. 36–7.
4 Ibid., p. 38.
5 Ibid., p. 39.
6 Ibid., p. 39.
7 *L'Etre et le néant*, Paris, 1953, pp. 44–6.
8 *Knowledge and Reality*, London, 1885, p. 220.
9 *Tractatus Logico-Philosophicus*, London, 1961, 5.513.
10 *Logic*, vol. II, ch. vii, para. 5.
11 'The Theory of Meaning,' *Collected Papers*, vol. II, London, 1971, pp. 362–3.
12 'Types and Meaninglessness,' *Mind*, 1960, p. 47.
13 'What Nonsense might be,' *Philosophy*, January 1981, p. 14.
14 *Philosophical Investigations*, para. 500.
15 *Tractatus Logico-Philosophicus*, 5.4733.

IX

Inference

The reader of the *Principles of Logic* will be struck by the amount of space Bradley devotes to the topic of inference. In the first edition there are 282 pages on the subject, compared with 210 on the nature of judgment. A further feature is evident from the chapter headings; Bradley seems to go over the same ground several times. Book II is devoted to the topic, but book III begins with 'The Enquiry Reopened,' and its penultimate chapter is entitled 'The Final Essence of Reasoning.' Nevertheless, this does not stop Bradley from adding a second part to that book which runs to 59 pages and closes with a famous sceptical passage. Bosanquet, it is worth noting, devotes only 37 per cent of his *Logic* to inference, whereas Bradley devotes 57 per cent. Given that inference is little discussed in modern treatments of logic, the proportion is striking, particularly when it is realized that it is logical, not scientific, inference which is mainly discussed. Obviously inference was a major problem for Bradley, in a way in which it had not been for previous logicians and was not for subsequent ones, even though he claims that there is no sharp dividing line between it and judgment. Hence I shall divide my discussion of Bradley's views on inference into three sections; book II will be examined in this chapter, and book III, part I in the next. Finally, I will look at the sceptical passages of the concluding chapters.

Bradley devotes so much space to inference because he regards it as more common than do some logicians. There is no gulf between judgment and inference; the two fade into one another. Indeed, one problem for logic is to separate the two, to discover if a particular judgment is direct or mediate. For logic is not solely concerned with what Hegel called 'ceremonial syllogising,' occasions when an argument is consciously expressed as such. In many cases it would be impossible or otiose to express an inference in a standard form. There is, however, a single thread running through all Bradley's discussion of logic; the problem of the *Principles of Logic* is how judgments can be true of reality. Some seem to reach reality through a connection with experience, and their problems have already been discussed. Others are believed as the result of a process of inference. Hence it might seem that their relation to reality is more tangential. But what is asserted is the same in this group as in the former: 'reality is such that S – P.' Bradley has already pointed out that many apparently ordinary judgments are arrived at through inference, for example the 'synthetic judgments of sense:'

It is thus by inference that we transcend the given through synthetic judgments. . . . (*PL*, p. 73)

Or

In synthetic judgments there is always an inference, for an ideal content is connected with the sensible qualities that are given us. In other words we have always a construction, which depends on ideas, and which only indirectly is based on perception. (*PL*, p. 62)

Even the past and the future are not 'given directly, but inferred from the present' (*PL*, p. 55). Thus we are always inferring; it is an activity which is as common as judging and performed in the same unthinking manner. The task of the logician is to show how truth can be transmitted through mental operations, for it is clear that Bradley accepts the normal notion that inference preserves truth. However, this could seem to mark an important difference between judgment and inference, for the former involves the notion of truth, the latter that of validity. This seems to direct the attention of the logician to the relation which must hold between two propositions in order that one can be inferred from the other, normally called 'implication.' Russell expressed the point:

But it is plain that where we validly infer one proposition from another, we do so in virtue of a relation which holds between the two propositions whether we perceive it or not: the mind, in fact, is as purely receptive in inference as common sense supposes it to be in perception of sensible objects.[1]

We are passive, Russell thinks, in both cases; inference involves the seeing of relations that exist independently of us.

Logicians, since the turn of the century at least, have been interested mainly in implication. Ryle, in one of the rare modern discussions of the topic, remarks:

Logicians say oddly little about inferences. They prefer to change the subject and talk instead about hypothetical statements. For instance, they shy off discussing what we do with such dicta as 'Today is Monday, so tomorrow is Tuesday' and discuss instead such dicta as 'If today is Monday, tomorrow is Tuesday.[2]

It is a hypothetical or relation of implication which entitles us to make inferences. Implication is a relation which holds between propositions; the logician is concerned with formal implications, i.e. ones that do not depend upon the particular subject-matter of the propositions in question. It is not denied that we can make inferences that depend on what the proposition is about; we frequently do. It is just that these are not the concern of logic, a fact which is now often marked by the prefix 'formal' attached to the term 'logic.' 'Symbolic logic' makes much the same point; the use of symbols instead of the words of ordinary language emphasizes the formal nature of the relations to be considered. Bradley, it is clear, was not a formal logician.

The formal or symbolic view of logic played an important role in the 'revolution in philosophy.' It also led to the belief that there was a close connection between logic and mathematics, exemplified in the early work of Russell. Bradley thought his ignorance of mathematics no great obstacle to the study of logic (cf. *PL*, p. 387n); this marks him off from the vast majority of those who have subsequently studied it. He was concerned with the question of how it could be that the results of inferences were true of reality; he would not have understood the question 'Why are the calculuses of logic and arithmetic applicable to reality?'[3] This is because he does not think of his study of inference as aiming at a set of rules. Ryle described the work of logicians as issuing in:

mainly [of] two kinds of pronouncements. One kind is composed of explanatory observations and these are expressed chiefly in ordinary prose. The other kind is composed of formulae, which are ordinarily expressed in a code. What do these formulae declare? They are formulations of rules of inference or consistency-rules. They express what fallacies are breaches of.[4]

Logic, then, is thought of as a calculus, a device or 'machine' for achieving results.

I have called it a 'machine' interpretation because the idea of logic implicit here has analogies to the use of computers, where the 'logic' is embodied in the mechanism; feeding in true premises will, if the machine is functioning correctly, produce a true output. It would seem that a remark of Wittgenstein about mathematics would also apply to logic:

Indeed, in real life, a mathematical proposition is never what we want. Rather, we make use of mathematical propositions *only* in inferences from propositions that do not belong to mathematics to others that likewise do not belong to mathematics.[5]

Bradley discusses the question of machines in the chapter on 'Jevons' Equational Logic.' This was a method of dealing mechanically with syllogisms. If *A*, *B* and *C* are the three terms of a syllogism, and the negation of a term is represented by the corresponding lower-case letter, then we can write out all eight possible combinations of the three terms: *ABC*, *ABc*, *AbC*, *Abc*, *aBC*, *aBc*, *abC*, *abc*. Any pair of premises will eliminate some of these possibilities, and those remaining will represent the conclusion that can be drawn. For example, 'All *A* is *B*' eliminates *AbC* and *Abc*, 'No *B* is *C*' removes *ABC* and *aBC*, so no combinations of *A* and *C* are left; hence we can conclude that 'No *A* is *C*.' This method is formally equivalent to the use of Venn diagrams. Jevons' 'Logical Machine' was a device to provide the alternatives and to eliminate some of them automatically. It incorporated all combinations of four terms, sixteen possibilities. Pressing the appropriate keys removed some, and those that were left represented the conclusion. Bradley says:

It is easy to exaggerate the powers of the machine. But I think it is impossible to deny that it executes such work as must otherwise be done by a process of thinking. For myself I do not hesitate to say that it performs mechanically an operation which, if performed ideally, would be an inference. And in this sense I think Professor Jevons is justified in his claim to have made a reasoning machine. (*PL*, p. 383)

The qualification 'if performed ideally' is the vital one, as is shown by what Bradley goes on to say. After running through the machine's operations in four steps, he says:

5. The assertion that what is left is true, and that, if but one possibility remains, that is fact. This is absolutely necessary to complete the inference, and *this is done entirely by the operator*. (*PL*, p. 384, Bradley's italics)

The passage is less than clear, but I take it that Bradley means that the judgment 'No *A* is *C*' is something which the operator has to assert. The appearance of certain letters on the face of the machine is not enough to constitute an inference. Whatever the machine may have done, it is the operator who is responsible for asserting the conclusion. The principle at stake here retains its validity even if the machine is vastly more complex and sophisticated than Jevons'. All too often nowadays, someone who has suffered inconvenience from the actions of a large organization is told 'It was the result of a computer error.' But what follows from, e.g., the print-out of '*X* has not paid his bill' is the result of human decisions about how to deal with the print-out, not the fault of the computer. And, it is generally believed, the machine's 'conclusion' is itself the result of bad programming or mechanical error, which are human responsibilities.

There is a sense in which the construction of computers merely emphasizes the nature of the problem; it does not create it. Care is necessary in stating exactly what the problem is. Bosanquet argued that many scientific instruments could also be regarded as 'reasoning machines;' he saw no fundamental difference between them and Jevons' apparatus:

In experimental instruments we find the attempt made to generate actual consequences which shall also be consequents, as arising from conditions precisely known in respect of the mode and degree of their combination. Any instrument which does this may be called a reasoning machine, whether it deals with combinations and eliminations of letters as logical symbols, or with the same relations of actual numbers, or of any definite motions with their effects.[6]

Though he agrees with Bradley that 'we must ourselves *make* the conclusion,'[7] he sees no difference between a spectroscope (to use his example) and a 'logical machine.' The former enables us to discover, perhaps in a way which we could not otherwise do, the composition of some substance; it does this by the use of natural laws. Its results could not, even in theory, be attained by thinking. The logical machine, on the other hand, is doing something that could in principle be done by thought alone. The 'in principle' is necessary here to cover the case of computers which can do calculations that are out of human range, owing to the time they would take. In principle they could be worked out by a human mathematician. The same applies to any conceivable 'logical machine.' One point at issue here is the kind of thinking involved. Bradley stresses that inference is in some sense a 'mental' operation; it is not just that it cannot in fact be done by a machine but is not in any way 'mechanical.' If logic could be reduced to the mere application of rules, to a version of the multiplication tables, then it would be different from what it at present is and of little philosophical interest. Hegel had no doubts in this respect:

Calculation being so much an external and therefore mechanical business, it has been possible to construct machines which perform arithmetical operations with complete accuracy. A knowledge of just this one fact about the nature of calculation is sufficient for an appraisal of the idea of making calculation the principal means for educating the mind and stretching it on the rack in order to perfect it as a machine.[8]

This need not be to deny that the discovery of algorithms may be a difficult intellectual operation; once discovered, however, they can themselves function as 'machines' and relieve the user of mental effort. The same thing goes, of course, for an improvement in notation; Russell once remarked that 'a good notation is a substitute for thought;' it is easier to do arithmetic in Arabic figures than it is in Roman, though the results are the same in both cases.

This discussion could be seen as an earlier version of the controversy over whether machines can think, with Bradley coming down on the negative side. He would argue that a computer is only a more complex version of Jevons' 'Logical Machine.'' Its operator had to transform the letters presented to him back into the verbal form of the original problem; a modern machine could give him the actual words, perhaps prefixed with 'Therefore.' Bradley would claim that the machine still had not concluded anything, but merely provided evidence on the basis of which the operator could draw a conclusion. Here a machine is implicitly defined as a device to assist us in what we want to do. For example, a car can assist me in travelling around the country, but it is I who go from Southampton to Bristol, who make the journey. Insofar as this kind of definition is accepted, the question of whether a machine could think becomes quite uninteresting, a mere matter of words. It would become a substantive issue if converted into the form 'Could there be constructed an artificial device that would make inferences? Because we are unclear about inference, it is hard to know what the question actually means, or what could count as an instance of such a device inferring. Would the print-out envisaged above be adequate? Without going into that issue, if anyone believes in the theory of evolution, then he must also believe that at one time there were no living creatures capable of reasoning, and, as a result of a long series of transitions, there later came to be such. Given what Bradley says about the development of logic within the individual, there seems no reason why he should deny the possibility of artefacts coming to emulate some or all of his properties. Certainly he could have no logical reason for ruling out the possibility. And as it becomes possible to produce human infants, and hence human beings, by 'artificial' means, e.g. conception *extra utero*, the line between the natural and the artificial becomes ever harder to draw. The only way to retain a rigid distinction between the two is to evoke a transcendent entity, a soul, as the guarantor of the separation of the two categories. But this could hardly be acceptable to the majority of believers in evolution. In talking of the reasoning powers of animals, Bradley remarks:

One very great obstacle to the study of animals is defective psychology propped by bad metaphysics (*PL*, p. 511).

Substitute 'computers' for 'animals' and the saying remains true.

Though there have been many definitions of logic in the period since Aristotle first 'invented' the study, there is widespread agreement that it is primarily concerned with separating valid from invalid inferences. Recently it has also been accepted that it does this by providing implication schemata, which themselves may be systematically deduced from axioms or accepted definitions. The Kneales conclude their *Development of Logic* in the following way:

. . . our science is best defined as the pure theory of involution, that is to say, the theory of the general form of principles of involution without regard to the special natures of the propositions contained in the classes between which the relation holds.[9]

Bradley takes an opposite view:

> It is impossible that there should be fixed models of reasoning; you cannot draw out exhaustive *schemata* of valid inference. . . . The popular belief in logic endows it with ability to test all reasonings offered it. In a given case of given premises the logician is thought to be a spiritual Director who, if he can not supply, at least tests right and wrong. . . . But, understood in this sense, logic has no existence, for there is and there can be no art of reasoning. Logic has to lay down a general theory of reasoning, which is true in general and in the abstract. But when it goes beyond that, it ceases to be a science, it ceases to be logic, and it becomes, what too much of it has already become, an effete chimaera which cries out for burial. (*PL*, pp. 268–9)

He uses the term 'spiritual Director' advisedly, for he follows with a 'purple' attack on casuistry, which he regards as an analogous perversion of ethics. One reason he gives is the infinite number of possible cases; these could not be accommodated by a code, which must remain abstract and general. It is not difficult to agree with Bradley's strictures in the case of ethics, for we are willing to allow that moral rules require sensitivity in their application, that it is not enough to apply given formulae mechanically to be moral. But we do not think this in the case of mathematics; there it is enough to know the appropriate formula and to bring the instance under it. Ever since Frege tried to unite logic and mathematics, most philosophers have believed that they were radically dissimilar to ethics; even though they accepted Bradley's condemnation of casuistry, they would still maintain that logic involved the application of rules.

Bradley is serious about the impossibility of finding rules which govern the majority of inferences that are actually made:

> Unless you artificially limit the facts, then models of reasoning can not be procured, since you would need in the end an infinitude of schemes to parallel the infinitude of possible relations. (*PL*, p. 270)

It is an inference to say 'Today is Monday, so tomorrow is Tuesday.' This could be represented as an application of the rule (or hypothetical) 'If today is Monday, then tomorrow is Tuesday.' But that would hardly constitute anything other than a verbal reformulation of the inference as made; it is not something that is likely to have been learnt independently. One way of dealing with the problem would be to say that the inference is not a formal one, that it depends on our knowledge of the order of the days of the week, for if we had to justify the inference, it would be that to which we would naturally refer. Because it is not a formal inference, it is of no interest to the formal logician. Bradley would say 'So much the worse for formal logic.' If it is admitted that logic cannot cope with the majority of inferences that we actually make, then there is still room for a philosophical study of them. It will not be 'formal logic' but nevertheless logic, for the topic introduced by Aristotle dealt with the way people reason. There is a philosophical puzzle about how reasoning is possible, how we can get from truths to further truths without observation, and this would seem to be a topic which logicians have traditionally dealt with.

Hence what Bradley means by 'inference' seems different from what most philosophers now mean by it. They would accept that logic was the 'science of reasoning' and attach little importance to its 'art.' Further, they would find unclear what Bradley means by his contrast between a 'general theory of reasoning' and something that goes beyond it. If all he means is that most inferences actually drawn are not made in strict formal manner, then most modern logicians would agree with him. But they would say that this fact was accidental; all could be reduced to a strict form if they were valid inferences in the first place. Indeed, it would be asked, what could be meant by a 'valid inference' if not one that was correct in virtue of its form alone? 'Today is Monday, so tomorrow is Tuesday' is not true in virtue of its form; hence it is a piece of 'material reasoning' not governed by formal rules. There is no reason to suppose that such inferences could be formalized. To say this is to accept Bradley's point that there cannot be 'models of reasoning,' that logic is not in the business of providing such models. Part of the problem is that nowhere in the *Principles of Logic* does he clearly state how he conceives logic; his views have to be deduced from his polemics against rival theories.

I have already mentioned (p. 47) his emphasis on the way in which ideas, judgment and inference pass into one another, and this remark both gives a clue to the length and nature of his discussion of the latter as well as indicating the source of his difference from contemporary examinations of the subject. Nowadays the fundamental logical relation is implication, and the feature of an implication is that it is truth-preserving, i.e. given a set of true propositions and a series of valid implications, other true propositions will be found to emerge.

Bradley's objection to such truth-functionality is that it depends on external relations, whereas in actual thinking we deal with internal ones. At one time a similar problem exercised the followers of the new logic; when I was a student a frequent worry was the so-called 'paradox of implication' which arose from the truth-table definition of 'implies.' This seemed to show that a false proposition implied any proposition. Various ways round were suggested, such as defining a relation of 'strict implication,' but analogous paradoxes arose for this as well. Nowadays no one is worried about such examples as 'If $2 + 2 = 5$, then the moon is made of green cheese.' for it is clear that if false premises are used in a truth-preserving system, then falsehoods will emerge. This is the logical equivalent of the computer operator's 'garbage in, garbage out.' However, even if we forget this old-fashioned worry, it is still possible to construct a modus ponens of the form 'If $2 + 2 = 4$, then Socrates is mortal, $2 + 2 = 4$, therefore Socrates is mortal.' It might be objected that no one would want to make such an inference. But this is precisely to grant Bradley's point that external relations are not enough for logic. The point could be put in the form that although the logical relations are themselves truth-functional, we in fact rely on something more than this when we actually infer.

Bradley's point could also be made by saying that the connectives of ordinary language, such as 'and' or 'or' are not truth-functional either. We do not use them to join sentences at random. When we put 'and' between two sentences that could stand alone from the point of view of grammar, it is because we see some connection between the two conjuncts, which may be a temporal one. He would perhaps make the point by saying that it was possible to judge the whole conjunction. Similarly, as I mentioned above, disjunction is of the form 'A is either b or c,' which again emphasizes the connection between the two disjuncts. The subject-matter of both halves is the same. This is, for him, equivalent to saying that such connectives can only be used where internal relations are in question; the connection arises from the content of the conjuncts or disjuncts. It is not the result of an arbitrary act of combination on our part, of uniting them by an external relation. Inference from such compound sentences depends on internal relations, as indeed does all inference. Because internal relations depend on content, not on form, the possibility of a purely formal logic is ruled out.

Book II of the *Principles* inaugurates the discussion of inference, but it is a preliminary clearing of the ground:

Instead of going at once from the facts to the truth, and from that to the removal of erroneous theories, I shall aim at reaching an easy vantage-ground, from which we may disperse the mass of mistakes which bar our progress and harass each movement. (*PL*, p. 243)

Although the conclusions reached are not totally rejected in book III, they are qualified and extended. He begins by stating three character-istics of inference:

1　Inference is different from observation: 'An inference can not wholly come in from without or be passively received. It is not mere vision, it is more than observation.' (*PL*, p. 245)
2　Inference is the result of a mental process; it is an advance from a truth to a further truth. (*PL*, p. 245)
3　It must give us new knowledge, add to our stock of infor-mation. (*PL*, p. 246)

He makes use of what he calls a 'discrepant metaphor' to summarize these:

The truth which is seen in the mirror of inference has not wandered in through the window-pane of sense, nor yet is it merely a reflection cast by an article of furniture already in the mind. (*PL*, p. 246)

Bradley expects general agreement on these characteristics, and regards them as equally important.

The third has given rise to the problem of what is to count as 'new knowledge.' For there seems to be a sense in which if a person knows two facts and a rule of inference that enables him to draw a conclusion from them, it is only a psychological point that there is something new. It was for the inferrer a discovery, but the relation of entailment must have existed prior to its employment; the conclusion was entailed by the premises, and this is the justification for the inference. The problem is that talk of entailment implies a relation which exists between propositions. Either this implies that propositions exist inde-pendently of whether anyone is asserting or thinking of them, or that there are, in some sense, rules which result in such a relation holding between them. Neither of these alternatives was acceptable to Brad-ley, as will become clear in the course of the discussion.

Of the second point, that a mental process is involved, Bradley says:

> Let us take an instance from geographical position. A is ten miles north of B, B is ten miles east of C, D is ten miles north of C; what is the relation of A to D? If I draw the figure on a piece of paper that relation is not inferred; but if I draw the lines in my head, in that case I reason. (*PL*, p. 258)

At first sight this looks extremely odd. Even Bosanquet thought that Bradley had made a mistake here; he believed that both were equally cases of inference:

> But in both cases the inference consists in the intuition which sees how the lines *must* go (the mere drawing them results from this and does not give it), and therefore how A must be related to D.[10]

Most readers will be inclined to agree with Bosanquet, and it seems that Bradley himself did when he came to write the second edition of the *Principles*: in a footnote to the passage I have just quoted he says 'This and what follows is seriously wrong' (*PL*, p. 261). But to get at Bradley's earlier views, it is necessary to see why he did think in 1883 that drawing was not inference; this can be best brought out by looking at the way in which Bosanquet develops his attack. He takes a slightly different example: 'Will a wall AB seriously obstruct an ancient light L?'[11] There are, he suggests, three different ways of dealing with this problem. One is drawing a picture of the situation. The second is erecting a temporary hoarding on the proposed site. The third is to build a wall on the site and see what happens. This last will certainly reveal if the ancient light is obstructed, but it would be odd to say that the knowledge had been obtained by an inference, though it might, still rather oddly, be described as an experiment. The erection of a hoarding in the place where the wall was planned would more properly be described in that way. Both are ways of discovering if an obstruction would be caused, so both give new knowledge; we would not describe them as inferences. The proposition that inference gives new knowledge is not simply convertible. We would normally accept that the use of a drawing on paper or the use of a 'mental drawing' – i.e. working it out 'in our heads' – would be examples of inference. They would both seem to qualify as 'ideal experiments,' to use a phrase which Bradley later adopts to describe the nature of inference.

Bosanquet's discussion of his own example is subtle, and depends upon a distinction between '*the* figure' and '*a* figure.' It is the problem of what is being talked about. Only in the case of an actual wall are we entitled to say 'The wall obstructs the light,' but this is a judgment based on perception of what occurs. In the other two cases, of the hoarding and the drawing, what we are entitled to say is that *a* wall built according to the plan AB would obstruct the light. The conclusion is that if we were to build the wall, then we would be liable for obstruction, and this is the result of an 'ideal experiment.' But in the case of the hoarding we actually see that the light is obstructed; in that of the drawing, we only see that the light would be obstructed, for no light is actually intercepted by the drawn lines. Here the 'experiment' does seem to be 'ideal,' whereas the erection of the hoarding is an actual experiment. Bosanquet argues that these two cases qualify as inferences. Bradley thinks neither does, for he assimilates the drawing to the hoarding. Because the drawing is a physical representation of the situation, we can 'see' the result in a way analogous to the way we see it in the case of the experiment; we are in the realm of observation, not of inference. The issue raised by this case is that of the nature of representation. The reason I have spent some time on it is to show how Bradley regarded inference at the time of the first edition of the *Principles*; it is a mental activity. The significance of this is that his problem was how mental operations could come to give results that were true of reality.

The problem could be expressed in linguistic terms by asking how, if inferences are the result of relations between words, it can turn out that our conclusions are true. For it is truths about the world that we seek, not about our language. Just as in the case of simple judgments it is the state of the world which is judged, so in the case where the judgment is reached as a result of a mental process. In his discussion of judgment, it seemed that Bradley was willing to conclude that some succeeded in being true of reality; inference raises further problems, some of which reflect back on conclusions which we might have thought had been established. Although inference issues in judgments, the process of inference seems to cast doubt on the possibility that any judgment, however reached, is a correct representation of reality. Hence the well-known sceptical conclusion of the whole work, which I will discuss in detail below (chapter XI). Here I only note that part of the reason for that scepticism is the mental nature of inference, which has a vital role to play in all of Bradley's discussions of the topic.

The talk of inference (and of judgment) as 'mental acts' has seemed to some contemporary philosophers to be misleading, for example to Ryle in *The Concept of Mind*.[12] This charge is true if 'acts' are taken as equivalent to 'actions,' as reports of something that was done, not in the public realm but 'behind locked doors.' There is no necessity to construe talk of 'acts' in this manner, no need to assume that a process of a ghostly kind is referred to. Most people would accept that something was happening in the brain when a judgment or inference was made, but they do not think of these terms as ways of talking of whatever was going on in neural circuits. Judgments and inferences have authors, i.e. they are normally attributed to a person. They may be accepted by others on the authority of that person, in which case the attribution of responsibility is a necessary step. But to say that is to say that the judgment or inference issued from that person, or that his was his 'act.' Bradley's discussion of the nature of the mental is designed to distinguish it from the psychical, from episodes that might occur in a biography or autobiography. Talk of 'acts' need only be an abstract way of referring to situations where an active verb is used; it need involve no 'ontological commitment' and clearly does not in the case of Bradley. Ryle's strictures in *The Concept of Mind* do not tell against anything Bradley says here.

The three general principles are meant to cover all types of inference. He concludes the exceptionally brief first chapter of book II by giving eight examples, which he accepts as standards throughout the discussion, and uses to show that many of the traditional theories must be wrong, for they would lead to a denial that one or other was an inference. But cases like these, he implies, are the kind of examples from which we learn the word 'inference' and hence cannot easily be rejected. They are:

   (i) A is to the right of B, B is to the right of C, therefore A is to the right of C.

  (ii) A is due north of B, B is due west of C, therefore A is north-west of C.

 (iii) A is equal to (greater or less than) B, B is equal to (greater or less than) C, therefore etc.

 (iv) A is in tune with B, and B with C, therefore A with C.

  (v) A is prior to (after, simultaneous with) B, B to C, therefore A to C.

(vi) Heat lengthens the pendulum, what lengthens the pendulum, makes it go slower, therefore heat makes it go slower.

(vii) Charles I was a king; he was beheaded, and so a king can be beheaded.

(viii) Man is mortal, John is man, therefore John is mortal.

(viii) is an example of the traditional syllogism, though many of the others are chosen to represent what would count as fallacies in the formal logic that was current at the time. Bradley later (*PL*, p. 401) explicitly mentions arithmetical reasoning as one type that has to be included in any satisfactory theory of inference; (iii) is an example of it. The formula that Bradley has in mind is 'datum – operation – result,' so presumably the first two sections of the above examples would be taken as the data, the third as the result, and the operation would be represented by the intervening 'therefore.' Incidentally, it is clear that Bradley does not attach any significance to the fact that all of these contain three sections. For him an inference can contain more or less. They do not all contain three 'terms,' for the first five commit the syllogistic fallacy of 'four terms.'

On a similar example of Bradley's, 'A is due north-west of C, because B is five miles south of A and again the same distance west of C' (*PL*, p. 268), Bosanquet comments 'This is more like a conundrum than an inference.'[13] Though this remark is somewhat unfair, most readers will be struck by the narrowness of the range of Bradley's examples. They may make the points that are needed, but it would seem that the diet is somewhat restricted, partly by the preponderance of relational inferences. It is perhaps worth pointing out that there is no expression of worry about relations; they are accepted as unproblematic in the context of inference. Bradley chose them because they could not be represented in the old logic but even in the new an inference of the form *aRb*, *bRc*, therefore *aRc* is not in general valid. Restrictions must be placed on the type of relation, for if A loves B, and B loves C, the relation between A and C is indeterminate. In the first of the examples, its validity depends on A, B, and C being in a line; if they were sitting round a table, C could be to the left of A. Bradley says 'We shall see hereafter that every inference may be taking as holding within the identity of one subject . . .' (*PL*, p. 296). He means that the subject need not be the grammatical one. In the first two instances it is space that he takes to be the real subject, in which case it might be claimed that this shows the inference is not formal; it depends on knowledge of the nature of space.

Bradley in fact nowhere distinguishes between formal and other types of inference, whereas both the old and the new formal logicians are concerned solely with the former. Books on logic may include sections on induction or scientific inference, but these are discussed in quite different terms. Many of the oddities of Bradley's account spring from the fact that he includes all 'going beyond what is given' under the heading of inference. His problem is that of the relation of judgments to reality. Hence the fact that the results of inference, i.e. new judgments, seem to have an indirect relation to reality, one mediated by the mind, is the source of a single problem for him. That there are different types of inference does not affect the relation of inferred judgments to reality. It even looks as if Bradley ignores some of the conclusions he had reached in his discussion of judgment when he turns to inference. He appears to hold to a view not unlike that of the empiricists he is attacking. In an article in *Mind*, Bosanquet explicitly makes this charge:

I will merely add as a corollary – that *of course* I find the same pernicious influence of 'common sense' and popular realism in Mr. Bradley's acceptance of Sigwart's teaching that 'all mediate certainty must stand in the end on immediate knowledge; the ultimate premises of proof cannot be proved.' I did think that all this was behind us[14]

Hypothetical judgments certainly did not seem to rest on immediate knowledge. In fact it appeared that they were themselves the result of inference. Unfortunately, the problems of grasping what Bradley means by 'inference' seem to become more acute as his discussion progresses; this problem is one which we shall meet again.

One thing which is clear from the list of examples is that Bradley does not believe that inference requires a major premise. His argument for this was accepted by Russell, who refers in the *Principles of Mathematics* to page 227 (2nd edn. p. 247) of the *Principles of Logic*.[15] Bradley devotes a purple passage to it:

Begotten by an old metaphysical blunder, nourished by a senseless choice of examples, fostered by the stupid conservatism of logicians, and protected by the impotence of younger rivals, this chimaera has had a good deal more than its day. Really dead long since I can hardly believe that it stands out for more than decent burial. And decent burial has not yet been offered to it. Its ghost may lie quiet when it sees that the truth, which lent it life, can flourish alone (cf. book III). (*PL*, pp. 247–8)

Bradley presents the believer in the major premise with a dilemma: either the major premise will have to rest on another major *ad infinitum,* as Lewis Carroll argued in 'What the Tortoise said to Achilles'[16] or it will be an abstract restatement of the original inference (*PL*, pp. 525–6.[17] In the latter case it will do no work because if the force of the original inference is not seen, neither will that of the premise, and the addition of a further premise will put us back on the other horn. Thus no manipulation will put all the instances of reasoning that he has given into anything approximating to syllogistic form. The syllogism may be a valid form of inference; it is not the only one.

Thus not all inference is subsumption. If a universal affirmative proposition is taken in extension, then either the syllogism embodying it involves a *petitio principii,* for if we know all men are mortal, we already know that John is, or if the conclusion refers to the whole collection, it is invalid (*PL*, pp. 249–50). However, the syllogism was correct in one respect; it required that at least one premise should be universal, though Bradley admits that it looks odd to say this of many of his examples, e.g. A is to the right of B, B to the right of C, therefore A to the right of C (*PL*, p. 295). In one sense, as we saw in the chapter on judgment, *every* judgment is universal, but he does spend some time on this case. He claims:

'B is to the right of C' is an universal judgment because B is an identity which has the differences of its spatial relations to A and C. It transcends the context B – C and is therefore universal. Or, from another point of view, the relation B – C is true of a subject which extends itself beyond those limits and is the identical subject of which the relation A – B is also true. (*PL*, p. 296)

There seem to be in fact two claims in this passage; either B itself is a universal, presumably a concrete one, or the real subject not mentioned in the argument, is universal. The difficulty which Bradley finds himself in here is due, perhaps, to the fact that he is using as example not an inference but an inference-schema; only if we substitute actual individuals or objects for the letters do we obtain an inference in his sense of the word. For 'A is to the right of C' is not a judgment that anyone is likely to make unless A, B and C are taken as names. I could infer 'Joseph is to the right of Whitelaw' from 'Joseph is to the right of Thatcher and Thatcher is to the right of Whitelaw.' Bradley is himself impaled on a dilemma; either the letters are names or he has obtained a principle of inference whose truth we can see independently of any actual inference made in accordance with it. But the truth is not 'A is to the right of C,' because this could not be a piece of knowledge in the sense in which he uses the words, it is that the formula is a principle of valid inference. At this point Bradley's cavalier attitude to symbolism catches up with him.

The discussion, however, was directed also to the belief that 'it is impossible to reason except upon the basis of identity' (*PL*, p. 285). He says that it is impossible to reason from S – M and M – P to S – P unless in both premises M is the same. And, for this to occur, M must be (stand for) the sort of thing that could be related both to S and to P. We normally think that the sameness is given by the use of the same letter. The 'principle of Identity' is used, for M is the same as M, but it does not need to be stated explicitly; it is 'shown' by the use of the same letter in two places. However, Bradley means something more by this remark about identity, which is not made fully explicit until book III. I will quote the whole of the passage he refers to (*PL*, p. 296):

All depends on our looking in a proper way at the premises we begin with. If for instance we have certain spaces and combine them, or two subjects and compare them, then in the middle operation, it may be said, the unity is imported from the outside. And so it is, if you take the spaces or the subjects as they wrongly appear in complete independence. But in that case you would never by any machinery force them together. The true starting-point is the total space as qualified by these points in relation, the common reality which appears in both subjects, the one ideal integer in which any given numbers exist as fractions, the underlying whole which presents itself as complex, and by abstraction is shown with a simpler predicate. This *implicit* subject is what supports the change brought in by our process. And it also serves as a centre of activity in the process itself. (*PL*, pp. 492–3)

There are problems with such a description, as the story told by Bosanquet in his discussion of this point will show. An abbé tells a group of guests that this first penitent was a murderer. A local nobleman enters and exclaims: 'I was the abbé's first penitent.' Those present draw the conclusion that the nobleman was a murderer. The middle term 'the abbé's first penitent' leads the audience to their conclusion without any special activity of synthesis on their part. And this would seem typical of many inferences actually drawn. Bradley may have been misled by his examples, for if we take one of the spatial cases from his list, it does seem that 'the true starting-point is the total space as qualified by these points in relation.' But this single space is normally given by the use of the same letters.

Perhaps I am unfair to Bradley here. He may mean that the fact that we see the symbols as referring to the same thing *is* the reference to 'an implicit subject' which validates the inference. But if the 'implicit subject' is the subject-matter of the inference, then it looks as if the very possibility of *formal* inference is denied. This is a point which will have to be considered below. The general conclusion he reaches in book II is that an inference 'is always an ideal construction resulting in the perception of a new connection' (*PL*, p. 285). 'Ideal' refers to the fact that it is something that takes place in the mind, involves ideas; 'construction' to the fact that an active process is involved. The word 'connection' is misleading. The next sentence reads 'So far as this *perception of the conclusion* (my italics) is concerned, there is no possibility of laying down rules . . .' (*PL*, p. 285). This general conclusion is meant to sum up the results of book II insofar as they are constructive. It is also taken to demolish much of what passed as logic in the textbooks of the time, and to establish that the syllogism is not the pattern of all inference. But after all his attacks on it, Bradley says that his differences with its friends are trivial as compared with his agreement, for 'against the enemy our cause is the same' (*PL*, p. 285). The enemy is the logic of J. S. Mill, and most of the second part of book II is taken up with its detailed demolition. Chapter I treats the association of ideas; I have already dealt with its substance in the discussion of ideas. As far as inference is concerned, Bradley has little difficulty in showing that the 'chemistry of ideas' fails to explain it. The second chapter deals with Mill's discussion of inference from particulars to particulars, which in a sense Bradley has already disposed of. In the third chapter he deals with Mill's account of induction, and has little difficulty in showing its defects. There seems no reason to discuss these in detail here.

NOTES

1 *Principles of Mathematics*, Cambridge, 1903, p. 33.
2 *Collected Papers*, London, 1971, vol. II, p. 234.
3 Title of a symposium at the Joint Session in 1946.
4 *Collected Papers*, vol. II, p. 226.
5 *Tractatus Logico-Philosophicus*, 6.211.
6 *Logic*, Oxford, 1888, pp. 153–4.
7 *Knowledge and Reality*, London, 1885, p. 327.
8 *Wissenschaft der Logik*, S, vol. V, p. 249.
9 *The Development of Logic*, Oxford, 1962, p. 742.
10 *Knowledge and Reality*, p. 297.
11 Ibid., p. 298.
12 *The Concept of Mind*, London, 1949, pp. 292–309.
13 *Knowledge and Reality*, pp. 314–15.
14 *Mind*, 1885, p. 265.
15 *Principles of Mathematics*, p. 41.
16 *Mind*, 1895, pp. 278–80.
17 Cf. G. S. Robinson, 'Following and Formalization,' *Mind*, 1964, pp. 48–9.

X

Inference: Further Investigations

Wollheim, in a passage quoted above, described Bradley as like a 'man forced backwards, step by step, down a strange labyrinth, in self-defence . . . .'[1] Perhaps a better description of his procedure in the discussion of inference would be that of a man taking a spiral path which leads to a summit, stopping from time to time to look again, from a higher vantage-point, at things which had earlier been examined. From the new position the picture does not appear quite as it did lower down; some things which were then clear begin to lose their firm outline; others which were almost invisible become obvious. All the time the relations between various features of the landscape change; new connections are seen and old ones turn out to be mere tricks of perspective. This is a general feature of Bradley's style of thought; he may have a definite map of the territory, though it is hard to be sure that he has; it should not be forgotten that each of his major works closes with a sceptical passage which constitutes a denial that a final position has been reached. But if he has, he does not show it to the reader at the outset; rather he leads him on the route that he had taken, indicating paths that had been followed by other philosophers and which fail to reach the goal. His method in the *Principles* is not unlike that described by another philosopher:

The same or almost the same points were always being approached afresh from different directions, and new sketches made. Very many of these were badly drawn or uncharacteristic, marked by all the defects of a weak draughtsman. And when they were rejected, a number of tolerable ones were left, which now had to be arranged and sometimes cut down, so that if you looked at them you could get a picture of the landscape.[2]

Bradley wants the reader to accompany him wherever the argument leads.

Bradley believes that in book II he has demolished many of the doctrines of previous logicians. But the conclusion about the nature of inference reached there turns out in the first part of book III to be inadequate; it requires supplementation in a variety of ways. A number of different lines are pursued:

(a) Consideration of types of inference which were not dealt with in book II; these include both the mathematical and the dialectical.

(b) An attempt to differentiate judgment from inference, for the new definition of the latter appears also to cover the former.

(c) An examination of the psychological background of both judgment and inference. This question has been discussed in chapter III above, but it is worth remarking here that Bradley's denial of psychologism does not lead him to underrate the importance of psychology. Although logic cannot be explained by psychology, any account must be in harmony with it. For the human mind has evolved; at an earlier stage it was incapable of judgment and reasoning; hence these abilities must be in some sense implicit in more primitive activities. The basic differences, he insists in a note to the 2nd edition (*PL*, p. 479) is that logic involves truth.

(d) Finally, Bradley inserts some preliminary warnings that the conclusions reached may not be as firm as appears, e.g. 'The general relation of the ground of knowledge to the ground of reality will vex us hereafter, and we will not anticipate' (*PL*, p. 404).

Bradley thinks that the examples he used in book II were undoubtedly inferences, but they did not include all cases in which we might be said to reason. It has been claimed, e.g. by Berkeley, that all cases of illusion must involve inference, because the senses only present data. Bradley does not accept this as a criterion that inference has occurred, though he does say that it is useful to look for an inference whenever there is a mistake (*PL*, p. 395). A better test is provided by the appearance of a 'must' in a judgment; 'wherever we have a *necessary* truth, there is reasoning and inference' (*PL*, p. 394). He says the same is true in cases where 'Why?' is answered by 'Because.' The answer is given by pointing to a truth, not to a fact and is thus 'ideal,' a word which for Bradley is always the adjectival form of 'idea.' In rearranging objects in the world we may be struck by a new quality of the whole. Similarly, in rearranging our ideas we may discover a quality which before we had not noticed. Hence we have here an 'ideal experiment:'

> the construction, being got by an ideal process, is itself an inference, and its result is nothing but a conclusion. But it is not any fresh relation of the original *data;* it is an issuing quality. (*PL*, p. 397)

The word is not particularly happy in this context, for experiment does not consist in moving objects to see what will happen but rather in trying out a suggestion that has already been thought of. Bradley's talk seems to suggest something arbitrary both in the physical and the mental sphere.

In the context of his argument he needs the notion to move from the result reached in book II, 'inference is an ideal synthesis round a centre of identity,' to cases where 'reasoning does not . . . give us a new relation of the terms we began with' (*PL*, p. 397).

Instead it gives us a new quality of the whole. Bradley instances identifying a series of points on a coast-line which, when combined on a map, establish that we have sailed round an island. Their relation is the datum, the inference that it is an island. It would, I think, be tedious to go through all of Bradley's examples in this section, so I will confine attention to two, mathematics and dialectic. Nowadays the former would constitute the clearest case of reasoning, if not the model of all types. Equally clearly, it fits neither the older logic nor Bradley's original formula. His approach to arithmetic is indirect; given the lines $A - B$, $B - C$, and $C - A$, we can infer that they form a triangle. We can also infer that the lines $A - B$, $C - D$ and $E - F$ can be combined to make a triangle. In other words, if I combine them, then the result is a triangle; my combining them gives rise to a quality which does belong originally to the lines so combined. The same is true of mathematical operations.

Bradley is satisfied that addition and subtraction are inferences (*PL*, p. 401); the difficulty is in seeing what exactly happens in such processes. One problem which exercises him is the nature of a unit and, consequently, what is meant by saying that two sets of units are equal, as in $2 + 2 = 3 + 1$. For the integer 2 is not two units, but one number. Units cannot be identical with one another, for then one plus one would be one (*PL*, p. 402). But, and here Bradley is not too distant from Frege's discussion of the same point,[3] there must be something which is the same and yet different, otherwise it is hard to understand what is going on. Normally we do not notice such difficulties, for 'when a product has been learnt before it was understood, [it] now comes to the mind . . . ready-made, self-apparent and obvious' (*PL*, p. 404). To have learnt numbers is also to have learnt how to apply them, so arguments like '1 + 1 does not always equal 2, because putting two drops of water together results in one larger drop' do not count against the principle used in normal addition. We know what it is to count and this is to know what sort of things can be counted. Equality is not the same as identity:

It is certainly not the same as mere identity, nor would it be safe for any one except a 'powerful thinker' to be guilty of such an elementary confusion. Because things are the same they need not be equal; and when they are equal, they need not be the same in more than one aspect. (*PL*, p. 402)

Later he amplifies this point (*PL*, p. 459); to say A = B is to admit that they are different, for otherwise there would be no point in saying it ('A = A' is always a tautology). But it is to compare them in one respect, that of quantity. It is only in that respect that it makes sense to say A = B. This is the core of his objection to Jevons' 'Equational Logic' (cf. *PL*, pp. 370–8). In other words, the sign '=' always refers to what can be counted or measured; it is this which gives sense to talk of 'units.' Bradley would not have understood such 'equations' as 'Cicero = Tully' because he would want to know in what respect they were equal. Normally it is either stated or obvious what the basis of comparison is, so problems do not arise. Bradley does not consider the higher branches of mathematics; he seems to assume that no new principles are introduced in them. He does say that mathematics will not fit the original formula for inference, for 'it establishes no relation between the terms of the premises. On the contrary the relation, which appears in the conclusion, has one terminal point which never appeared in the *data* at all' (*PL*, p. 404). By this Bradley means that the process, e.g., of addition, involves a recombination of the given units and the perception that they, when so combined, constitute a different number; it is held that this result is true of reality. What is said in this section may not seem very satisfactory as a 'foundation' for mathematics, but that was far from his purpose. It is the nature of inference which is at issue, and hence all he needs to show is that mathematics does provide examples that fall under his principle.

I turn next to what Bradley terms the 'Dialectic Method.' He does not consider whether Hegel intended the 'dialectic' to be a contribution to logical theory, or indeed a replacement for the traditional logic. The latter has been argued by many Marxists, perhaps most conspicuously by Engels. The evidence presented in chapter II above would seem decisive against the latter claim. It also seems clear that Hegel never thought it was an original discovery, but rather a recognition of a process that was actually used in thinking, particularly by philosophers. Bradley opens his discussion with a careful expression of his own approach to the topic (*PL*, p. 408), and rejects the normal 'thesis-antithesis-synthesis' account (*PL*, p. 410), on the grounds that insistence on the 'antithesis' being the negation of the 'thesis' is unnecessary, though he admits the suggestion is 'heretical' (*PL*, p, 410). Dialectical inference occurs when a *datum* is felt to be one-sided, and is supplemented by an additional, though contrary, idea. Unfortunately, he gives no examples and the language is abstract. I think what he means is that when a particular datum is contemplated, it is found to be lacking in some respect. This absent feature is responsible for the feeling of insufficiency because it is already present in the mind. Hence the original datum needs it, and it needs the original datum, in order to exist. So reasoning has taken place and a new result been achieved. Thus dialectic falls under the heading of inference. Bradley comments:

This great ideal of self-development and natural evolution led in Hegel's hands to most fruitful results, and in the main these will stand when the principle of negativity is rejected as error. (*PL*, p. 410)

But, like mathematics and the other cases considered in chapter II of book III, it will not fit the original formula. I have only considered two of the examples he uses, because they represent opposite poles of inference. What is important is that these considerations lead to a new formula which includes all types of reasoning and does not include those things which are not reasoning, such as memory and judgment. He expresses it:

And when . . . we approach our array of ideal operations, we see that they fall under analysis and synthesis. (*PL*, p. 470)

Further, these operations are two sides of one coin:

Analysis is the synthesis of the whole which it divides, and synthesis the analysis of the whole it constructs. The two processes are one. (*PL*, p. 471)

Ryle once described Bradley as possessing an 'exiguous logical alphabet,' of spelling the world out of a 'penurious selection of letters.'[4] It would seem rather that here Bradley's trouble is that he has produced a formula of such generality that it tells us little, besides seeming either to be contradictory or else to rob the words 'analysis' and 'synthesis' of meaning. In addition, the inferences that we actually make appear to have dropped from view at this level of generality.

It is perhaps best to quote the examples, themselves abstract, which he gives:

Take an act of analysis in which A becomes A(bcd). The elements in this result come to us as separate, but this very separation involves a relation. They are distinguished by virtue of a central identity, and they stand thereby in some kind of relation with one another. But this relation is synthetical. It did not exist before the operation, and has resulted from it. Thus the analysis, whilst analyzing, has shown itself synthesis. (*PL*, pp. 470–1)

This certainly appears an act of verbal legerdemain. I presume the kind of example he has in mind is the discovery that this figure, recognized by shape as a triangle, has three sides linked to one another. Similarly in the case of the example he gives of the other process, we are given A – B and B – C, so we go to A – B – C, of which he says 'Thus the synthesis has analyzed while it seemed but to conjoin' (*PL*, p. 471). The given, in both cases, is sense-experience. Bradley's claim is that in performing an 'ideal operation' on it we are discovering what is there, but was not given; the result is a judgment true *of* reality, but one which is not given directly *by* reality. It should not be forgotten that this is not a new formula to instruct us how to infer, but an attempt to characterize all those instances of inference which have already been accepted to be such. The aim is not to reduce all to a single pattern nor to establish their validity upon its basis, for the starting point of the whole exercise was acceptance that the examples were valid. Whatever he is doing, Bradley is not trying to construct a deductive system.

What he means can best be seen by looking at two things which are not inferences, judgment and memory. Of judgment he says that it can look like both an analysis and a synthesis, but this does not make it an inference. Inference is an ideal experiment performed on a datum, but in judgments of perception there is no datum, which sounds a surprising claim to us who are prone to think in terms of 'sense-data' (*PL*, p. 479). However, the datum for an inference is already ideal, i.e. the result of a prior judgment which has, so to speak, 'intellectualized' what was given to sense. 'Data' for Bradley are always ideas; the senses give us sensations, though there is already something mental about these. In a typical sentence he sums it up: 'We may say then that our senses give us sensations; but their gift contains traces of something like thought' (*PL*, p. 482). Nevertheless, it is not thought. The same applies to memory, for that does not present us with an idea connected by association or any other mechanism with our present thoughts, but with another fact, e.g. that something similar had occurred in previous experience (*PL*, p. 441). Perhaps the best way of regarding analysis and synthesis is as characterizations of the notion of 'ideal experiment,' Bradley's previous attempt to find a term to cover all inferences.

However, these two are not sufficient; there is a third feature involved, connected with the 'Axiom of Identity.' It is also related to the 'concrete universal.' Knowledge, he claims 'advances from the abstract to the concrete' (*PL*, p. 474), though he admits that this sounds like a paradox. He explains it:

The confused whole, that is, which comes before our senses and pours out its riches, goes bankrupt when we refuse to accept such payment and insist on receiving universal truth. Or we may say, the felt concrete, when distilled by thought, yields at first but a thin and scanty result. The intellectual product, which first comes over, is a connection whose actual truth holds only of a fraction of the subject. It is not until we have gone down further to principles, that our intellectual results spread over the whole field and serve to unite the mass of detail. In becoming more abstract, we gradually reach a wider realm of ideas; which is thus not sensibly but intellectually concrete. What is abstract in one world is concrete in the other. (*PL*, p. 474)

This move is clearly Hegelian; the first concepts which we use are abstract, they become more concrete with increasing knowledge.

But the question that the passage from Bradley seems to raise is 'What is concrete about the concrete universal?' Hegel seems to identify knowledge and reality; here Bradley keeps them separate, as the final sentence of the quotation reveals. The 'intellectually concrete' is not concrete because it is real in the sense of being a feature of the external world, but because it is adequate to its object in the sense that inferences which start from it turn out to be true of reality. The self-development of the idea matches that of reality, and it is this feature that makes possible the validity of analysis and synthesis and hence of logical inference. For analysis and synthesis themselves have defects (*PL,* pp. 487–9).

The standard which we use to see that they are defective is contained in a long section which it is desirable to quote in full:

If we realized our ideal, what then should we get?

We should get a way of thinking in which the whole of reality was a system of its differences immanent in each difference. In this whole the analysis of any one element would, by nothing but the self-development of that element, produce the totality. The internal unfolding of any one portion would be the blossoming of that other side of its being, without which itself is not consummate. The inward growth of the member would be its natural synthesis with the complement of its essence. And synthesis again would be the movement of the whole within its own body. It would not force its parts into violent conjunctions, but, itself in each, by the loss of self-constraint would embrace its own fulfilment . . . Nor would the process cease till, the whole being embraced, it had nought left against it but its conscious system. Then, the elements knowing themselves in the whole and so self-conscious in one another, and the whole so finding in its recognized self-development the unmixed enjoyment of its completed nature, nothing alien or foreign would trouble the harmony. It would all have vanished in that perfected activity which is the rest of the absolute. (*PL*, p. 489)

To say the least the passage is obscure; it seems that it is Hegelian; in the final sentence there is an echo of a well-known passage from the preface to the *Phenomenology*:

The true is thus the bacchanalian whirl in which no member is not drunken; and because each, as soon as it detaches itself, dissolves immediately – the whirl is just as much transparent and simple repose.[5]

The ideal, which serves as the 'canon and touchstone of reason'

(*PL*, p. 489) is Hegelian 'Absolute Knowledge.' It is that expressed in a passage from *Appearance and Reality* quoted above (p. 119). With perfect knowledge, starting from any one point it would be possible to go on to grasp everything else. There would be internal connections between any one piece of knowledge and all others.

Whatever may be the status of that remark in its original context, it is clear that here Bradley is talking of knowledge and not of what is known; the nature of reality itself is not in question. The opening sentence contains an ideal of the complete systematization of knowledge. But it is an ideal which is implicit in our ordinary attitude to knowledge, not one imposed on it by the philosopher. We are dissatisfied with an isolated fact, particularly if it does not square with the rest of what we think we know. When it can be connected with other facts in a systematic way, it is more likely to be accepted as true. The same applies to whole bodies of knowledge; there was a time when physics appeared to have no connection with chemistry. To discover their interconnection via atomic theory is to reach a deeper understanding of both. The ideal in question is that used by scientists in their ordinary operations.

A firm adherence to this ideal is manifested in Bernard Bosanquet's *Logic*, which appeared five years after Bradley had published the *Principles*:

For logic, at all events, it is a postulate that 'the truth is the whole.' The forms of thought have the relation which is their truth in their power to constitute a totality; which power, as referred to the individual mind, is its power to understand a totality. The work of intellectually constituting that totality which we call the real world is the work of knowledge.[6]

Whatever may be the difficulties in achieving this ideal, Bosanquet sees it as philosophically unproblematic. If we were to achieve a total and coherent system of knowledge, then it would be true of reality, and it is this which he thinks he has learnt from Hegel. He does not think any problems for logic arise for such a notion of knowledge. Hence he is a less philosophically interesting writer than Bradley. The passage from the *Principles* I have quoted might be said to mark the high point of Bradley's Hegelianism, as well as the culminating point of his discussion of inference. His difference from Bosanquet is revealed in the grammatical structure of the two passages; Bosanquet uses the indicative throughout, Bradley the subjunctive; the whole passage is hypothetical. And this is reinforced by the opening of the next paragraph 'This crown of our wishes may never be grasped.' At his stage of the argument he does not say that it is an ideal impossible of attainment; he does stress that it would satisfy us were we to attain it.

The way in which he discusses this ideal is an example of those preliminary warnings of the final conclusion to the *Principles* which I mentioned at the beginning of this chapter. It is also interesting because he makes a general statement about the nature of philosophy or of the impulse to philosophize:

There has come in to us here, shut up within these poor logical confines, and pondering on the union of two abstract functions, a vision of absolute consummation. In this identity of analysis and synthesis we recognize an appearance of our soul's ideal, which in other shapes and other spheres has perplexed and gladdened us; but which, however it appear, in Metaphysics or Ethics or Religion or Aesthetic, is at bottom the notion of a perfected individuality. (*PL*, p. 490)

The status given to logic is noteworthy. The discussion was not a digression because this idea of 'self-developing perfection' lies at the base of our every-day arguments. The missing principle, which lay below analysis and synthesis, is that of self-development.

The term is perhaps misleading; the prefix 'self' refers not to the individual who is reasoning but to the idea which is the basis of the inference. It is this idea, which is itself a meaning and not a 'psychic fact,' which is responsible for the movement of thought. There is a sense in which inferring is something we do; there is another in which the inference is forced on us. In the earlier stages of his discussion, Bradley seemed to concentrate on the former; here it is the latter that takes precedence. The negative expression of this is the formula 'I must because I can not otherwise' (*PL*, p. 491); the positive runs 'I must *so* because I will *somehow*' (ibid.). (The positive version already hints at doubts about the ultimate validity of inference. It seems to render its necessity somehow arbitrary.) The striving for totality drives us to infer, to connect together our ideas and judgments, but it is a self-development because the inference, if it is valid, is not of our making:

Our apparatus of proof has been compared to a scaffolding, which is removed when the edifice of reason has been built; yet, if *we* have but placed the parts in conjunction, there is nothing which will hold when the scaffolding has gone. If our process is not to end in a ruin, the apparatus we have used must be simply a prop, supported on which the argument has grown up, till strong enough at last to support its own fruit and stand by itself. . . . Every inference we make would prove unstable, unless, at least to this poor extent, it were self-development. (*PL,* p. 494)

Both in judgment and in inference we feel that the result is something that is forced on us; what we say is true of reality. In the case of judgment the pressure comes from what is given to the senses. The twists and turns of Bradley's discussions of inference arise from the attempt to discover the equivalent driving force in the case of inference. It must lie in the 'ideal realm' because inference is an ideal process; all he can find to fit the role is 'self-development.'

In order to make judgments it is necessary to have a notion of a 'reality' independent of the person judging. The problem that remains for Bradley is what the equivalent 'reality' is in the case of inference. It might be said that in some of our contemporary thoughts about this we attribute the role of an independent reality to language; our inferences are validated by appeals to 'rules for the use of words.' These are external to the individual. The danger of talking in terms of 'ideas' is that it seems to make the basis of reasoning something internal and hence removes its independence. For Bradley, taking language to be an independent reality would not solve the problem, for the result of an inference is thought to be true of the same reality about which judgments are made. To put the point in a different way, such a solution would still leave open the problem of the relation between language and reality. In fact, although he expresses himself in terms of ideas, this is the problem that occupies him in the second part of book III.

To say that inference depends on form raises the same problem, which might then be expressed as a question about what it is that possesses the form. It cannot be reality, because there is no obvious way in which its 'form' could be discovered. If it is the form of our discourse which is at issue, then the same problem about the relation of that to reality arises. Bradley is, as we have seen, the enemy of 'formal logic,' and he devotes the first chapter of the second part to finally settling his accounts with it, concluding that, in logic as in all sciences, there is a 'relative distinction of form and content' (*PL,* p. 532). Nevertheless, form cannot account for the truth which we attribute to the results of our inferences. To say that inference depends on the self-development of ideas does not solve the problem either. We do infer, and accept the results of inference as true of the one reality. Even though Bradley thinks he has successfully described inference, he does not think that he has so far justified it.

NOTES

1 *F. H. Bradley*, London, 1959, p. 18.
2 *Philosophical Investigations*, Oxford, 1953, p. ixe.
3 *The Foundations of Arithmetic*, tr. J. L. Austin, Oxford, 1950, pp. 39e–67e.
4 'Logic and Mr. Anderson,' *Collected Papers*, vol. I, London, 1971, p. 243.
5 tr. W. Kaufmann in his *Hegel*, London, 1966, p. 424.
6 *Logic*, Oxford, 1888, p. 3.

XI

Ultimate Doubts

The argument of the last three chapters of the *Principles* is difficult to follow, but there is a careful and subtle train of thought running through it. The conclusion is sceptical, and seems to cast doubt on all that has gone before, to destroy the claims of logic to give any insight into the ultimate nature of reality as well as to cast doubt on the very possibility of inference. The chapter in which the expression of ultimate doubt occurs is entitled 'The Validity of Inference.' The concluding chapters also appear to be the most 'metaphysical' of the book. In the preface to the first edition, Bradley briefly deals with this issue. Some will think the metaphysical content excessive, others that he ought to have gone further. But, he claims, he only went as far as was necessary or as he could. It should not be forgotten that his relation to metaphysics has a certain ambiguity. In the preface to *Appearance and Reality* he comments:

Metaphysics is the finding of bad reasons for what we believe upon instinct, but to find these reasons is no less an instinct. (*AR*, p. xii)

Here much the same thought occurs:

This does not mean that, like more gifted writers, I verify in my own shortcomings the necessary defects of human reason. (*PL*, p. xi)

Philosophy, or metaphysics, is an enquiry we have to undertake; we must follow the argument wherever it leads and not be surprised if it ends in 'doubts and perplexities.' Bradley may have a vision of what would satisfy our desires in this respect, but he is certain that he has not achieved an account of that vision which will stand firm in the face of philosophical doubts. He is not a 'system-builder' who can believe that in the structure he has conceived all human life can be comprehended. If he were, he thinks, his work would be easier to grasp: 'If I saw further I should be simpler' (*PL*, p. xi). It is easier to argue to a conclusion which has already been accepted on other grounds.

Chapter II of part II begins the discussion of the problem which was hinted at earlier, the relation of the ground of knowledge to the ground of reality, how inference can be true of reality. Bradley has hitherto been concentrating on how inference takes place; it is 'an ideal operation which gives us a result' (*PL*, p. 535). We argue 'A = C because A = B and B = C.' This gives the reason for our conclusion; is it also the cause, either in the sense of the psychic operations which must take place in our minds or in the sense of what is the case in the real world outside our minds? In the latter case, 'the connection of truths and the course of events would be one and the same.' This leads Bradley into a discussion of the nature of causation or, more accurately, into the nature of what we are saying when we say 'A causes B.' It is not necessary to follow the details, but will suffice to say that he concludes that the judgment. 'A causes B' is itself the result of inference. We are never presented with a cause because cause is an instance of a law; it hence involves abstraction and universals, which cannot be given in the phenomenal sequence:

The thread of causation is nothing visible. It is not seen till it is demonstrated; and it is demonstrated solely by the ideal unity which *we* discover and make within the phenomenal flux of the given. But it has no actual existence within that flux, but lives first within the world of universals. (*PL*, p. 540)

The cause, as we know it, is always a 'because.'

It might be thought that every 'because' is also a cause, but this is an 'obstinate confusion' (*PL*, p. 545) which depends on a failure to separate the 'psychical event' and the 'logical judgment.' There must be some kind of 'mental mechanism' which is operative in thinking; any conclusion which is asserted is the result of operations in the mind. In this sense the premises are the cause of the conclusion; it is they that cause me to assert it. But this causal chain has no connection with the truth of the assertion. As far as the mental process is concerned, the result as an event has nothing to do with the truth or falsity of the judgment; we must always carefully distinguish, says Bradley, the 'cause in psychology and the ground in logic. The two series may run parallel, and may partly coincide, but they are never identical' (*PL*, p. 546). The same argument could be expressed in the 'linguistic mode;' indeed, given the difficulty of the argument of this section of the *Principles*, it is frequently necessary to make this translation in order to be clear what Bradley is saying. In this case it would seem possible to distinguish the rules of language from the truth of premises and conclusion. 'A is bigger than B' and 'B is bigger than C' imply 'A is bigger than C.' This is what might be termed a 'linguistic' rule. But that we can assert the conclusion 'A is bigger than C' depends on the truth of the premises, not simply on the fact that the premises themselves imply the conclusion. It is, Bradley would say, because A is bigger than B etc. as a matter of fact that the conclusion is true; it is not because our words are related in a certain way.

It is this which leads him to a 'dire suspicion:'

If in inference the conclusion is made what it is by an arbitrary act, how can any such process be true of reality? Our knowledge of the cause will itself be dragged down in the common ruin of all our reasoning, and in the end we must doubt if there is such a thing as a valid inference. (*PL*, pp. 547–8. It is a worry of this type which gradually grows throughout the remaining pages of the *Principles*.)

When the subject of inference was first discussed in chapter IX, it may well have seemed arbitrary of Bradley to dismiss the common notion of 'rules of inference.' It is now possible to see the source of his rejection. We can distinguish an argument which logically proves its result from one which is also true of reality, in other words we can distinguish validity from truth. A valid argument can exist in a hypothetical mode; indeed it must, for the correct formula is of the form 'If A – B and B – C, then A – C.' when '–' stands for any transitive relation. In order to make use of this formula, it must be possible to find things which will fill the slots represented by capital letters. In particular, 'B' must stand for the same thing in both premises; if it does not, then the actual inference fails. At this point his problem seems to be one of identifying actual objects (*PL*, p. 571). Earlier, as we have seen, he had argued that a logical formula is only arrived at by abstracting from actual inferences that we make. Here he seems to be talking as if the formula had an independent validity. He even says:

Our main result may be so summed up. Arguments, so far as they amount to demonstration, have been found to depend on logical postulates. (*PL*, p. 570)

By 'postulates' he means 'assumptions we are forced to accept, but which cannot be proved' (*PL*, p. 552).

It looks as if he has changed his ground; in fact he has not. He did not deny the validity of formal arguments within logic but merely the adequacy of the notion of form to justify our actual practices. For the validity of the form cannot, of itself, guarantee the truth of an inference. If we make use of Ryle's metaphor of the 'inference-ticket' to describe a valid implication, then Bradley's underlying doubt is whether the lines on which the ticket is to be used exist in reality or whether it is possible to identify the station from which the ticket starts. For if we say that language is what guarantees the truth of inference, it must either be maintained that there is a necessary correspondence between language and reality or we arrive at a linguistic monism in which language is reality. The former view gives rise to many problems, including that of how this correspondence comes about; the latter is a version of Hegel's view which Bradley cannot accept. It is not enough, he thinks, to say 'Our idea of what belongs to the realm of reality is given for us in the language that we use.'[1] As regards the first view, Bradley criticizes such a notion of a 'pre-established harmony:'

We must admit that, although a valid inference in some way must answer to the nature of things, yet at least some reasoning does not show that nature. It exhibits a process essentially different from the actual course of real existence. . . . Unless you revolutionize your belief about reality (and perhaps you ought to revolutionize that belief), you cannot maintain the strict correspondence of thought and of things. (*PL*, p. 583)

For it is clear that not all our thought is even meant to represent reality; much of it is consciously 'bracketed off' by a variety of devices, and some of it is simply wrong. Nevertheless, we do accept that logical relations hold between items that are 'bracketed off;' there can be inferences within stories. Further, we make use of implications that are thought of as holding independently in order to decide which judgment to assert. Both imply that logical relations exist in language and independently of individual language users.

As for the second point, we need a notion of reality in order to get language or thinking off the ground, because it is an essential feature of either that they need not represent reality. Bradley goes further, and denies that they can ever represent it:

> But ideas do not exist, and they can not exist, if existence means presence in the series of phenomena. I do not mean merely to press the obvious consequence that a thing can not be in two places at once. I do not mean that ideas, being inside my head, can not also and at once be found outside it. I mean much more than this. Neither outside my head, nor yet inside it, can ideas have existence; for the idea is a content which, being universal, is no phenomenon. The image in my head exists psychologically, and outside it the fact has particular existence, for they are both events. But the idea does not happen, and it can not possess a place in the series. (*PL*, p. 584)

This is a repetition of his earlier argument about the nature of ideas, which was discussed in chapters III and IV. There are images, just as there are words, but when we are using them in discourse it is meanings, not the psychical or physical objects, which are used. Judgment or inference may be true of the world, and for ordinary purposes this may be sufficient. But in trying to understand the nature of logic this ordinary purpose is not adequate. Language or thought can never give 'that tissue of relations, it can not portray those entangled fibres, which give life to the presentations of sense' (*PL*, p. 586). Thus consideration of the claims of logic leads in the end to a denial that thought does represent reality as it is. Bradley's arguments which he thinks lead inexorably to this point have not depended on his use of some alternative view, he would claim. They arise out of the attempt to get clear about the assumptions that seem necessary in order to proceed as we normally do.

The only alternative that will save logic is a Hegelian view, and it is this which Bradley rejects in the closing 'purple passage:'

> Unless thought stands for something that falls beyond mere intelligence, if 'thinking' is not used with some strange implication that never was part of the meaning of the word, a lingering scruple still forbids us to believe that reality can ever be purely rational. It may come from a failure in my metaphysics, or from a weakness of the flesh which continues to blind me, but the notion that existence could be the same as understanding strikes me

as cold and ghost-like as the dreariest materialism. That the glory of this word in the end is appearance leaves the world more glorious, if we feel that it is a show of some fuller splendour; but the sensuous curtain is a deception and a cheat, if it hides some colourless movement of atoms, some spectral woof of impalpable abstractions, or unearthly ballet of bloodless categories. Though dragged to such conclusions, we can not embrace them. Our principles may be true, but they are not reality. They no more *make* that Whole which commands our devotion, than some shredded dissection of human tatters *is* that warm and breathing beauty of flesh which our hearts found delightful. (*PL*, pp. 590–1)

I have quoted the passage at length to bring out its flavour; it appears that some parts point towards the argument of *Appearance and Reality*. But more important for the present discussion is the fact that it constitutes an attack on Hegel's ideal of Absolute Knowledge. This is often expressed in the form 'the real is the rational and the rational the real.' Bradley explicitly refers to this just before this passage, when he says 'Since the rational and the real in truth are one. . . . ' (*PL*, p. 590). Again, in the first edition preface he talks of his relation to Hegel and says:

but I never could have called myself an Hegelian, partly because I can not say that I have mastered his system, and partly because I could not accept what seems to be his main principle, or at least part of that principle. (*PL*, p.x)

I take it that it is the identity of the real and the rational that he refers to.

Absolute Knowledge, as Bradley interprets it, and there is no space here to go into the issue of how far this is what Hegel meant, involves the identification of knowledge and reality. Hegel reached this position because he denied that immediate experience was the source of richness and variety; it was rather an impoverished realm of universals (cf. chapter I of the *Phenomenology*). Bradley seems to be referring to this when he writes:

Why should not the result of the deepest philosophies be after all the truth, and our sensuous presentment be misrepresentation that can not give fact? In this case, if our logic diverged from the given, it perhaps after all has been wiser than it knew of. Unawares it has followed the hidden reality, and against itself has throughout been true. (*PL*, p. 589)

If Hegel's claims were correct, then there would be no problem about the validity of logic. Our inferences and judgments would not just be true *of* reality, they would *be* reality. And this is the claim that Bradley cannot accept. Reality, that reality which we all experience through our senses and which is a necessary starting-point for all our judgments, that reality which forces itself on us when we misjudge, cannot be the same as thought, however much philosophical arguments which we cannot refute seem to lead to that position.

What Bradley expresses in this final passage is not so remote from an analogous expression by a rather different philosopher:

Just now I was in the park. The root of a chestnut tree buried itself in the earth under the seat. I could no longer remember that it was a root. Words had disappeared, and, with them, the meanings of things, their uses, the feeble bench-marks that men had scratched on the surface. . . .

It took my breath away. Never, before these last few days, had I understood what 'to exist' means . . . existence had been unveiled. It had lost its inoffensive manner of being an abstract category; it was the very stuff of things. . . . But this root . . . existed in so far as I could not explain it. . . . Its function explained nothing; it allowed you to understand in general what a root was, but not *this*.[2]

Sartre is attacking a view which he thought led to a form of 'idealism,' the phenomenology of Husserl, which seemed to reduce all objects to 'intentional objects,' things in the mind. Sartre's argument, in this passage, is that there is a radical difference between things which have only an 'intentional' existence, like circles or songs, and things in the world which escape our attempts at conceptualization.

Bradley seems to be making the same point, albeit in a rather different context, that of a discussion of logic. It is wrong to see in the passage I have quoted any presentiment of the doctrines of *Appearance and Reality*. This is explicitly denied by many of the notes added to the second edition, and by the Terminal Essays themselves. In a note to this final chapter, he says that he did not attempt to solve the problem of whether truth was ever identical with fact, and sketches in a dozen lines the argument of both *Appearance and Reality* and *Essays on Truth and Reality* (*PL,* p. 595). The difference between the philosophical position he held in 1883 and his later metaphysical views is made clear in the final paragraph of the first edition. This starts by rejecting a 'cheap and easy Monism' on the grounds that 'enquiry into logic' renders it impossible. For the result of the investigation is that we are left in a dualist position, with the 'parallel series of sense and of thought, phenomena presented by simple observation and reasoning that retraces the chain of presentations' (*PL*, p. 591). Neither of these can be reduced to the other nor can both be seen as the result of a single underlying Monistic principle. This position is itself unsatisfactory:

> The desire to comprehend our Universe as the double outgrowth and revelation of a single principle, depends on a genuine impulse of philosophy. (*PL*, p. 591)

That impulse cannot be satisfied by logic, but must await the results of a metaphysical enquiry.

There are in this concluding paragraph some indications of the form that such a metaphysics will take:

> If the string of appearances could possibly appear, if conceivably their sequence could be given as fact, yet assuredly logic could never reproduce them, or supply us with a truthful counterpart and copy. (*PL*, p. 591)

The point about the first phrase of this quotation is that the string or interconnection of appearances is not what appears. What we are presented with is 'This,' or a series of separate 'thises;' it is we who try to go beyond what is actually given in memory and inference. Our judgments are intended to be true of reality, but they always miss their goal by their very nature:

> The past can not be restored in its sensuous fulness; the detail is literally not present to the mind. It is judged to be there; but such judgment is nothing but a general indication, a symbolic reference to a context, whose main character and import still survives, but whose complex particulars have perished irrevocably. (*PL*, p. 588)

The same applies to the net that science casts across reality. It is not that these judgments are false in the sense that different ones would be true; Bradley is not a simple sceptic. For the ordinary purposes of everyday life they will serve, and indeed must serve because there is nothing better that we might achieve by any further application of the principles with which we work. But if we philosophize we cannot find them satisfactory; we are driven to go beyond them.

This is a starting point for metaphysics, not its conclusion. However, even the conclusion of the metaphysical enquiry is not as clear and confident as might be expected. The final chapter of *Appearance and Reality* is entitled 'Ultimate Doubts,' and closes with something not so different from the conclusion of the *Principles*:

To repeat–in its general character Reality is present in knowledge and truth, that absolute truth which is distinguished and brought out by metaphysics. But this general character of Reality is not Reality itself, and again it is not more than the general character even of truth and knowledge. (*AR*, pp. 484–5)

One difference, however, is that in the later work 'reality' always has a capital letter. Even here there is no coincidence between thought and reality. It is not my purpose to investigate Bradley's later metaphysics; I have mentioned this passage only to indicate that even the later Bradley is not a simple minded metaphysician.

As far as the first edition of the *Principles of Logic* is concerned, it seems clear that we can say that if idealism proclaims the identity of thought and reality, then it is not an idealist work. By the same token, it is not an expression of Hegelian ideas. In addition, Hegel wanted to replace metaphysics by logic. Bradley thinks that logic is on a lower level than metaphysics and that by considering logic we are driven to philosophize further. Thus I disagree with a remark of Ryle's:

So far from his logic being the stairway up to his ontology, Bradley's ontology is the beam off which dangle the rope-ladder and hangman's nooses of his logic.[3]

If he had accepted in full the legacy of Hegel, then this judgment would be applicable, and Bosanquet, perhaps a genuine Hegelian, would have been more content with the general tenor of the *Principles*. It seems to me that the arguments of the *Principles* deserve attention even by those who have no interest in Bradley's later metaphysics. No 'cheap and easy Monism,' nor even a cheap and easy holism, will stand against them.

NOTES

1 P. Winch, *The Idea of a Social Science*, London, 1958, p. 15.
2 *La Nausée*, Paris, 1938, pp. 161–4, tr. ARM.
3 Review of R. Wollheim, *F. H. Bradley, The Spectator*, 15 January 1960.

XII
New Certainties

The second edition of the *Principles of Logic* is a remarkable work. Many writers reissue their books late in life, either with a preface saying that their views have now changed or with substantial revisions to bring them into line with their latest thoughts. Bradley does neither of these things. The actual changes made in the original text are minute; he refers to alterations in punctuation and the removal of misprints and grammatical errors. I noted only two verbal alterations; 'disparate' was, on two occasions, changed to 'discrepant' in the second edition (*PL*, p. 414). He leaves the original text as it was, and adds to each chapter what he describes as a 'Commentary,' which consists of a series of notes on individual words or arguments, varying in length from a line to several pages. In addition, he appends twelve 'Terminal Essays' which deal with particular topics, notably Inference and Judgment. Altogether, 192 pages are added to the original text, so the new edition is over one-third longer than the old. It is also hard to read 'the text' of the second edition. The notes do not form a connected commentary, but deal with individual points, for example

'There is an axiom &c.' This and what follows is erroneous. Section 28 also is largely mistaken. See once more ibid [which refers to a previous note]. (*PL*, p. 430)

The Terminal Essays are coherent, but it is not always clear how closely they are related to the original. I suspect that they are only fully comprehensible to someone who is conversant with what Bradley had said in *Appearance and Reality* and the *Essays on Truth and Reality,* to which both the notes and the Essays constantly refer.

The fact that a second edition of the work was called for forty years after its publication in 1922, and that it was issued in a corrected impression six years later, is evidence of that continuation of Anglo-Hegelianism into the 'contemporary' period of philosophy which was discussed in chapter I. The critical notice of the book in *Mind* for 1923 describes it as the 'long demanded second edition.'[1] This review also explains the corrected printing; it concludes by saying 'the proof-reading, particularly in the second volume, has been less careful than the importance of the work demanded.'* The text was also reprinted in 1950, at the height of the 'revolution in philosophy,' though this may have been more an act of piety on the part of the Oxford University Press than a response to a continuing demand. Although *Ethical Studies* was then, and is still, used as a text for undergraduate courses, ·and George Paul lectured on *Appearance and Reality* during the late 1940s and early 1950s, I do not recall the *Principles* receiving any mention in Oxford at that period. The nearest thing to an 'idealist' logical text considered, and it is not very close to Bradley or to Bosanquet, would have been H. W. B. Joseph's *Introduction to Logic* (1906). And that book was presented as an example of an 'old-fashioned' view of the subject.

Bradley certainly talks in the preface to the second edition as if the re-issue was called for. He adds:

On the other hand I regret that, while Logic during this interval has lived and moved, I myself have failed, except partially, to follow its advance. My available energy has been expended mainly in fields which more or less fall outside Logic proper. And it is too late for me now to make good my shortcoming, and to endeavour to master those recent works which have succeeded in throwing, at the lowest estimate, much light on their subject. (*PL*, p. vii)

Russell's major logical writings had all been published by this time, but Bradley does not even mention them in the notes and essays, though he does refer to Russell in some of his other writings; these references, however, are mainly to places where Russell has criticized Bradley's theory of relations. Nowhere in the second edition does Bradley squarely confront the new logic. In almost the only

---

* *Mind*, 1923, p. 356. The proof-reading is still not perfect; at least there is some uncertainty about the spelling of the word 'development.' In the Terminal Essays this occurs sometimes as 'developement' e.g. p. 597. It is spelt normally on p. 599. Similarly 'developes' is found on p. 603, which also has 'development.'

reference to recent developments, he says in the Terminal Essay on Inference:

In the above I have urged once more against 'Formal Logic' the criticism which, nearly forty years ago, appeared in this volume. But how far the position taken by Dr. Bosanquet and myself, has since been destroyed by the defenders of Formal Logic, or again perhaps strengthened or even superseded by logical discoveries due to later innovators, I do not attempt to discuss. (*PL,* p. 619)

The development of Bradley's thought in the forty years after completing the *Principles* is adequate to account for the change in the status he allots to logic, but I think there is also, in the Terminal Essays, an implicit recognition that the work of Russell and others has made logic into a technical subject to an extent which was not possible for those working in the old tradition of the syllogism. Essay X is entitled 'A Note on Implication,' and it is significant that the word occurs only in the Essays. That it is Russell to which this essay is directed is made more likely by the opening remark, which refers to the necessity of calling things by their proper names. It continues:

And to employ the term 'implication' where you assume that there is no more than an external conjunction, is to my mind a case of indefensible misnomer. It is surely misleading to speak of B as implied in A, if A cannot be said in some sense to contain B. (*PL,* p. 695)

This seems a direct criticism of the example of material implication which Russell gives in the *Principles of Mathematics,* that 'Socrates is a triangle' implies both 'Socrates is mortal' and '2 + 2 = 4.' For Bradley implication occurs only within a whole or totality. The presumption that it is Russell he has in mind is increased by his reference to 'a single "asymmetrical" relation' (*PL,* p. 697).

The example he uses brings out the difference between his view and that of the new logic. It is said, he claims, that A can imply B without B implying A; e.g. that the taking of a certain amount of arsenic implies death, but death can also come from other causes. He regards this as 'monstrous,' as 'ruining the genuine fact which is before us.' It involves taking 'B' as an abstraction, as an example of 'death in general,' whereas if it is to be implied by taking arsenic, it must be that particular sort of death:

And the reason why and how a man can imagine that the taking in the abstract of arsenic implies factual and concrete death, while he rightly insists that more than mere death is needed to show the antecedent taking in fact of arsenic – seems to myself to be a matter more for psychology than for logic. (*PL*, pp. 697–8).

Implication is a relation that exists within a concrete whole, and which is reached by analysis of that whole. It is because we experience the complex event '*A* taking such an amount of arsenic and dying in this manner' that we are entitled to say that 'taking arsenic implies death.' The evidence for this would equally allow the opposite implication, 'this sort of death implies arsenic.' The attempt to generalize this involves 'falsification' or 'mutilation.'

In spite of this passage, the main burden of the additions and Terminal Essays is autobiographical; he indicates the ways in which his metaphysical doctrines have altered his earlier views on logic. Hence, for the point of view from which I have been writing, an examination of what Bradley says about logic in the strict sense of the word, the new version is not of great interest. To deal adequately with the changes would involve an investigation of Bradley's metaphysics in some detail. This I am not qualified to undertake, even if space to pursue these questions were available. Also, I suspect that it is hard to understand his later metaphysics without a clear idea of their origin in logic, and it is this that I have aimed to supply. Hence in this chapter I will only indicate some major points of difference and add some comments on the reasons which led him to them.

One logician to whom Bradley constantly refers in the second edition is Bosanquet. He concludes the new preface:

I regret that Dr. Bosanquet's *Implication and Linear Inference* came too late to be used. But I cannot end this Preface without some expression of my gratitude to Dr. Bosanquet for all that, since 1883, I have owed to him, and without some acknowledgement of how deeply this reissue is in debt to his invaluable works on Logic. (*PL*, p. viii)

This is not merely a pious expression of indebtedness. The new notes contain some sixty references to Bosanquet, of which the following is typical:

This chapter contains some serious errors. I have since accepted in the main Dr. Bosanquet's account of negation. See his *K & R* and *Logic*. I have briefly discussed the whole matter in T.E.VI. (*PL*, p. 125)

The Terminal Essays contain further references to Bosanquet. The problem of reading the second edition lies not only in trying to make sense of a note which flatly denies the position maintained in the text, but also in following up the numerous references to other of Bradley's works and to those of Bosanquet. The latter wrote a great deal on logic in the period immediately following the publication of the *Principles,* and much of it was directly critical of what Bradley had said. In *Mind* for 1885 there was a ten-page article, entitled 'Mr. F. H. Bradley on Fact and Inference.' In the same year there appeared *Knowledge and Reality,* a polemical work by an author clearly steeped in the arguments of the *Principles*. It might be described as the longest review ever written; it runs to 333 pages. In 1888 Bosanquet published his own *Logic,* which contained 638 pages. The year before he had brought out a translation of Lotze's *Logic*. Some of the work was done by other hands, but he was the editor and revised the whole; the two volumes comprise over 700 pages. Thus in the five years following the publication of the *Principles* Bosanquet produced a great mass of material on the subject of logic. In all of it there was frequent mention of his debt to Bradley.

It has been suggested that there was, at the end of the nineteenth century, a great English philosopher named 'Bradley-Bosanquet.' This exaggerates the similarity of their views. However, they do seem to constitute a small mutual admiration society, though at a deeper level perhaps neither understood the other's views fully. The relation between them might be compared to that of Marx to Engels; Bosanquet often thought he was following Bradley, but sometimes he misunderstood him, or took him to be saying what Bosanquet thought should be said. He was not entirely uncritical, however; *Knowledge and Reality* was written to recall Bradley to the true Hegelian line:

It is my object in the following pages to show how Mr. Bradley's essential and original conception might be disengaged from some peculiarities which he apparently shares with reactionary logic.[2]

The 'reactionary logic' is that of some contemporary German thinkers, notably Sigwart and Lotze. Bosanquet thought them reactionary because they had failed to grasp Hegel's arguments against empiricism, and seemed to a large extent to have accepted Mill's views. He detected undercurrents of empiricism even in the text of the *Principles;* these were incompatible with the main line of argument and needed to be removed.

In many cases, it seems that Bosanquet did not fully understand Bradley's arguments; at best he gives them a somewhat shallow interpretation. For, as I said above, he had few worries about the metaphysical implications of his version of Hegelianism. For him the study of logic becomes almost a self-contained exercise:

The conception of logical science, which has been my guide in the present work, is that of an unprejudiced study of the forms of knowledge in their development, their inter-connection, and their comparative value as embodiments of truth.[3]

He even compares the 'study and analysis of judgment forms' to the 'study and analysis of the forms of flowers or plants.'[4] He concludes the book with a passage that can be taken as an expression of a pure version of Idealism:

And because our intelligence creates and sustains our real world by a continuous judgment which embraces these forms, in their concrete connection, within the unity of its system, it is further true that Logical Science is the analysis, not indeed of individual real objects, but of the intellectual structure of reality as a whole.[5]

Bradley, at the time he wrote the *Principles,* did not think that 'reality as a whole' had an intellectual structure; it existed, and we could make judgments about it. These might cohere into a whole. Such knowledge was not reality. We do not make 'our real world,' though what we say may be true of '*the* real world' to some degree. Bosanquet can be considered an Idealist; I have already argued that Bradley was not. Further, Bosanquet was primarily concerned with the influence of logic and of philosophy on the world of practice. Bradley is more a 'philosophers' philosopher,' willing to follow the argument wherever it leads even though the final conclusion seems impossible to maintain and remote from what the common man believes.

The difference between the two philosophers might be summed up in this way: Bosanquet remained largely within the Hegelian scheme, though he developed and refined it, adapting the system to changed conditions, both historical and philosophical, at the end of the nineteenth century. He was more responsive to the intellectual currents of the time, as can be seen from one of his last books, *Implication and Linear Inference,* which deals with many of his contemporaries, including Russell and Husserl. Nevertheless, he deals with them from his own point of view. Bradley, on the other hand, starts his intellectual progress from a position like that of Bosanquet; both had learnt much from Green. But Bradley develops an independent line. I have already pointed out that *Ethical Studies* is more Hegelian than the *Principles.* His first publication, the 'Presuppositions of Critical History,' is equally Hegelian, and was considered to be an example of the Oxford 'high *a priori* road.' Later he did express doubts about his deviation:

Now this whole doctrine may of course be mistaken in principle. I have failed, I know well, to grasp it and carry it out as it should have been carried out. Nay, if I had been able to keep closer to a great master like Hegel, I doubt if after all I might have not kept nearer to the truth. (*CE,* p. 687. The reference is to *Appearance and Reality*)

Nevertheless, in the second edition any lingering empiricism has been purged, and Bradley returns to the 'high *a priori*' style. If a metaphysician were asked to choose between a principle or absolute truth, and the 'knowledge that England was conquered by the Normans or that Belgium was invaded by the Germans' (*PL,* p. 685), he would reply: 'Without doubt or hesitation, I take my stand with the . . . high abstract principle' (*PL,* p. 686).

In general, the Terminal Essays can be characterized as accepting the negative criticism of traditional logic that was offered in the main text. The difference lies in the fact that whereas he had previously expressed a 'lingering doubt' about the truth of his results, now he has reached negative certainty. At the beginning of the first essay, he sets out the programme:

Everywhere inference, I shall argue, must be more or less defective, and, since logic must be abstract, the defect, I shall go on to urge, is in principle irremovable. . . . Passing on, I will deal next with the question as to how far all inference is arbitrary, and again how far it is unreal. Its reality, I shall contend, is genuine, but on the other hand that reality is relative only. Every inference, I shall further point out, is in principle fallible, and there is no remedy to be found in any search for Forms of reasoning. The Criterion, it follows, is not be found not here but elsewhere, and I will conclude by remarking on the true aim and purpose of logic. (*PL*, pp. 597–8)

'The Criterion' is that developed in *Appearance and Reality*. Its application to the nature of truth is set out in that book:

The essential inconsistency of truth may, perhaps, best be stated thus. If there is any difference between *what it means* and *what it stands for*, then truth is clearly not realized. But, if there is no such difference, then truth has ceased to exist. (*AR*, p. 482n)

Logic can only deal with a representation of reality, or, to put the same point in another way, language is about reality, and hence cannot *be* reality. If it is thus separated from its object, then it is to that extent false. But if it were to be united with it, it would no longer be language; there would be no gulf between, as it were, sense and reference. It would have passed into something higher, that unified system of experience which is Reality. In so far as it cannot do that and retain its character as logic or as language, it is only an appearance. But it is an appearance of the Absolute, for all appearances are so to a limited degree. It is their limitations which make them only such.

Paradoxically, this metaphysical conclusion makes it possible for Bradley to accept the Hegelian view which he rejected at the end of the final chapter of the *Principles*, albeit in a relative form. As far as logic is concerned, the systematic nature of knowledge is a mark of its relative truth:

Our actual criterion is the body of our knowledge, made both as wide and as coherent as is possible, and so expressing more and more the genuine nature of reality. And the measure of the truth and importance of any one judgment or conclusion lies in its contribution to, and its place in, our intelligible system. This is the doctrine which, though in the present volume I failed to insist on it, I inherited and have always held. For its consistent and valuable advocacy the reader is referred to Dr. Bosanquet's writings. (*PL*, p. 620)

It is significant that 'reality' in this passage does not have a capital;

this marks the fact that the whole is still in the realm of appearance. It was the apparent failure of logic that led to the doubts and worries of the main text. Because he now thinks that its failure is in a sense complete, because, in other words, he believes that he has succeeded in characterizing the nature of Reality, that he can accept logic at a lower, more mundane, level.

Hence he states its object in words that belong to Bosanquet, the study of 'the general essence and main types of inference and judgment' (*PL*, p. 620). Within the ideal realm, the realm of intelligible system, we can set out:

The degree to which the various types succeed and fail in reaching their common end, gives to each of them its respective place and its rank in the whole body. Such an exposition is in my view the main purpose of Logic, but for an attempt to realize this object I can not refer to the present volume. The reader must be directed once more to the works of Dr. Bosanquet. (*PL*, p. 620)

Logic thus is reduced to the status of a special science, on a level with psychology (*PL*, p. 613). It no longer seems to have the philosophical importance which Bradley gave it in the main text of the *Principles*. This new view perhaps explains why he can conclude this essay by saying 'In my actual reasonings I myself certainly have never troubled myself about any logic; but I do not know the conclusion which should follow from this' (*PL*, pp. 620–1). Logic is classification, a kind of botanizing among forms of thought instead of forms of plants. Absolute truth is the province of metaphysics, which now becomes the central concern of philosophy.

However, a closer look at some of the details may serve to make his earlier views clearer in some respects. For, not unsurprisingly, the majority of the changes are due to his new conception of Reality. I will use the capitalized form to refer to that discussed in the second edition, whilst plain 'reality' means the element so often mentioned in the first edition. There are three main changes in his views:

1 The existence of 'floating ideas' is denied.
2 Reality is no longer an undifferentiated whole.
3 His view of inference changes, because truth depends on a systematic whole.

I have already referred to (1) in chapter III, but there I was concerned only with the fact that even within the main text there were problems if ideas were allowed to 'float freely' because an idea depended on its meaning, its reference to something outside itself. Bradley extracted more from his denial of their possibility. In discussing negation, he says:

> My book is faulty here owing to its acceptance of 'floating ideas,' and through its failure to recognize that in its own sphere every idea has reality. (*PL*, p. 665)

By this he means that every idea is, at the same time as it is an idea, also a 'psychic content,' an existent in some sense. He continues the passage by saying that all negation is real:

> The content which it denies is never excluded absolutely. Far from falling nowhere, that content qualifies elsewhere the Universe. In this other region it owns positive truth and reality – whatever may be the amount and final character of these, and whatever the conditions under which, however much transformed, the denied content finds its goal. (*PL*, p. 665)

The reason that Bradley gives is that an idea always involves a 'loosening of "what" from "that" ' (*PL*, p. 640). This can only occur if the 'what' has a reference to something else. For it to have such a reference, there must be, in some sense, an object to which it refers. Patently many ideas do not refer to *the* real world, so there must be a number of 'worlds' which are, or must be, in some sense 'real.' The clearest expression of this view comes from *Essays on Truth and Reality:*

> Then there is my present actual world, and the ambiguous existence of what has been and is about to be. There are the worlds of duty and religious truth, which on the one side penetrate and on the other side transcend the common visible facts. And there are the regions of hope, desire and dream, madness and drunkenness and error, all 'unreal,' if you please, but all counting as elements in the total of reality. The various worlds of politics, commerce, invention, trade and manufacture, all again have their places. Above the sensible sphere rises the intellectual province of truth and science, and more or less apart from this, the whole realm of the higher imagination. Both in poetry and in general fiction, and throughout the entire region of the arts and artistic perception, we encounter reality. (*ETR*, p. 33)

I have quoted this at length to bring out the 'Meinongian' character of this plurality of 'worlds.' In a sense Bradley is here more extreme than Meinong, for he maintains that 'every idea qualifies the real' (*ETR*, p. 35). It would seem that no one of these realities has any precedence over the others: they are all equally valid in their own spheres.

To discuss this view in the detail it deserves would take us too far into metaphysics. Here I am only concerned with the effect it has on logic. The result is that there are no 'mere ideas;' every idea involves a judgment, because to refer an idea to reality is to judge. To think, as we would normally say, of a centaur is to judge that there is, in some realm, a centaur. In ordinary discourse we distinguish between 'thinking of a centaur,' which has no judgmental character, and saying that a centaur had a man's trunk on a horse's body. The latter is counted as true because there is a public definition of the word, whereas 'a centaur' is neither true nor false, just an image or 'idea.' We normally think it possible to imagine any number of entities without judging as to their existence; this seems to be denied by Bradley at this stage. Presumably on this account even a dream consists of a series of judgments. Bradley's 'holism' becomes extreme at this point. Apparently the various 'worlds' even contain self-contradictions:

On the other hand, if even in an imaginary world you seek to unite round and square simply in one subject, they once more cease to qualify this 'real' world. They are once more exiled to a further outlying world of mere imagination, in which, being again somehow merely conjoined, they can both together be real. . . . I would, however, once more remind the reader that in any case, by even speaking of contradictories, we tacitly assume them to be somehow conjoined, and I would add that any view of contradiction which fails to deal with this aspect of the case is at best incomplete and is probably defective. (*ETR*, pp. 41–2n)

The passage is less than clear, and the fact that to envisage two things as contradictory involves putting them together, in some sense, hardly establishes that there is a world in which they are conjoined. It is a consequence of his metaphysical views that all partial realities are, in the last resort, contradictory because they involve self-contradictions. This is the criterion which he uses throughout *Appearance and Reality* to deny the ultimate reality of all finite 'realities.' Hence in some sense self-contradictory things do exist, for otherwise the separate realities would already be Reality.

There is one class of exceptions to this, namely aesthetic objects; these cannot be 'true' in the sense that is of interest to logic, for they 'go beyond truth in the narrower and stricter sense of the word' (*PL,* p. 627n). In the body of the text he says of them:

For an aesthetic object, left merely as such, does not come to me as true, nor does it offer itself as mediated by any link of internal necessity. Such an object, I fully agree, is never a mere fact. It is always an ideal in the sense of something set free from mere existence. (*PL,* p. 627)

The words 'set free from mere existence' as applied to a musical air, which is Bradley's example here, will remind some readers of another tune which had the same property attributed to it, 'Some of these days' in Sartre's *La Nausée.* Sartre, or his character Roquentin, says this for rather different reasons than moved Bradley. Nevertheless, for both it is an 'ideal object' without reference to anything beyond itself. For both it can be analysed and so treated as a fact, but when this is done its character is falsified, and for Bradley, 'as aesthetic it has ceased to be itself.' Thus there is one type of object which is not a member of a special reality, and presumably not of Reality either.

This doctrine of a plurality of worlds has consequences for judgment. It requires a distinction between 'reality' and 'Reality,' if only because there are many of the former and only one of the latter. Hence there is a philosophical problem of the relation between them. Bradley's distinction between 'appearance' and 'Reality' is not between the unreal and the real, for the various appearances are 'realities' which somehow make up 'Reality.' Thus Reality is not an undifferentiated whole, only divided up by our judgments, as it was in the main text; it is a totality of all 'realities:'

In Judgment the Reality to which we in fact refer is always something distinguished. It *is* Reality, as our whole world, but, at the same time and none the less, it is also *this* reality. It is a limited aspect and portion of the Universe, it is some special and emphasized feature in the total mass. (*PL,* p. 629)

The stress which he puts on this point in the Terminal Essays serves to show that in the main text he did not treat the reality there discussed as differentiated or distinguished in itself. For everyday truth all that is required is that judgments refer to *a* reality: 'Reality as the subject of our judgment is always a selected reality' (*PL,* p. 629).

Nevertheless, it is necessary for him to say something about the relation between a 'selected reality' and 'Reality' as a whole, for ultimately truth would seem to depend on a reference to the latter, insofar as that is possible. Though we normally judge of a selected reality:

yet, on the other hand, however much content passes over, as an idea, into what we call the predicate – this content still, as an immediate qualification, makes part of the entire subject. However much emphasized it remains still in one with the unbroken Reality. . . . Hence the matter of our separated predicate is continuous with and in one with the presented Universe which is our ultimate subject. . . . This two-fold nature of Reality, by which it slides away from itself into our distinction, so as there to become a predicate – while all the time it retains in itself, as an ultimate subject, every quality which we loosed from and relate to it – is, if you please, inexplicable. (*PL,* p. 629)

In a sense Reality is both divided and undivided, and for this reason 'inexplicable.' However, insofar as judgment is concerned, it is its division which is important. There is, in the argument here, an echo of the doctrine of 'degrees of truth and reality.' Bradley even seems to make use of what is very like the Hegelian distinction between a proposition and a judgment (cf. p. 36 above), for a mere S – P is different from an S(R) – P in which reality is explicitly mentioned (cf. *PL,* pp. 624–6). Thus

The judgment which offers itself as simple affirmation is really, we found, an abstraction from fact. (*PL,* p. 640)

As such, it is not really a judgment. But if it contains the ground of the connection between its elements within it, it is more than a judgment; it is an inference.

He defines inference as he did in the main text, 'the ideal self-development of an object.' But he immediately continues that inference is always defective and that the defect is irremovable (cf. pp. 200–1 above). It arises from the 'two-fold nature of Reality.' For inference is correct 'in its own world, and so far as it succeeds in maintaining its proper character' (*PL,* p. 617). Within a special or selected reality, self-development can occur, for we can establish relatively isolated intelligible systems. If inference is considered to give ultimate truth, then it is inadequate. Logic can exist at a certain level, but in a metaphysical sense it too is inadequate:

Logic in a word assumes that *Implication* exists, and that implication, where genuine, is also real. It assumes the reality of an ideal Universe, and of subordinate wholes and systems within this Universe. (*PL,* p. 600)

He continues:

Hence . . . , where you have a system, you can, starting at a given point within the system, develope this by a necessity which is the real intrinsic nature of your beginning. (ibid.)

This can take place within an 'ideal Universe,' which, by that very token, is not the same as 'the Universe' or 'Reality.'

However, the object we develop is an ideal content before us, taken to be real as being in one with Reality, the real Universe. And our inference, to retain its unity and so in short to be an inference, must, further, remain throughout within the limits of its special object. But what in any particular case this object is, and how its limits really are defined, cannot be taken as appearing in those forms of language which serve as its expression. (*PL,* p. 598)

It is rare for Bradley to express himself as linguistically as he does in this passage. The object is ideal, but what we want to consider is the self-development of the real object, that which is 'in one with Reality.' Only that would give ultimate truth. Because the object is an element in the whole Reality, it only is itself as so contained (*PL,* p. 600); it is modified by the rest of Reality. But in inference it is only considered as modified in that ideal reality within which we consider it. Hence the defectiveness of all inference.

However, there is a further complication which Bradley adds, 'our inability in logic to take account of the psychical aspect inseparable from all thinking' (*PL,* p. 597). Here again we are confronted by the abstract nature of logic, for it cannot take this mental aspect into account and still remain logic. Bradley says 'truth must happen and occur, and must exist as what we call a mental event' (*PL,* p. 612). Similarly, psychology has to neglect the logical aspects of the psychical events it deals with. In the argument he presents it is clear how logic has been demoted to the status of a special science, on a par with psychology; it is now a matter of the classification of judgment-forms. Metaphysics has taken over its original tasks. In the text Bradley had been content to admit that truth must exist as a mental event, but there he did not think that it raised any great problems. It is hard to see in the Terminal Essays what these new problems actually are, or why logic is at fault if it fails to take psychology into account. It looks as if he were saying that I cannot rely on my pocket calculator if I do not understand its mechanism fully. Arithmetic itself is caught up in the general ruin, for the 'world of number' that it must assume is one which 'we do not understand, and which, at least, as we have it there, seems self-contradictory' (*PL,* p. 604). Arithmetical inferences cannot involve genuine self-development because the steps are 'merely external.' These conclusions are the result of his belief that truth is a whole, and because logic is partial, it cannot arrive at truth. How any other study can, even inadequately, do this I shall not enter into here.

I have only glanced cursorily at the Terminal Essays and Additions of the second edition of the *Principles,* though I think I have said sufficient to show that they involve a radical rethinking of the province of logic. To follow the details would be tedious and confusing. The second edition marks the decline of Bradley's interest in logic as an independent subject. Hence its constant reference to *Appearance and Reality* and the rest of his late works. I do not want to deny that there may be in these works points which are of importance to logic, though I do maintain that they are not adequately spelt out in the text under consideration.

My concern has been with the main text, which I do think is of importance to logic, if only because it presents a point of view so radically different from that which is customary at present. Because this was my purpose, I have been expository rather than critical. It has not been any part of my intention to claim that Bradley was correct in the many places in which he differs from what is now, in logic, held to be true. However, I do think that an examination of the differences between him and contemporary writers may lead some of the latter to revise their views. My subsidiary aim has been to restore Bradley to his rightful place in the history of British philosophy. *The Principles of Logic* is an important text for this purpose, because there is a danger that he will be regarded only as a metaphysician, and as a consequence those who think he is an important figure will do so on the grounds that they disapprove of contemporary trends in philosophy. Such a move seems to me disastrous for Bradley's reputation. If a philosopher has nothing to offer those who are in the forefront of contemporary thinking, then he is dead, however much he may be praised by reactionaries.

NOTES

1 James Gibson, *Mind*, 1923, p. 352.
2 *Knowledge and Reality*, London, 1885, p. vii.
3 *Logic*, Oxford, 1888, p. v.
4 Ibid., p. vii.
5 Ibid., vol. II, p. 236.

Appendix
Pagination of the First and Second Editions of the *Principles*

Bibliography

BOOKS

Abbott, E. and Campbell, L., *The Life of Benjamin Jowett,* London, 1897.
Anschutz, R. P., *The Philosophy of J. S. Mill,* Oxford, 1953.
Bain, Alexander, *The Emotions and the Will,* London, 1859.
Black, Max, *Caveats and Critiques,* London and Ithaca, 1975.
Bogen, J., *Wittgenstein's Philosophy of Language,* London, 1972.
Bosanquet, Bernard, *Essays and Addresses,* London, 1889.
Bosanquet, Bernard, *The Essentials of Logic,* London, 1895.
Bosanquet, Bernard, *Implication and Linear Inference,* London, 1920.
Bosanquet, Bernard, *Knowledge and Reality,* London, 1885.
Bosanquet, Bernard, *Logic,* Oxford, 1888.
Bosanquet, Bernard, *The Principle of Individuality and Value,* London, 1912.
Caird, Edward, *Hegel,* London, 1883.
Cameron, J. M., *The Night Battle,* London, 1962.
Collingwood, R. G., *Autobiography,* London, Penguin Books, 1944.
Dummett, M., *Frege,* London, 1973.
Eliot, T. S., *Knowledge and Experience in the Philosophy of F. H. Bradley,* London, 1964.
Ensor, R. C. K., *England, 1870–1914,* Oxford, 1936.
Fodor, J. A., *The Language of Thought,* Hassocks, 1976.
Frege, G., *Conceptual Notation,* trans. T. W. Bynum, Oxford, 1972.
Frege, G., *The Foundations of Arithmetic,* trans. J. L. Austin, Oxford, 1950.
Frege, G., *Philosophical Writings,* trans. Peter Geach and Max Black, Oxford, 1952.
Frege, G., *Posthumous Writings,* trans. P. Long and R. White, Oxford, 1979.
Frege, G., *Wissenschaftlicher Briefwechsel,* ed. G. Gabriel *et al.,* Hamburg, 1976.
Green, T. H., *The Works of T. H. Green,* ed. R. L. Nettleship, London, 1890.

Hegel, G. W. F., *The Subjective Logic of Hegel*, trans. and ed. H. Sloman and J. Wallon, London, 1855.

Hegel, G. W. F., *Werke in zwanzig Bände*, Theorie Werkausgabe, Suhrkamp Verlag, Frankfurt am Main, 1969–72.

Hume, David, *A Treatise of Human Nature*, ed. L. A. Selby-Bigge, Oxford, 1896.

Jowett, Benjamin, *The Dialogues of Plato*, Oxford, 1871.

Kant, I., *Critique of Pure Reason*, trans. N. Kemp Smith, London, 1929.

Kaufmann, Walter, *Hegel*, London, 1966.

Keynes, J. N., *Formal Logic*, London, 1887.

Kneale, W. and M., *The Development of Logic*, Oxford, 1962.

Leibniz, G. W., *Leibniz's Logical Papers*, ed. and trans. G. H. Parkinson, Oxford, 1966.

Lotze, Hermann, *Logic*, trans. and ed. Bernard Bosanquet, Oxford, 1888.

Mansel, H. L., *Letters, Lectures and Reviews*, ed. H. W. Chandler, London, 1873.

Marx, Karl, *The German Ideology*, London, 1965.

Mill, J. S., *Autobiography*, New York, n.d.

Mill, J. S., *Examination of Sir William Hamilton's Philosophy*, London, 1872.

Muirhead, J. H., *Bernard Bosanquet and his Friends*, London, 1935.

Newman, J. H., *The Idea of a University*, London, 1889.

Passmore, J., *A Hundred Years of Philosophy*, London, 1957.

Pattison, Mark, *Memoirs*, London, 1885.

Pears, D. F., *Bertrand Russell and the British Tradition in Philosophy*, London, 1967.

Ramsey, F. P., *The Foundations of Mathematics*, London, 1950.

Richter, Melvin, *The Politics of Conscience*, London, 1964.

Russell, Bertrand, *Logic and Knowledge*, ed. R. C. Marsh, London, 1956.

Russell, Bertrand, *Philosophical Essays*, London, 1910.

Russell, Bertrand, *My Philosophical Development*, London, 1975.

Russell, Bertrand, *The Principles of Mathematics*, Cambridge, 1903.

Ryle, Gilbert, *Collected Papers*, London, 1971.

Ryle, Gilbert, *The Concept of Mind*, London, 1949.

Ryle, Gilbert (ed.), *The Revolution in Philosophy*, London, 1956.

Sartre, J.-P., *L'Etre et le néant*, Paris, 1953.

Sartre, J.-P., *La Nausée*, Paris, 1938.

Strawson, P. F., *Introduction to Logical Theory*, London, 1952.

Stirling, H. S., *The Secret of Hegel*, London, 1898.

Wallace, William, *The Logic of Hegel, with Prolegomena*, Oxford, 1874.

Warnock, Geoffrey, *English Philosophy since 1900*, Oxford, 1958.

Wiggins, David, *Identity and Spatio-temporal Continuity*, Oxford, 1967.

Wilson, J. Cook, *Statement and Inference*, ed. A. S. L. Farquharson, Oxford, 1926.

Winch, Peter, *The Idea of a Social Science*, London, 1958.
Winch, Peter (ed.), *Studies in the Philosophy of Wittgenstein*, London, 1969.
Wittgenstein, L., *Tractatus Logico–Philosophicus*, trans. D. F. Pears and B. F. McGuinness, London, 1961.
Wittgenstein, L., *Philosophical Investigations*, Oxford, 1953.
Wollheim, Richard, *F. H. Bradley*, Pelican Books, London, 1959.

ARTICLES

Ayer, A. J., 'Internal Relations,' *Supplementary Proceedings of the Aristotelian Society*, vol XIV, 1935.
Bosanquet, Bernard, 'Mr. F. H. Bradley on Fact and Inference,' *Mind*, vol. X, 1885.
Carr, H. Wildon, 'Is the "Concrete Universal" the true Type of Universality?' *Proceedings of The Aristotelian Society*, vol. 20, 1919–20.
Carroll, Lewis, 'What the Tortoise said to Achilles,' *Mind*, vol. IV, 1895.
Davidson, Donald, 'True to the Facts,' *Journal of Philosophy*, vol. 66, 1969.
Davidson, Donald, 'Truth and Meaning,' *Synthese*, vol. 17, 1967.
Diamond, Cora, 'What Nonsense might be,' *Philosophy*, January 1981.
Foster, Michael, 'The Concrete Universal,' *Mind*, 1931.
Geach, Peter, Review of Michael Dummett's *Frege*, *Mind*, 1976.
Gibson, James, Review of second edition of the *Principles of Logic*, *Mind*, 1923.
Lindsay, T. M., 'Recent Hegelian Contributions to English Philosophy,' *Mind*, 1877.
Manser, Anthony, 'Games and Family Resemblances,' *Philosophy*, 1967.
Manser, Anthony, 'Hegel's Teleology,' Philosophy Department, University of Southampton.
Moore, G. E., 'External and Internal Relations,' *Proceedings of the Aristotelian Society*, 1919–20. Reprinted in *Philosophical Studies*, London, 1922.
Moore, G. E., 'The Nature of Judgment,' *Mind*, 1899.
Pap, Arthur, 'Types and Meaninglessness,' *Mind*, 1960.
Pattison, Mark, 'Philosophy at Oxford,' *Mind*, 1876.
Robinson, G. S., 'Following and Formalization,' *Mind*, 1964.
Ryle, Gilbert, 'Internal Relations,' *Supplementary Proceedings of the Aristotelian Society*, vol. XIV, 1935.
Ryle, Gilbert, Review of R. Wollheim, *F. H. Bradley*, *The Spectator*, 15 January, 1960.
Smith, N. Kemp, 'The Nature of Universals,' *Mind*, 1927.

Sommers, Fred, 'Do we need Identity?' *Journal of Philosophy,* vol. 66, 1969.

Sommers, Fred, 'Leibniz's Program for the Development of Logic,' *Essays in Memory of Imre Lakatos,* ed. R. S. Cohen, P. K. Feyerabend and M. W. Wartofsky, Dordrecht, 1976.

Taylor, A. E., 'F. H. Bradley,' *Proceedings of the British Academy,* 1926.

Index